Learning to Pass

CLAiT Plus

2006

- Integrated e-document production •
- Manipulating spreadsheets and graphs •
- Creating and using a database •

Units 1–3

**Ruksana Patel
& Penny Hill**

www.heinemann.co.uk
✓ Free online support
✓ Useful weblinks
✓ 24 hour online ordering

01865 888058

Heinemann

Inspiring generations

Heinemann Educational Publishers
Halley Court, Jordan Hill, Oxford OX2 8EJ
Part of Harcourt Education

Heinemann is the registered trademark of Harcourt Education Limited

First published 2006

10 09 08 07 06
10 9 8 7 6 5 4 3 2 1

British Library Cataloguing in Publication Data is available
from the British Library on request.

10-digit ISBN: 0 43508270 1
13-digit ISBN: 978 0 435 082703

Typeset by

Original illustrations © Harcourt Education Limited, 2006

Cover design by Wooden Ark

Printed in the UK by Bath Press

Cover photo: © Getty Images

Acknowledgements

Every effort has been made to contact copyright holders of material reproduced in
this book. Any omissions will be rectified in subsequent printings if notice is given to
the publishers.

The authors would like to express their grateful thanks to Stephe and Mur Cove,
Rebecca Hill and Abdul Patel for working through the books and providing invaluable
feedback and for their support. Thank you to Fayaz and Fozia Roked and Brian
Hill for their help, encouragement and support. Thank you to the Lake District
Mountain Rescue Association for allowing us to use their statistics for Chapter 2 of
Unit 2. Thank you to Gavin Fidler for his expert input and to Lewis Birchon for his
invaluable input which has improved the quality of the books and for his constant
support, advice and patience during the production process. And finally, we would
like to thank each other for 'being there for each other'.

Microsoft product screenshots reprinted with permission from Microsoft Corporation.

Tel: 01865 888058   www.heinemann.co.uk

Contents

This book has been designed to cover the syllabus for Unit 1 Integrated e-document production, Unit 2 Manipulating spreadsheets and graphs, and Unit 3 Creating and using a database of the OCR Level 2 Certificate/ Diploma for IT Users (CLAiT Plus) and can also be used as a basis of learning the skills for the ITQ qualification. Unit 1 is the core unit and is required by candidates who would like to achieve the Level 2 Certificate or Diploma for IT Users (CLAiT Plus).

Learning outcomes for Unit 1: Integrated e-document production

A candidate following a programme of learning leading to this unit will be able to:

- *use a computer's system hardware and software safely and securely to create a variety of business documents*
- *use an input device to enter and manipulate data accurately from a variety of sources*
- *work with data files using database and/or spreadsheet facilities to select and import data*
- *use mail merge facilities*
- *create, format and print a mail merge master document and mail merged documents*
- *create and print an integrated document, combining text, numeric and tabular data, an image and a graph*
- *format page layout and manipulate text according to a house style.*

Learning outcomes for Unit 2: Manipulating spreadsheets and graphs

A candidate following a programme of learning leading to this unit will be able to:

- *identify and use spreadsheet and graph software correctly*
- *enter, edit and manipulate data*
- *create formulae and use common functions*
- *format and present data*

- link live data from one spreadsheet to another
- select and control data sources
- present data using graphs and charts
- format axes and labels
- format the presentation of graphs and charts
- use graphs to extrapolate information to predict future values
- use spreadsheets to solve problems and project results.

Learning outcomes for Unit 3: Creating and using a database

A candidate following a programme of learning leading to this unit will be able to:

- Create a database file, set up fields and enter a range of information
- import datafiles, update and interrogate databases using complex search criteria
- plan and produce database reports in a variety of report formats
- format and present database reports.

CLAiT Plus

The OCR Level 2 Certificate/Diploma for IT Users (CLAiT Plus) is a qualification designed to recognise the skills, knowledge and understanding of IT users in employment, education or training. It aims to provide a nationally recognised standard in IT assessment that is accessible and flexible whilst also being reliable, consistent and valid. It is designed to fit the needs of the learner, employer and training provider.

The redeveloped qualification

CLAiT Plus has been redeveloped to produce a qualification that provides a clear progression route from Level 1 to Level 3, at both unit level and whole qualification level. It will equip learners with the range of transferable skills necessary to meet the demands of the modern workplace, and will prepare learners for progression to further training and accreditation in IT User skills at Level 3.

The new qualification maps to the National Occupational Standards for IT Users created by e-skills UK. This takes account of recent software developments and provides greater flexibility, ease-of-use and relevance.

Aims of the qualification

The qualification aims to develop:

- *knowledge of IT hardware and software and the ability to operate equipment correctly and safely*
- *knowledge of a range of different software applications and the ability to use different applications effectively to complete complex tasks*
- *ability to manage and manipulate complex documents and data in a variety of applications*
- *ability to manipulate and integrate data across different applications*
- *ability to enter data accurately*
- *skills and knowledge in contexts that are directly relevant to employment situations*
- *a natural progression route for candidates who have completed a Level 1 qualification or have basic computer skills.*

Structure of the qualification

UNIT STATUS	UNIT TITLE
Core unit	Unit 1: Integrated e-document production
Optional units	Unit 2: Manipulating spreadsheets and graphs Unit 3: Creating and using a database Unit 4: e-publication design Unit 5: Design an e-presentation Unit 6: e-image manipulation Unit 7: Website creation Unit 8: Electronic communication

All units are equally weighted. Candidates may work towards the units in any particular order and learning programmes can be tailored to meet individual needs.

Guided learning hours

An average candidate that has the stated recommended prior learning suggested by OCR should take around 30 guided learning hours per unit to acquire the knowledge, understanding and skills necessary to pass that unit. However, this figure is for guidance only and will vary depending on individual candidates and the mode of learning.

Recommended prior learning

There are no formal requirements for CLAiT Plus, but the CLAiT Plus units assume familiarity with IT concepts at Level 1. There are no minimum entry requirements, however, it is expected that candidates will be working at around Level 2 of the National Qualifications Framework. Candidates will benefit from development of skills assessed through the OCR Level 1 for IT Users (New CLAiT) qualification.

Candidate profile

CLAiT Plus caters for the full range of learners in IT, whether in school, college, training, further education or employment. The qualification is suitable for those who already possess basic skills in the use of IT and who wish to further develop their ability.

It is suitable for those in full-time education who wish to gain a comprehensive qualification at Level 2. It is also suitable for those following part-time courses and those in employment who wish to develop skills in one or more specialist areas in order to meet the needs of their workplace situation.

Assessment

Units 1 to 8 are assessed in a centre by a centre assessor and are then externally moderated by an OCR examiner-moderator. OCR sets the assessments however, OCR will allow centres/candidates to produce a suitably appropriate personalised scenario and tasks which allow the candidate to achieve all assessment objectives as listed in individual unit specifications. Candidates are allowed a notional duration of 3 hours for each assessment. If candidates do not pass an OCR-set assignment at the first attempt, they may have other attempts at a unit using a different OCR-set assignment. In order to achieve a unit pass, candidates must make no critical errors and no more than six accuracy errors. For detailed marking criteria please refer to the OCR Level 2 Certificate/Diploma for IT Users (CLAiT Plus) Tutor's Handbook.

Alternative forms of assessment

Centres are able to purchase Microsoft Office Specialist tests through OCR and use these as an alternative assessment method towards the following units:

MICROSOFT OFFICE SPECIALIST TEST	OCR UNIT TO BE CLAIMED
Word core	Unit 1: Integrated e-document production
Excel core	Unit 2: Manipulating spreadsheets and graphs
Access core	Unit 3: Creating and using a database
PowerPoint core	Unit 5: Design an e-presentation
Outlook core	Unit 8: Electronic communication

Certification

Candidates may achieve individual unit certificates, an OCR Level 2 Certificate For IT Users (CLAiT Plus) or an OCR Level 2 Diploma For IT Users (CLAiT Plus).

Each unit is regarded as a worthwhile achievement in its own right. Candidates have the option of achieving as many or as few units as are appropriate for their own learning needs or employment situation. Candidates will be awarded a unit certificate for each individual unit achieved.

To achieve the Level 2 Certificate for IT Users (CLAiT Plus) qualification, candidates are required to achieve **three** units including the core unit (Unit 1).

Candidates who achieve **five** units including the core unit (Unit 1) will be awarded an OCR Level 2 Diploma for IT Users (CLAiT Plus).

Progression

CLAiT Plus is part of a suite of qualifications in IT User skills offered by OCR. Other IT User qualifications offered by OCR are Level 1 (New CLAiT) and Level 3 (CLAiT Advanced).

Candidates who are successful in achieving accreditation at Level 2 will be able to progress to the OCR Level 3 Certificate/Diploma for IT Users. CLAiT Plus also provides a basis for progression to the NVQs which form part of the ITQ suite, NVQ Levels 1, 2 and 3 for IT Users.

This book covers the syllabus for Units 1, 2 and 3 of CLAiT Plus. The skills you are learning through this study are important for employment – skills in the use of IT are needed in 9 out of 10 new jobs in the UK. This foreword explains how you can make your study even more valuable. Your successful completion of this CLAiT Plus unit can contribute to achieving an ITQ, and your progress towards an ITQ (including your completion of this unit) can be recorded in an e-skills Passport.

The ITQ qualification and e-skills Passport

Both the ITQ and the e-skills Passport have been created by employers. The **ITQ** is a flexible IT user qualification and training package that can be tailored to ensure you are trained in the IT skills that you need for your job. The ITQ is the New National Vocational Qualification (NVQ) for IT Users. It forms part of the new Apprenticeship Framework for IT Users and is based on the e-skills UK[1] National Occupational Standards.

The **e-skills Passport** is an online tool which helps you build your IT user skills profile. The e-skills Passport provides a simple means for you to assess the level of your IT skills, plan your ITQ and demonstrate your progress and achievements to date. It is not a qualification, nor is it a formal appraisal system but it is a means to steer you towards the right mix of training and/or qualifications that suit you and your employer. This will give you your personal record of achievement, presented in a form that is widely understood and recognised by employers.

Although the e-skills Passport provides an essential understanding of the IT user skills you need prior to undertaking ITQ, it is also recommended before embarking on CLAiT Plus 2006. For more information visit the e-skills Passport website (www.e-skillspassport.com)

CLAiT Plus 2006 and the ITQ

CLAiT Plus 2006 units can contribute towards the optional units for the ITQ qualification at level 2 as shown in the following table. The knowledge, understanding and skills content for CLAiT Plus 2006 units are also based on the National Occupational Standards.

---

[1] e-skills UK is the Sector Skills Council for IT and Telecoms (www.e-skills.com)

ITQ UNITS	CLAiT PLUS 2006 UNIT
Word processing level 2 (WP2)	Unit 1 Integrated e-document production
Spreadsheet software level 2 (SS2)	Unit 2 Manipulating spreadsheets and graphs
Database software level 2 (DB2)	Unit 3 Creating and using a database
E-mail level 2 (MAIL2)	Unit 8 Electronic communication
Presentation software level 2 (PS2)	Unit 5 Design an e-presentation
Website software level 2 (WEB2)	Unit 7 Website creation
Artwork and imaging software level 2 (ART2)	Unit 6 e-image manipulation

This book covers the syllabus for Units WP2: Word processing, SS2: Spreadsheet software and DB2: Database software of the ITQ at Level 2. You can use other units from CLAiT Plus 2006 and New CLAiT 2006 (which are published in Heinemann's *Learning to Pass New CLAiT/CLAiT Plus* 2006 series) as well as other popular IT user qualifications to count towards your ITQ.

Therefore, if you are embarking on the ITQ and you have selected this unit then this book can provide the underpinning knowledge required to help you to successfully complete the unit.

The ITQ calculator

The ITQ can be achieved at three levels. Each component unit at each level has been allocated a number of points. The tables below also show the total number of points that need to be achieved for ITQ at each level. You can select units from different levels in order to achieve the desired number of points, provided that you take the mandatory unit (Make Selective Use of IT) and at least 60% of your unit choices are at the ITQ level that you wish to achieve.

	ITQ LEVELS		
	Level 1	Level 2	Level 3
Total required	40	100	180
Total points to come from optional units at level of qualification	15	40	75

For example, for a Level 2 qualification:

- *overall points total of 100*
- *25 points come from mandatory unit*
- *75 points come from optional units*
- *of the 75 optional points 40 must be achieved at Level 2.*

ITQ internal credit matrix

UNIT TITLES	UNIT VALUES		
	Level 1	Level 2	Level 3
Mandatory unit			
Make selective use of IT	15	25	35
Optional units			
Using IT systems	5	15	25
Operate a computer	10	20	30
IT troubleshooting for users	5	15	25
IT maintenance for users	5	15	25
IT security for users	5	15	25
Use IT to exchange information	5	15	25
Internets and intranets	5	15	25
E-mail	5	15	25
Word processing	10	20	30
Spreadsheets	10	20	35
Databases	10	20	35
Websites	10	20	35
IT artwork and images	10	20	35
IT presentations	10	20	30
Specialist or bespoke software	10	20	30
Evaluate the impact of IT	5	15	25
Sector specific unit	10	20	30

For more information about ITQ, visit the ITQ website (www.itq.org.uk).

Who this book is suitable for

This book is suitable for:

○ *candidates working towards: OCR Level 2 Certificate/ Diploma for IT Users (CLAiT Plus), and OCR ITQ qualification*

○ *use as a self-study workbook – the user should work through the book from start to finish*

○ *tutor-assisted workshops or tutor-led groups*

○ *individuals wanting to learn to extend their skills of Microsoft Office Word 2003, Excel 2003 and Access 2003 (default settings are assumed).*

Although this book is based on Windows XP, Microsoft Office Word 2003, Excel 2003 and Access 2003, it may also be suitable for users of Microsoft Office 2002 (XP) and Microsoft Office 2000 applications. Note that a few of the skills may be slightly different and some screenshots will not be identical.

How to work through this book

This book assumes knowledge of Level 1 skills in file management, creating documents using Microsoft Word, Excel and Access 2003, and Level 1 word processing, spreadsheet, database and file management terms.

1 Before you begin this book, make sure that you feel confident with the basics of using a computer and Windows XP. These skills are covered in Chapter 1 of the Unit 1 book *Learning to Pass New CLAiT: File management and e-document production*.

2 If there are some terms that you do not understand, refer to the Definition of terms section at the end of each unit.

3 Work through each unit in sequence so that one skill is understood before moving on to the next. This ensures thorough understanding of the topic and prevents unnecessary mistakes.

4 Read the ▶▶ *How to...* guidelines which give step-by-step instructions for each skill; do not attempt to work through them. Read through the points and look at the screenshots – make sure that you understand all the instructions before moving on.

5 To make sure that you have understood how to perform a skill, work through the **Check your understanding** that follows. You should refer to the How to... guidelines when doing the task.

6 At the end of each section is an **Assess your skills** box. Read though these lists to find out how confident you feel about the skills that you have learned.

If you need help, you may refer to the How to... guidelines or Quick reference guides whilst doing the Build-up tasks. Whilst working on the Practice tasks, you should feel confident enough to use only the Quick reference guides if you need support. These guides may also be used during an assessment.

7 Towards the end of each unit are **Quick reference guides**. You should refer to these whilst doing the **Build-up** and **Practice tasks** that follow them, and also during an assessment.

8 A CD-ROM accompanies this book. On it are the files that you will need to use for the tasks. The solutions for all the tasks can be found on the CD-ROM in the unit folders.

9 If you need practice on a particular skill, you may use the worked files to complete the appropriate Practice task(s).

Note: there are many ways of performing the skills covered in this book. However, this book provides guidelines that have proven to be easily understood by learners.

Contents

UNIT 1: Integrated e-document production

How to use this book

In Unit 1, you need to combine a number of files saved in a variety of file formats to create an integrated document, amend a document, create a mail merge master document and perform a mail merge.

This book is divided into 6 sections:

- *in Section 1 you will learn how to work with documents saved in generic and non-generic (native) file formats*
- *in Section 2 you will learn how to format a document and integrate files*
- *in Section 3 you will learn how to format tabular data*
- *in Section 4 you will learn how to amend a document*
- *in Section 5 you will learn how to create mail merge documents and protect files*
- *in Section 6 you will learn how to archive files.*

You will use a software program called Microsoft Office Word 2003 which is part of Microsoft Office 2003. Word is a program that allows you to produce a wide variety of business documents, including integrated documents and mail merge. We will refer to it as Word from now on. You may also work with file compression software such as WinZip.

Files for this book

To work through the tasks in this book, you will need the files from the folder called **L2U1IDP_files**, this folder is on the CD-ROM provided with this book. Copy this folder into your user area before you begin.

▶▶ How to... *copy the folder L2U1IDP_files from the CD-ROM*

1 Insert the CD-ROM into the CD-ROM drive of your computer.

2 Close any windows that may open.

3 From the desktop, double-click the **My Computer** icon.

4 Double-click the **CD-ROM drive** icon.

5 A window will open displaying the contents of the CD-ROM.

6 Click once on the folder **L2U1IDP_files**.

7 The folder will be highlighted (usually blue).

8 In the **File and Folder Tasks** section, click **Copy this folder**.

9　A **Copy Items** dialogue box will open.

10　In this dialogue box click on the user area where you want to copy the folder **L2U1IDP_files** to.

11　Click the **Copy** button.

12　The folder **L2U1IDP_files** will be copied to your user area.

TIP!

It is advisable to copy and paste a second copy to another folder in your user area as backup.

Preparing your work area

You are advised to prepare your user area to keep your files organised.

○ *Create a folder for your CLAiT Plus work*

○ *In this folder, create a subfolder for all the CLAiT Plus units that you will be doing*

○ *In each unit subfolder, create further sub-folders, for example:*

U1 IDP working – your working folder in which all working files will be saved.

L2U1IDP_files – the source files from the CD-ROM.

L2U1_worked – this folder should also be copied from the CD-ROM.

Terms and symbols used for instructions in this book

INSTRUCTION	METHOD
Click	Press and release the **left** mouse button once.
Double-click	Quickly press the left mouse button **twice** then release it.
Select	Click on an item or highlight text.
Right-click	Press the right mouse button once.
+ e.g. Ctrl + P	Used to indicate that two keys should be held down together. Hold down the **Ctrl** key then press the **P** key.
→	Indicates a new instruction follows.

Useful keyboard shortcuts

SHORTCUT	ACTION
Ctrl + A	Select all
Ctrl + C	Copy the highlighted text or object
Ctrl + V	Paste the highlighted text or object
Ctrl + X	Cut the highlighted text or object
Ctrl + Z	Undo the last action
Ctrl + Y	Redo the last action
Ctrl + 1	Apply a single line space to the highlighted text
Ctrl + 1.5	Apply one and a half line (1.5) spacing to the highlighted text
Ctrl + 2	Apply double line spacing to the highlighted text
Ctrl + B	Make the selected text bold
Ctrl + I	Make the selected text italic
Ctrl + U	Underline the selected text
Ctrl + S	Save the document using the same filename
F7	Display the Spelling and Grammar dialogue box

UNIT 1: Integrated e-document production

Work with generic and non-generic file formats

LEARNING OUTCOMES

In this section you will learn how to:

- understand generic and non-generic files
- open a generic file from My Computer or Windows Explorer
- open a .txt file or .rtf file from within Word
- save files in generic and non-generic formats
- work with several open files
- close files from the taskbar.

Generic files

A generic file is a file saved in a format that can be read by most computer systems (e.g. PCs, Apple Macs) and in a large number of software applications (e.g. Word). Some formatting may be lost but the data can still be read. Files with the extension .txt, .rtf and .csv are examples of generic file formats.

A generic file can usually be opened from Windows Explorer, My Computer or from within Word.

▶▶ How to... *open a generic file from Windows Explorer or My Computer*

1 Locate the file to be opened.

2 Position the mouse pointer over the file.

3 Right-click, a menu displays.

4 From the menu, select **Open With**.

5 A submenu displays (Figure 1.1).

6 If the program that you want to open the file with displays in the submenu, click on it (in Figure 1.1 the program is Microsoft Office Word).

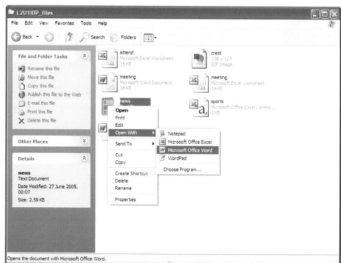

FIGURE 1.1 Opening a generic file from My Computer

7   The file will open in the program selected.

8   If the program you want to open the file with does not appear in the submenu, click on **Choose Program**.

9   The **Open With** dialogue box will be displayed (Figure 1.2).

10 Select the required program (in Figure 1.2 Microsoft Office Word).

11 Click on **OK**.

12 The file will open in the program selected.

▶▶ How to... open a .txt or .rtf file from within Word

1   On the **Standard** toolbar, click on the **Open** icon.

2   The **Open** dialogue box will be displayed (Figure 1.3).

3   In the **Look in** box, click on the drop-down arrow to locate the folder in which your file is stored.

4   Click on the drop-down arrow to the right of **Files of type**.

5   Click on **All Files**.

6   Select the file from the list displayed in the main window.

7   Click on **Open**.

8   The file will now open in Word.

▶▶ How to... save files in generic and non-generic formats

1   Click on the **File** menu.

2   Click on **Save As**. The **Save As** dialogue box will be displayed (Figure 1.4).

3   Click on the drop-down arrow next to the **Save as type** box.

4   From the list of file types, select the file type required (e.g. **Word Document** or **Rich Text Format**). **Word Document** will be at the top of the list.

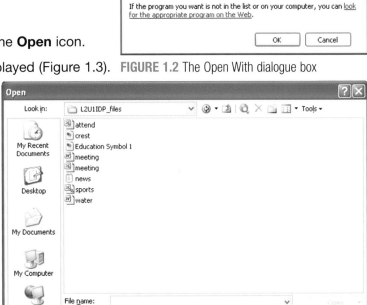

FIGURE 1.2 The Open With dialogue box

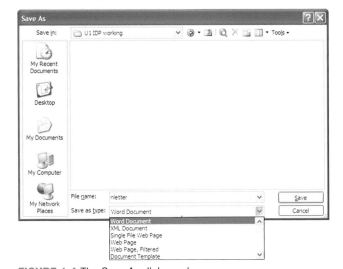

FIGURE 1.3 The Open dialogue box

FIGURE 1.4 The Save As dialogue box

5 Click the drop-down arrow next to the **Save in** box and locate the folder in which you want to save the file.

6 In the **File name** row, enter the required filename.

7 Click on **Save**.

> **TIP!**
>
> All formatting will be lost if a file is saved as a text file (.txt). Therefore, you must ensure that you select **Word Document** (.doc) if you want to retain the formatting. Documents saved as rich text files (.rtf), however, will retain some formatting (e.g. fonts and margins).

Check your understanding *Open and save a text file in Word*

1 Open Word.

2 From within Word, open the text file **news**.

3 In your working area, save the file as a Word document using the filename **nletter**.

4 Close the document.

Multitasking

Working with several open files is often referred to as multitasking.

How to... *work with several open files*

1 From **Windows Explorer** or **My Computer**, open the folder containing the files.

2 From within the folder, open the first file.

3 On the **taskbar**, click on the folder containing the other files. The **Folder** window will be displayed.

4 Open another file.

5 On the **taskbar**, click on the folder containing the other files. The **Folder** window will be displayed.

6 Open the next file.

7 All the open files will appear on the taskbar (Figure 1.5).

> **TIP!**
>
> To show files on the taskbar, select **Options** from the **Tools** menu. Click on the **View** tab, click to insert a tick in the **Windows in Taskbar** box.

The open files are displayed on the taskbar

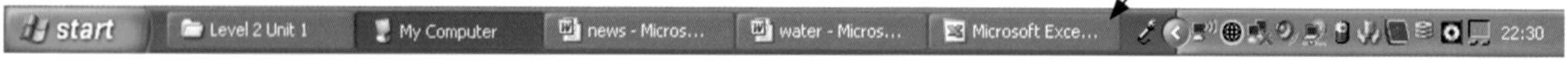
start
Level 2 Unit 1
My Computer
news - Micros...
water - Micros...
Microsoft Exce...
22:30

FIGURE 1.5 The open files on the taskbar

8 Click on the file you want to work with.

9 The file will be displayed on the screen.

10 Click on another file to switch between files.

How to... *close files from the taskbar*

1 On the **taskbar**, position the cursor over the file to be closed.

2 Right-click. A menu will be displayed.

3 Click on **Close**.

1 From **Windows Explorer** or **My Computer**, open the folder **L2U1IDP_files**.

2 Open the text file **news** with **Word**.

3 Open the rich text file **water** with **Word**.

4 Open the file **attend** with **Excel**.

5 Using the taskbar, switch between the three files.

6 Observe the difference in formatting of the .txt file **news** and the .rtf file **water**.

7 From the taskbar, close all open files.

ASSESS YOUR SKILLS – Work with generic and non-generic file formats

By working through this section you will have learnt the skills listed below. Read each item to help you decide how confident you feel about each skill.

- understand generic and non-generic files
- open a generic file from My Computer or Windows Explorer
- open a .txt file or .rtf file from within Word
- save files in generic and non-generic formats
- work with several open files
- close files from the taskbar.

If you feel that you need more practice on any of the skills in the above list, go back and work through those skills again.

If you feel confident, move on to Section 2.

2: Format a document and integrate files

LEARNING OUTCOMES

In this section you will learn how to:

- set margins and page layout
- format a document
- change line spacing
- copy formatting
- insert headers and footers
- print a document
- format a bulleted or numbered list
- insert a page break
- insert an image
- insert a graph
- resize images and graphs
- insert a data file as a table
- convert a data file to a table.

▶▶ How to... *set margins and page layout*

1 In a Word document.

2 Click on the File menu, click on **Page Setup**.

3 The **Page Setup** dialogue box will be displayed. Click on the **Margins** tab.

4 Enter the margins required in the Top, Left, Bottom and Right boxes.

5 Click to select **Portrait** or **Landscape** orientation.

6 Check the **Preview** section to ensure **Apply to** is set to **Whole document**. Click on the drop-down arrow to change if necessary.

7 Click on the **Paper** tab. Check that **Paper size** is set to **A4 210 x 297 mm**. Click on the down arrow to change if necessary.

8 Click on the **Print Options** button. The **Print** dialogue box will be displayed (Figure 1.6). Make sure **Allow A4/Letter paper resizing** is *not* ticked.

FIGURE 1.6 The Print dialogue box

9 Click on **OK** to close the Print dialogue box.

10 Click on **OK** to close the Page Setup dialogue box.

House styles

Many organisations have house styles that must be followed in the production of all documents. For example, a school or college may have a house style which states that all letters sent out by the school or college should be produced in the typeface Arial, 12 pt font size, single line spacing and one line space between paragraphs.

If an organisation uses house styles, it can be sure that all the documents the organisation produces will look the same and will contain the necessary information or graphics. Some house styles will also specify such things as the position, type and style of headers and footers.

You will be asked to apply a house style to documents. Before you format a document you should check how that document has been prepared. Check whether or not there are clear line spaces between paragraphs. Also check to see the spacing used after punctuation.

▶▶ How to... *format an entire document*

1 Open the document to be formatted.

2 Press **Ctrl** + **A**. The entire document will be highlighted.

3 Use the **Formatting** toolbar to set the required font, size, emphasis and alignment (Figure 1.7).

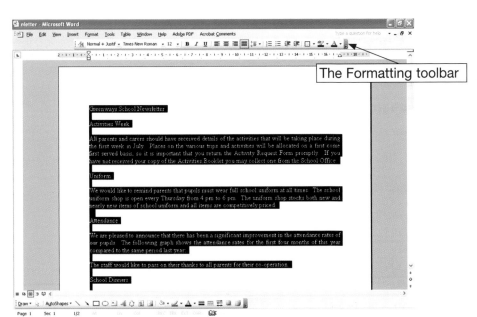

The Formatting toolbar

FIGURE 1.7 The Formatting toolbar

TIP!

To add toolbars, click on the **View** menu, click on **Toolbars**. Click on the required toolbar to select.

To add buttons (icons) to the toolbar, click on the drop-down arrow at the end of the toolbar. Choose from the selection shown or click on the **Add** or **Remove** buttons, choose the required button.

4 Click on the **Format** menu, **Paragraph**. The **Paragraph** dialogue box will be displayed (Figure 1.8).

5 Click on the **Indents and Spacing** tab. Check the **Indentation** box. **Left** and **Right** will normally be set to **0 cm** and **Special** to **(none)**. Change if necessary.

6 Check the **Spacing** box. **Before** and **After** will normally be set to **0 pt** and **Line spacing** to **Single**. Change if necessary.

7 Click on the **Line and Page Breaks** tab. Check that **Widow/Orphan control** is ticked. Click to tick if necessary.

8 Click on **OK**.

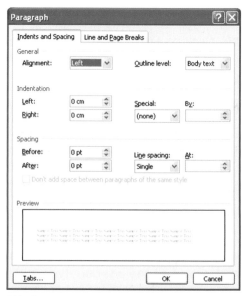

FIGURE 1.8 The Paragraph dialogue box

▶▶ How to... *change the line spacing*

1 Select the paragraph(s) to be changed.

2 Click on the **Format** menu, click on **Paragraph**. The **Paragraph** dialogue box will be displayed. Select the **Indents and Spacing** tab.

3 Under **Spacing**, click on the drop-down arrow next to **Line spacing** and select the spacing required.

4 Click on **OK**.

What does it mean?

A widow is a single line at the top of a page. An orphan is the first line of a new paragraph at the bottom of a page. Widows and orphans look untidy on the printed page. If the Widow/Orphan control is ticked, Word will automatically move single lines from the top of pages (widows) back to the bottom of the previous page and first lines of paragraphs (orphans) over to the next page.

Check your understanding *Format an entire document*

1 Open your saved file **nletter**. Format the entire document as follows:

Paper size	**A4 portrait**
All margins	**1.5 cm**
Alignment	**justified**
Font	**Times New Roman**
Emphasis	**none**
Font size	**12**
Line spacing	**single**

2 Save the file using the filename **nletter1**.

▶▶ How to... *format a line of text (e.g. a heading) or a paragraph*

1 Select the text to be formatted.

2 Use the **Formatting** toolbar to set the font, size, emphasis and alignment.

TIP!

To select a paragraph or a single line of text (e.g. a heading), click anywhere in the paragraph and then triple-click in quick succession.

1 Continue working in the file **nletter1**. Format the heading **Greenways School Newsletter** as follows:

Alignment	**centre**
Font	**Arial**
Font size	**24**
Emphasis	**bold**

2 Format the subheading **Activities Week** as follows:

Alignment	**left**
Font	**Arial**
Font size	**14**
Emphasis	**bold**, **italic**

3 Save the file keeping the filename **nletter1**.

▶▶ How to... *copy the formatting of a line or paragraph to other lines or paragraphs*

1 Select the formatted text.

2 Double-click on the **Painter** 🖌 icon on the **Standard** toolbar.

3 Select (highlight) the lines/paragraphs to be formatted in the same style.

4 When you have finished copying the format, click on the **Format Painter** icon again (or press **Escape**) to deselect it.

TIP!

Formatting can be copied to single words by clicking anywhere in the word. Formatting can be copied to a paragraph by triple-clicking anywhere in the paragraph.

1 Continue working with the file **nletter1**.

2 Copy the formatting of the subheading **Activities Week** to each of the subheadings listed below:

Uniform

Attendance

School Dinners

Homework Club

Sports

Quiz Night

PTA

3 Save the file keeping the filename **nletter1**.

1 Click on the **View** menu, click on **Header and Footer**. The **Header and Footer** dialogue box will be displayed.

2 In the **Header** box, key in the required information.

3 To switch to the footer, click on [icon].

4 To key in several items on the same line, press the **Tab** key [icon] on the keyboard. The tab position can be adjusted by holding down the Tab symbol and dragging it to the position required (Figure 1.9).

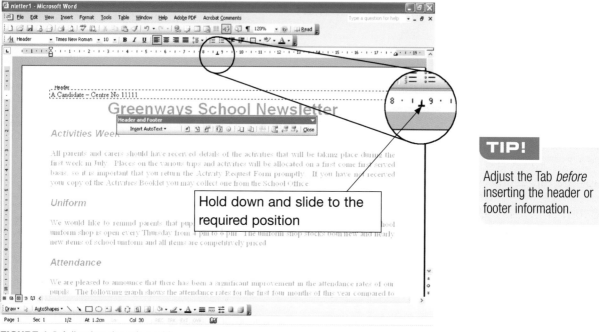

Hold down and slide to the required position

TIP!

Adjust the Tab *before* inserting the header or footer information.

FIGURE 1.9 Adjusting the tab position

5 The **Header and Footer** dialogue box allows you to add a number of automatic headers and footers (see Figure 1.10).

6 Click on **Close** when all headers and footers have been entered.

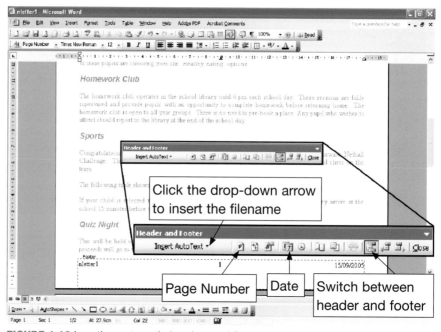

Click the drop-down arrow to insert the filename

Page Number

Date

Switch between header and footer

FIGURE 1.10 Inserting automatic headers and footers

1 Continue working with the file **nletter1**.

2 Insert your name and centre number in the header.

3 Using the Tab key to separate items, enter the following on one line, as a footer:

○ automatic filename

○ automatic page numbers

○ automatic date.

4 Save the file keeping the filename **nletter1**.

Printing a document

You should always check your document before printing. It is a good idea to view the non-printing characters. On the **Standard** toolbar, click on the **Show/Hide** icon ¶ to view the non-printing characters. Hard returns (**Enter** key presses) are represented by the paragraph marker ¶, spaces between words and sentences are represented by a dot •, indents and/or tabs are represented by an arrow →.

To turn off Show/Hide, click on the **Show/Hide** icon again. You should also view the document using **Print Preview** . Multiple pages can be viewed by clicking on the **Multiple Pages** icon (Figure 1.11). Hold down the left mouse button and drag to select how many pages you want to view on the screen.

TIP!

When files are imported between lines/paragraphs of text, there should always be one paragraph marker above and one paragraph marker below the inserted item. If a file has been inserted at the top of a page, there should be no paragraph marker above the inserted item.

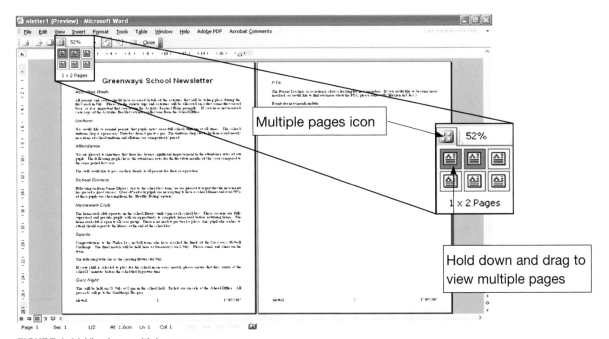

Multiple pages icon

Hold down and drag to view multiple pages

FIGURE 1.11 Viewing multiple pages

▶▶ How to... print a document

1 Check your document using **Show/Hide** and make any necessary changes.

2 View your document using **Print Preview**.

3 Check the layout. Close **Print Preview** to make any necessary changes. If changes have been made, view your document again.

4 Click on the **File** menu, click on **Print**. The **Print** dialogue box will be displayed.

5 Check the settings:

- ● **Page range** should be **All**
- ● **Number of copies** should be **1**
- ● **Pages per sheet** should be **1 page**
- ● **Scale to paper size** should be **No scaling**.

6 Click on **OK**.

7 Proofread the printout carefully. If you spot any mistakes, correct these on-screen and print the document again.

> **TIP!**
>
> Once you have checked your print settings, you can print the document quickly using the **Print** icon 🖨 on the **Formatting** toolbar.

Check your understanding *Print a document*

1 Continue working with the file **nletter1**.

2 Use **Print Preview** to check the formatting of the document. Make any necessary changes.

3 Save the document keeping the filename **nletter1**.

4 Print the document.

5 Proofread the printout carefully. Correct any errors if necessary and print the document again.

▶▶ How to... insert a bulleted or numbered list

1 Select the text to be numbered or bulleted.

2 To insert bullets, on the **Formatting** toolbar, click on the **Bullets** icon.

3 To insert numbers, on the **Formatting** toolbar, click on the **Numbering** icon.

> **TIP!**
>
> You can customise (choose different) bullets. Select the text, click on the **Format** menu, click on **Bullets and Numbering**. The **Bullets and Numbering** dialogue box will be displayed. Select the tab for **Bulleted** or **Numbered**, click on the style of your choice and then on **OK**.

▶▶ How to... insert a page break

1 Place the cursor in front of the first word in the line or paragraph that you want to move to the next page.

2 Hold down **Ctrl** and press **Enter**.

> **TIP!**
>
> When inserting a page break, make sure you do not position your cursor above the paragraph because this will create a blank line at the top of the new page.

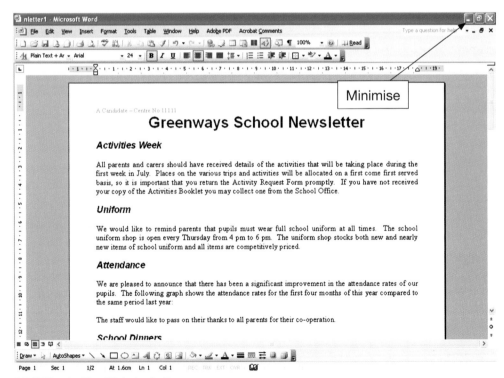

▶▶ How to... *insert an image*

1 Position the cursor in the place that the image is to be inserted.

2 Click on the **Insert** menu, click on **Picture**, click on **From File**. The **Insert Picture** dialogue box will be displayed. In the **Look in** box, locate the folder that contains the image.

3 Click on the image file.

4 Click on **Insert**. The image will now be inserted into the document.

5 Right-click on the image. A menu will appear. Select **Format Picture**. The **Format Picture** dialogue box will be displayed.

6 Click on the **Layout** tab. Select the **Wrapping style** (usually **Tight**). Select the **Horizontal** alignment. Click on the **Advanced** button for more wrapping options (e.g. to wrap the text above and below the image). Click on **OK**.

7 Check the spacing above and below the inserted image and amend if necessary.

▶▶ How to... *insert a graph*

1 Position the cursor in the place where the graph is to be inserted. Click on the **Minimise** button (Figure 1.12).

Minimise

A Candidate – Centre No 11111

Greenways School Newsletter

Activities Week

All parents and carers should have received details of the activities that will be taking place during the first week in July. Places on the various trips and activities will be allocated on a first come first served basis, so it is important that you return the Activity Request Form promptly. If you have not received your copy of the Activities Booklet you may collect one from the School Office.

Uniform

We would like to remind parents that pupils must wear full school uniform at all times. The school uniform shop is open every Thursday from 4 pm to 6 pm. The uniform shop stocks both new and nearly new items of school uniform and all items are competitively priced.

Attendance

We are pleased to announce that there has been a significant improvement in the attendance rates of our pupils. The following graph shows the attendance rates for the first four months of this year compared to the same period last year:

The staff would like to pass on their thanks to all parents for their co-operation.

School Dinners

FIGURE 1.12 The Minimise button

2 Locate and open the file containing the graph.

3 Click on the outside edge of the graph (or border). On the **Standard** toolbar, click on the **Copy** icon.

4 From the taskbar, switch to the Word document.

5 On the **standard** toolbar, click on the **Paste** icon. The graph will now be inserted into the document.

6 Check the spacing above and below the inserted graph and amend if necessary.

7 From the taskbar, close the file containing the graph.

▶▶ How to... *resize images and graphs maintaining proportion*

1 Click on the object to be resized so that the handles appear (Figure 1.13).

2 Position the cursor over any corner handle.

3 Hold down the left mouse button.

4 Drag the handle towards the centre to make the object smaller.

5 Drag the handle away from the centre to make the object larger.

FIGURE 1.13 Resizing pictures and graphs

▶▶ How to... *insert a data file as a table*

1 Position the cursor in the place where the data file is to be inserted.

2 Click on the **Insert** menu, click on **File**. The **Insert File** dialogue box will be displayed.

3 In **Files of Type** select **All Files**.

4 Locate the file to be inserted.

5 Click on the file.

6 Click on **Insert**. The data file will now be inserted into the document (Figure 1.14).

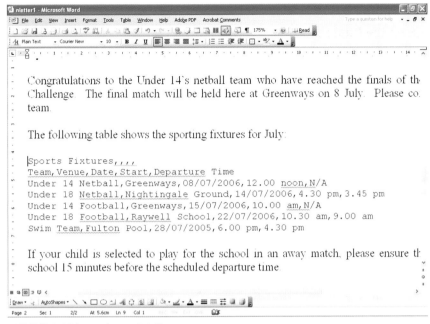

FIGURE 1.14 Importing a datafile

Note how the data in each column is separated by a comma.

▶▶ How to... *convert an imported data file to a table*

1 Select (highlight) all the imported data.

2 Click on the **Table** menu, click on **Insert**, click on **Table**.

3 Your data will now be displayed in a table (Figure 1.15).

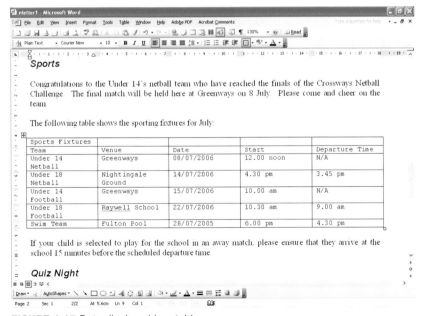

FIGURE 1.15 Data displayed in a table

TIP!

You can insert the data file by opening the file in Excel and copying the data from the file into Word. If you use this method, you may need to adjust the size of the table and/or the column widths when you have inserted the table into your document.

For more control over the layout of your table, you can use the **Convert Text to Table** facility. Once you have inserted your file, click on the **Table** menu, click on **Convert**, click on **Text to Table**. Choose the required settings. Click on **OK**.

4 Check the spacing above and below the inserted data file and amend if necessary.

The draft document on pages 20–22 shows the position where the files, page br eaks and bullets should be inserted. Refer to this when completing each step.

1 Open the file **nletter1** (from your working folder or from the worked copies folder).

2 Insert the image **crest**.

3 Centre the image between the margins.

4 Resize the image to make it smaller, but retain the original proportions.

5 Insert the graph **attend**.

6 Resize the graph to make it smaller, but retain the original proportions.

7 Insert the datafile **sports** as a table.

8 Insert the page break where shown.

9 Apply bullets and 1.5 line spacing to the three lines indicated in the draft document.

10 View your document using the **Show/Hide** facility. Check the following:

- all items have been inserted where specified
- there is one clear line space below the image (a paragraph marker)
- there is one clear line space above and below the graph
- there is one clear line space above and below the table containing the data file
- all pages start on the first line of the page (there are no paragraph markers above the first line of the page).

11 Make any necessary amendments.

12 View your document using the **Print Preview** facility. Your document should fit on to two pages.

13 Save the document as a Word document using the filename **nletter2**.

14 Print the document.

15 Proofread the printout carefully. If you spot any mistakes, correct these on-screen and print the document again.

Draft document

> Insert the image **crest** here

Greenways School Newsletter

Activities Week

All parents and carers should have received details of the activities that will be taking place during the first week in July. Places on the various trips and activities will be allocated on a first come first served basis, so it is important that you return the Activity Request Form promptly. If you have not received your copy of the Activities Booklet you may collect one from the School Office.

Uniform

We would like to remind parents that pupils must wear full school uniform at all times. The school uniform shop is open every Thursday from 4 pm to 6 pm. The uniform shop stocks both new and nearly new items of school uniform and all items are competitively priced.

Attendance

We are pleased to announce that there has been a significant improvement in the attendance rates of our pupils. The following graph shows the attendance rates for the first four months of this year compared to the same period last year:

Insert the graph **attend** here

The staff would like to pass on their thanks to all parents for their co-operation.

Page break

School Dinners

Following on from Jamie Oliver's visit to the school last term, we are pleased to report that the new menu has proved to be a great success. Over 60% of our pupils are now opting to have a school dinner and over 90% of these pupils are choosing from the 'Healthy Eating' options.

Homework Club

The homework club operates in the school library until 6 pm each school day. These sessions are fully supervised and provide pupils with an opportunity to complete homework before returning home. The homework club is open to all year groups. There is no need to pre-book a place. Any pupil who wishes to attend should report to the library at the end of the school day.

Sports

Congratulations to the Under 14's netball team who have reached the finals of the Crossways Netball Challenge. The final match will be held here at Greenways on 8 July. Please come and cheer on the team.

The following table shows the sporting fixtures for July:

Insert the datafile **sports** here

If your child is selected to play for the school in an away match, please ensure that they arrive at the school 15 minutes before the scheduled departure time.

Quiz Night

This will be held on 21 July at 8 pm in the school hall. Tickets are on sale at the School Office. All proceeds will go to the Sandthorpe Hospice.

PTA

The Parent Teachers Association is always looking for new members. If you would like to become more involved, or would like to find out more about the PTA, please contact Ms Morgan in Class 3.

Events for next month include:

Quiz Night
Car Boot Sale | Apply a bullet character to these three lines of text
Theatre Visit

ASSESS YOUR SKILLS – Format a document and integrate files

By working through this section you will have learnt the skills listed below. Read each item to help you decide how confident you feel about each skill.

- set margins and page layout
- format a document
- change line spacing
- copy formatting
- insert headers and footers
- print a document
- format a bulleted or numbered list
- insert a page break
- insert an image
- insert a graph
- resize images and graphs
- insert a datafile as a table
- convert a datafile to a table.

If you feel that you need more practice on any of the skills in the above list, go back and work through those skills again.

If you feel confident move on to Section 3.

3: Format tabular data

LEARNING OUTCOMES

In this section you will learn how to:

- set tab stops
- clear (remove) tabs
- display data in a table
- adjust column widths
- merge table cells
- set column/cell alignment
- set tabs in a table
- add or remove gridlines, borders and shading
- change font size
- change font colour.

When data is displayed in columns or rows, it is referred to as tabular data (i.e. it is in the form of a table). In Word, tabular data can be displayed using tab stops or by using the table facility.

Tab stops

A tab stop is a point on the horizontal ruler that indicates how far the text will be indented or where a column of text will begin. Tab stops allow you to line up text to the left, right or centre of the tab stop, or to a decimal point.

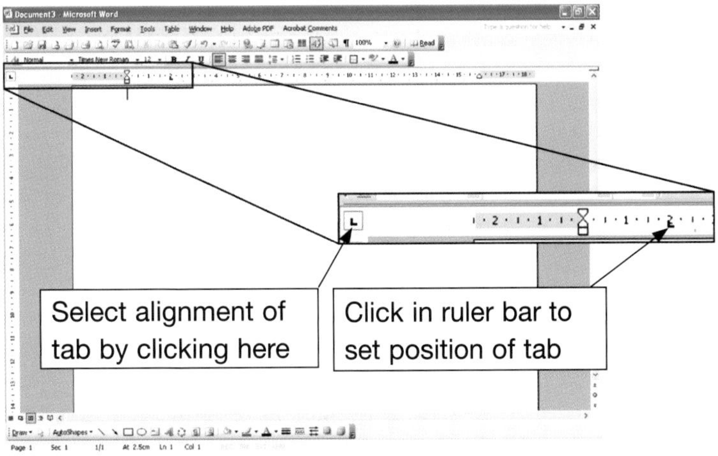

▶▶ How to... set tabs

To select the alignment you require, click on `L` at the end of the ruler bar until it displays the alignment you want (Figure 1.16).

Types of tab:

Left tab `L` *Centre tab* `⊥`
Right tab `⌐` *Decimal tab* `⊥·`

The **Tab** key `⇆` on the keyboard is used to move from one tab stop to the next. Once you have inserted a tab stop, you can adjust the tab by clicking and dragging the tab stop to the required position.

Select alignment of tab by clicking here

Click in ruler bar to set position of tab

FIGURE 1.16 Selecting the alignment of tabs

1 Position the mouse pointer over the tab stop to be removed.

2 Click and hold on the left mouse button.

3 Drag the tab stop away from the ruler (into your document).

4 Check that the tab stop has been removed.

You can set tab points to an exact measurement. Click on the **Format** menu, click on **Tabs**. The **Tabs** dialogue box will be displayed (Figure 1.17). In the **Tab stop position** box, key in the exact position of the tab stops you require (e.g. 2.5). In the **Alignment** box, select the alignment required. Click on Set. When you have set all the required tab stops click on **OK**.

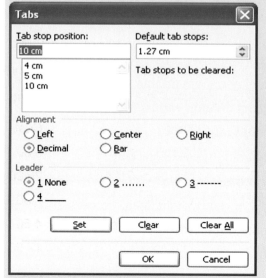

Figure 1.18 is an example of text displayed in columns with different tab stop settings.

FIGURE 1.17 The Tabs dialogue box

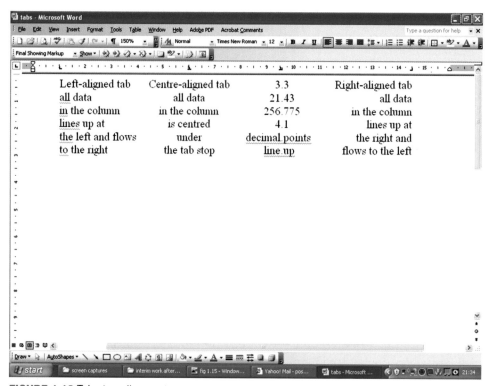

FIGURE 1.18 Tab stop alignment

1 Open a new document.

2 Set your left and right margins to **2 cm**.

3 Set a right-aligned tab stop at **4 cm** for the first column of data.

4 Set a left-aligned tab stop at **5 cm** for the second column of data.

5 Set a decimal-aligned tab stop at **10 cm** for the third column of data.

6 Set a centre-aligned tab stop at **13.5 cm** for the fourth column of data.

7 Key in the following information using the tab settings to align the data:

Number of Places	Event	Cost	Contact
120	Quiz Night	6.50	Mr Redburn
80	Car Boot Sale	25.00	Mrs Patel
200	Concert	3.50	Ms Pavett-Brown
150	Race Evening	4.50	Mr Strover
45	Theatre Visit	17.50	Miss Rashid

8 Format the headings **Number of Places**, **Event**, **Cost** and **Contact** as bold.

9 Enter your name and centre number as a header or footer.

10 Use **Print Preview** to check the layout of the document and amend as necessary.

11 Save the document using the filename **events**.

12 Print the document.

Displaying data in a table

A table is a simple way of displaying data in columns and rows. You can select a different alignment for each cell within the table (e.g. centre, left, right). You can also set tab stops within a table. You learnt how to insert a table in Section 2. In this section you will learn how to format the data in a table.

▶▶ How to... *adjust column widths*

1 Position the mouse pointer over the gridline or border of the column to be adjusted.

2 When the ◀||▶ symbol is displayed, hold down the left mouse button and drag the gridline or border to the desired position.

3 Release the mouse button.

TIP!

When the left mouse button is held down, you can use the arrow keys on the keyboard to adjust the columns instead of dragging the gridline or border.

▶▶ How to... merge table cells

1 Select the cells to be merged.

2 Click on the **Table** menu.

3 Click on **Merge Cells**.

▶▶ How to... set column and cell alignment

1 Select the column(s) or cell(s) to be aligned.

2 On the **Formatting** toolbar, click on the appropriate alignment icon.

▶▶ How to... set tabs in a table

1 Select the column(s) or cell(s) in which you wish to set a tab.

2 Select the alignment of the tab to be set.

3 Click on the ruler bar to set the tab point.

▶▶ How to... align text in a table to a tab stop

1 In the cell in which the tab has been set, click immediately in front of the data to be aligned to the tab point.

2 Hold down **Ctrl + Tab**. The data will move to the tab point.

3 Repeat for all cells containing data to be aligned to the tab point.

Gridlines, borders and shading

When you insert a table, Word will normally display the table with gridlines and borders. When the borders are removed, the gridlines will still be shown in grey on the screen – these gridlines will not print but allow you to adjust your rows and columns easily. The grey non-printing gridlines can also be hidden by selecting the **Table** menu, **Hide Gridlines**.

▶▶ How to... add or remove borders

1 Select the table/column/row/cell to which borders need to be added or removed.

2 On the **Formatting** toolbar, click on the drop-down arrow next to the **Borders** icon (Figure 1.19).

3 Select the required border (or select **No Border** if you do not wish to display any borders).

TIP!

If you have difficulty selecting the table/column/row/cell, click in the table/column/row/cell you wish to select. Click on the **Table** menu, click on **Select**. Choose from **Table/Column/Row/Cell**.

TIP!

If you select **decimal** alignment, Word will automatically align the data to the decimal tab. You will not need to use Ctrl + Tab.

TIP!

To display the ruler bar, click on the **View** menu, click on **Ruler**.

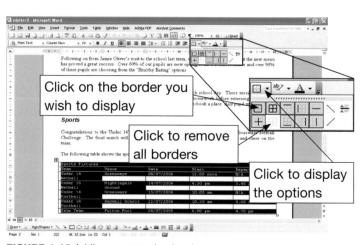

FIGURE 1.19 Adding or removing borders

How to... *change borders and apply shading*

1 Select the table/column/row/cell to which borders need to be added or removed.

2 Click on the **Format** menu, click on **Borders and Shading**.

3 The **Borders and Shading** dialogue box will be displayed (Figure 1.20).

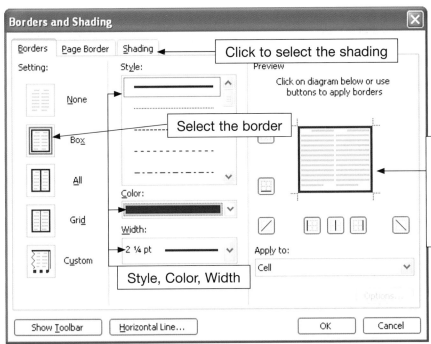

FIGURE 1.20 The Borders and Shading dialogue box

4 Select the **Style**, **Color** and **Width** of your border.

5 Click on the **Shading** tab.

6 Click on the shading required.

7 Click on **OK**.

How to... *change the font size to one not displayed in the drop-down list*

1 Select the text.

2 On the **Formatting** toolbar, click in the **Font Size** box.

3 Enter the font size required.

4 Press **Enter**.

TIP!

Check that your text can be read! If you select very dark shading Word will automatically change the colour of any text in the shaded area to white. You can change the colour yourself by clicking on the drop-down arrow next to the **Font Color** icon on the **Formatting** toolbar, and then selecting the colour required.

1 Select the text.

2 On the **Formatting** toolbar, click on the drop-down arrow next to **Font Color** (Figure 1.21).

3 Click on the colour required.

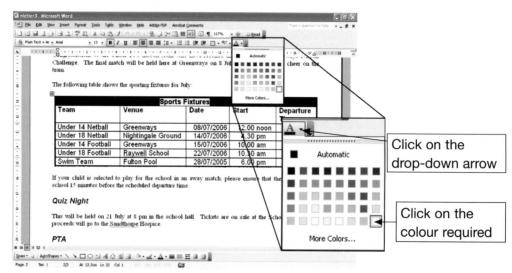

Click on the drop-down arrow

Click on the colour required

FIGURE 1.21 Changing the font colour

Check your understanding *Format tabular data using tables*

You are going to format data in a table

1 Open the document **nletter2**

2 Locate the table containing the **Sports Fixtures**.

3 Format all the data in the table as follows:

Font **Arial**
Font size **13**

4 Apply a thick (2 pt or more) dark border to the outside edge of the entire table.

5 Merge the five cells in the first row of the table only.

6 Apply dark shading to the first row of the table only.

7 Format the text **Sports Fixtures** to be:

white
bold
centre-aligned

8 Format all the data in the second row to be:

bold
left-aligned

9 Adjust the table width so that the left and right borders of the table are within the page margins.

10 Adjust the width of the last column in the table so that the heading **Departure Time** is displayed on two lines. Make sure that words are not split.

11 Adjust the width of the first, second, third and fourth columns so that no entry is displayed on more than one line.

12 Format all the data in the first and second columns to be left-aligned.

13 Format the dates in the third column to be right-aligned. The heading **Date** must remain left-aligned.

14 Format all the times in the fourth column to be aligned with a decimal tab. The heading **Start** must remain left-aligned.

15 Format all the data in the fifth column, under the heading **Departure Time**, to be centre-aligned. The heading **Departure Time** must remain left-aligned.

16 Make sure your name and centre number are displayed as a header.

17 View your document using the Print Preview facility. Your document should fit on to two pages.

18 Save the document using the filename **nletter3**.

19 Print the document.

ASSESS YOUR SKILLS – Format tabular data

By working through this section you will have learnt the skills listed below. Read each item to help you decide how confident you feel about each skill.

- set tab stops
- clear (remove) tabs
- display data in a table
- adjust column widths
- merge table cells
- set column/cell alignment
- set tabs in a table
- add or remove gridlines, borders and shading
- change font size
- change font colour.

If you feel that you need more practice on any of the skills in the above list, go back and work through those skills again.

If you feel confident, move on to Section 4.

LEARNING OUTCOMES

In this section you will learn how to:

- copy text
- insert a special symbol
- format text as superscript or subscript
- find and replace
- use spell check.

In the OCR assignment, you may be required to amend an existing document. This document is likely to be a rich text file. When you save this file, you may save it in the same format (.rtf) or you may save it as a Word document (.doc).

Basic editing techniques

You should already know how to perform basic editing techniques as these were covered at Level 1. You may, however, wish to refer to the Unit 1, Level 1 book to ensure you know how to move, delete and insert text. These skills are also covered in the Quick reference guides starting on page 46 of this book.

▶▶ How to... *copy text*

1 Highlight the text to be copied (make sure you include any punctuation marks after the text).

2 Right-click, a menu displays, click on **Copy**.

3 Click in the position that you want a copy of the text to be placed.

4 Right-click, a menu displays, click on **Paste**. The text will now be copied.

5 Check that the punctuation and spacing before and after the copied text is correct.

TIP!

To locate the text to be edited, use the **Find** facility. From the **Edit** menu, select **Find**. Key in the text to be edited.

TIP!

Use the **Show/Hide** icon to check the spacing.

▶▶ How to... *insert a special symbol*

1 Click in the position you wish to insert a symbol (or highlight the letter to be replaced by a symbol).

2 Click on the **Insert** menu, click on **Symbol**. The **Symbol** dialogue box will be displayed. Click on the **Symbols** tab.

TIP!

If you cannot find the symbol you wish to insert, click on the drop-down arrow next to the **Subset** box and select a different subset of characters to see more alternatives.

Special characters (such as the copyright symbol ©, the trademark symbol ™ and the section symbol §) can be inserted in the same way by clicking on the **Special Characters** tab.

3 Scroll down to find the symbol required.

4 Click on the required symbol, click on **Insert**.

5 Click on **Close**. The symbol will now be inserted into your document.

▶▶ How to... *format text as superscript or subscript*

1 Select the character to be made superscript or subscript.

2 Click on the **Format** menu, click on **Font**. The **Font** dialogue box will be displayed.

3 Click in the **Superscript** or **Subscript** checkbox, as required.

4 Click on **OK**.

Find and replace

At Level 2 you will need to use the more advanced features of find and replace (e.g. whole-word and case-sensitive searches). Although you could do this manually, it is more efficient to use the **Find and Replace** function as this is quicker and will ensure that all words are replaced.

▶▶ How to... *find and replace*

1 Click on the **Edit** menu, click on **Replace**.

2 The **Find and Replace** dialogue box will be displayed. Click on | More ≽ |.

3 More options are displayed (Figure 1.22). In the box next to **Find what** key in the text to be replaced.

4 In the box next to **Replace with** key in the replacement text.

5 In the **Search Options**, select how you want the replace to be performed (e.g. **Find whole words only**, **Match case**).

6 Click on **Replace All**.

7 A window will be displayed telling you how many replacements were made.

8 Click on **OK**.

9 Click on the **Close** button to close the Find and Replace dialogue box.

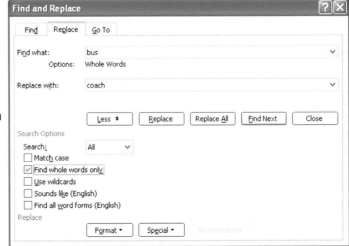

FIGURE 1.22 The Find and Replace dialogue box

Checking the spelling of a document

You will need to check the spelling of your documents. Always make sure that the language is set to English UK. From the **Tools** menu, select **Language**, click on **Set Language**, select **English (U.K.)**. Click on **OK**.

TIP!

Remember, the spell checker will only identify words that are incorrectly spelt. It will not identify errors such as 'in' instead of 'on'. You will need to proofread your work carefully to make sure that you have not made any errors like this.

1 On the **Standard** toolbar click on the **Spelling and Grammar** icon ✓ (or press **F7**). The **Spelling and Grammar English U.K.** dialogue box will be displayed.

2 Check that the box in front of **Check grammar** is *not* ticked.

3 Word will identify any incorrectly spelt or duplicated words in red.

4 Look at the word carefully to make sure that the spelling is incorrect.

5 If the word is incorrectly spelt, select the correct word from the suggestions listed. Click on **Change**.

6 If the word is a 'specialist word' (e.g. a name), click on **Ignore All**.

7 If there is a duplicated word, read the text to make sure it should be deleted.

8 Click on **Delete**.

9 When the spell check has been completed, click on **OK**.

> **TIP!**
>
> If a word is not displayed in the **Suggestions** box, you can edit the word in the Spelling and Grammar dialogue box and then click on **Change**. If the word is still not recognised, Word will give you a warning so that you can choose not to make the change.

Check your understanding *Amend documents*

1 Open the rich text file (.rtf) **water**.

2 In the first paragraph make the **2** in **H2O** a subscript character.

3 In the first paragraph delete the final sentence:

> **All glass containers will be confiscated.**

> **TIP!**
>
> Use the **Find** facility (**Edit** menu → **Find**) to locate the text to be edited.

4 At the end of the document enter the following text as the final paragraph under the subheading **Reminder**:

> **Please ensure that the final payment for this trip has been handed to Mrs José by the end of this week.**

5 Make sure you have inserted the special character in the word **José**.

6 Replace all instances of the word **bus** with the word **coach** wherever it occurs (three times in all). Ensure that you replace whole words only.

7 Spell check the document and correct any errors. Spellings must be in English UK.

8 Delete any duplicated words, but do not change the grammar of the document.

9 Do not change specialist words.

10 Insert your name and centre number as a header or a footer.

11 Check your document using Print Preview and correct as necessary.

12 Save your document as a Word file with the filename **tripinfo**.

13 Print the document.

14 Close the document.

ASSESS YOUR SKILLS – Amend documents

By working through this section you will have learnt the skills listed below. Read each item to help you decide how confident you feel about each skill.

- copy text

- insert a special symbol

- format text as superscript or subscript

- find and replace

- use spell check.

If you feel that you need more practice on any of the skills in the above list, go back and work through those skills again.

If you feel confident, move on to Section 5.

5: Create mail merge documents and protect files

LEARNING OUTCOMES

In this section you will learn how to:

- create a mail merge master document
- insert merge fields
- format mail merge documents
- produce a screen print
- password protect a document (protect files)
- open a previously saved mail merge master document
- find a data source
- reattach a data source
- create a mail merge query
- perform a mail merge.

Mail merge

Mail merge enables you to combine information that will be the same in every document you send out (e.g. the body of the letter) with information that will be unique in every document (e.g. the name of the person who will receive the letter).

Mail merge takes information from a *data source* (a file that contains information unique to each recipient of the message) and inserts this into a copy of the *master document* (the message that will be the same for every recipient).

The places in the master document that will contain the unique information are called *merge fields*. These fields are enclosed within brackets: << >>. In the examples shown in Figures 1.23 and 1.24, when the mail merge was performed, Word would take the information from the data source and insert it where shown in the master document to produce individual invitations.

We have pleasure in welcoming

<<First Name>> <<Last Name>>

to Birmingham

Mail merge master document

First Name	Last Name
Amir	Khan
Sarah	Smith
Michael	O'Regan

Data source

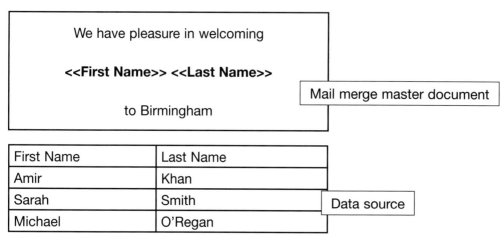

FIGURE 1.23 Extracting information from the data source to be inserted into the mail merge master document

We have pleasure in welcoming

Amir Khan

to Birmingham

We have pleasure in welcoming

Sarah Smith

to Birmingham

We have pleasure in welcoming

Michael O'Regan

to Birmingham

FIGURE 1.24 The individual invitations

The finished merged documents are not normally saved because they can be very large files that would take up a great deal of disk space. The mail merge, however, can be recreated very easily from the original master document and data source.

Before you begin any mail merge tasks make sure the Mail Merge toolbar is displayed.

▶▶ How to... *display the Mail Merge toolbar*

Click on the **View** menu, select **Toolbars**. On the drop-down list, click on **Mail Merge** (Figure 1.25).

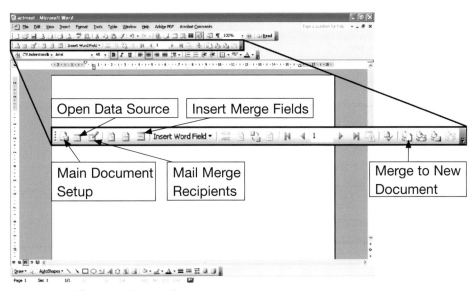

FIGURE 1.25 The Mail Merge toolbar

▶▶ How to... *create a mail merge master document*

1 On the **Mail Merge** toolbar, click on the **Main Document Setup** icon.

2 Click on the type of document required (this will usually be **Letters**).

3 Click on **OK**.

4 On the **Mail Merge** toolbar, click on the **Open Data Source** icon. The **Select Data Source** dialogue box will be displayed.

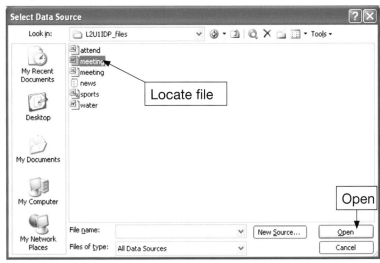

FIGURE 1.26 The Select Data Source dialogue box

5 Click on the drop-down arrow next to the **Look in** box. Locate the data file to be used (Figure 1.26).

6 Click on the file.

7 Click on **Open**.

Note: The file does not display, but some icons on the Mail Merge toolbar become active.

> ▶▶ **How to...** insert a merge field into a mail merge master document

1 With your mail merge master document open on the screen, click in the position you wish to insert the merge field.

2 On the **Mail Merge** toolbar, click on the **Insert Merge Fields** icon. The **Insert Merge Field** dialogue box will be displayed (Figure 1.27).

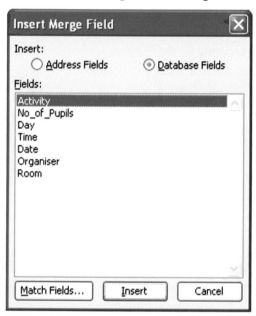

FIGURE 1.27 The Insert Merge Field dialogue box

3 Click on the field to be inserted.

4 Click on **Insert**.

5 Click on **Close**.

6 Repeat steps 2 to 5 to insert any other required fields.

7 Save the master document.

Formatting mail merge documents

The formatting that you select for the mail merge master document will be applied to all the documents in the mail merge. It is a good idea, therefore, to open the data source before you prepare your mail merge master document, so that you know how much information will be inserted when the documents are merged. You can format the document to suit the data.

TIP!

If you have a choice, use the .csv file as your data source. This may save you from having to reattach the data file when you perform your mail merge (see page 40).

TIP!

Check that the spacing before and after an inserted merge field is correct. If two merge fields are inserted next to each other they will appear as one word unless a space is inserted between the two fields.

TIP!

If you have a short document it will look better if it is centred vertically on the page. From the **File** menu, select **Page Setup**, click on **Layout** tab. Next to the **Vertical alignment**, click the drop-down arrow to select **Center**. Click on OK.

1 Create a new mail merge master document suitable for displaying a notice (Select **Letters**).

2 Use A4 portrait orientation. You may use any margins to suit your document.

3 Key in the following text, inserting merge fields from the **meeting** data file. Follow the line endings and ensure that there is at least one clear line or paragraph space where shown:

> [insert **Activity** merge field]
>
> **Please Meet In**
> [clear line space]
> [insert **Room** merge field]
> [clear line space]
> At [insert **Time** merge field]
> [clear line space]
> **On**
> [clear line space]
> [insert **Day** merge field]
>
> [insert **Date** merge field]

4 Format the entire document as follows:

Horizontal alignment	**centre**
Vertical alignment	**centre**
Emphasis	**bold**

5 You may use any legible font and font size.

6 Insert your name and centre number as a header or footer.

7 Save the master document using the filename **actmeet**.

8 Print a copy of the document **actmeet** on one page showing the merge fields.

9 Proofread the printout carefully. If you spot any mistakes, correct these on-screen and print the document again.

10 Close the document.

Protecting files

There may be occasions when you wish to protect documents from being amended or viewed by others. You can do this by setting a password for the document.

A password can be set to 'read-only' so that people are able to open and read the file but cannot make any changes unless they have the password, or the password can be set to 'password to open' so that only people with the password can open the file.

Passwords are case sensitive. This means that a letter is treated as a different character when it is in upper case (e.g. M) and in lower case (e.g. m).

A password should be something that other people would find very difficult to guess. For maximum protection, passwords should be a random combination of numbers, upper and lower case letters. Remember that you will not be able to open the document if you cannot remember the password you have set.

▶▶ How to... *produce a screen print*

1 Display the window or dialogue box that you wish to screen print.

2 To take a copy of the whole screen, press the **Print Screen** key on the keyboard (this will make a copy of the entire screen).

3 To take a copy of the active window only, press **Alt** + **Print Screen**.

4 Open a new Word document.

5 Right-click in the new document. From the menu, select **Paste**.

▶▶ How to... *password protect a document*

1 Open the document you wish to protect.

2 Click on the **Tools** menu, click on **Options**. The **Options** dialogue box will be displayed.

3 Select the **Security** tab.

4 If you do not want other people to access the file, in the box next to **Password to open** key in the password.

5 If you do not want other people to edit the file, in the box next to **Password to modify** key in the password.

6 Click on **OK**.

7 The **Confirm Password** window will be displayed (Figure 1.28).

8 Key in the password again.

9 Click on **OK**.

10 Save and close the document.

FIGURE 1.28 The Confirm Password box

> **TIP!**
>
> The Print Screen key may be labelled Prt Sc or Prnt Scrn (or similar).

> **TIP!**
>
> Don't forget to add your name and centre number to screen prints.
>
> You can save all your screen prints in one document and print when you have completed your assignment.

Check your understanding *Protect a file*

1 Open the document **actmeet**.

2 Using the password **Mo7mtg19**, protect the file **actmeet** from unauthorised access (Password to open).

3 Save the file using the filename **passmeet**.

4 Close the document.

open a previously saved mail merge master document

When you open a previously saved mail merge master document, Word may sometimes not find the data source that you had originally attached to the document. If the message shown in Figure 1.29 is displayed when you open your mail merge master document, you will need to follow the instructions under 'How to... find your data source' (below).

If your data source still fails to open, follow the instructions under 'How... to reattach your data source' (page 40).

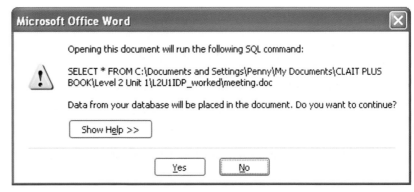

FIGURE 1.29 Find Data Source

1 Locate and open the mail merge master document.

2 If the message shown in Figure 1.29 is displayed, click on **Yes** (do not press Enter).

3 Your master mail merge document should now open.

4 Follow the instructions under 'How to... create a mail merge query' (page 41).

▶▶ How to... *find your data source*

If the message in Figure 1.30 displays when you try to open your master document:

1 Click on the **Find Data Source** button.

2 The **Select Data Source** dialogue box will be displayed (Figure 1.31).

3 Click on the drop-down arrow next to the **Look in** box. Locate the data file to be used.

4 Click on **Open**.

5 Your mail merge master document should now open.

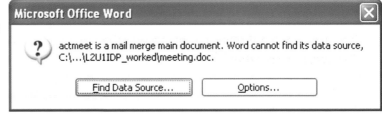

FIGURE 1.30 Opening the mail merge master document

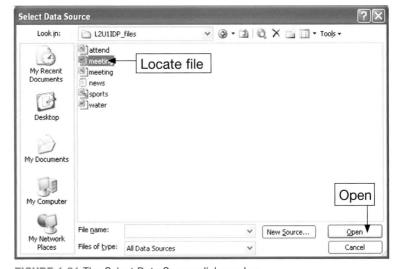

FIGURE 1.31 The Select Data Source dialogue box

If, after trying to find the data source, the message shown in Figure 1.32 is displayed again, you may need to reattach the file.

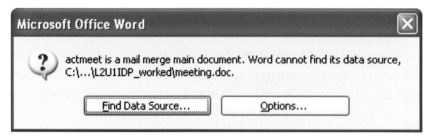

FIGURE 1.32 Opening the mail merge master document

1 If so, in the message window click on the **Options** button.

2 The message shown in Figure 1.33 will appear.

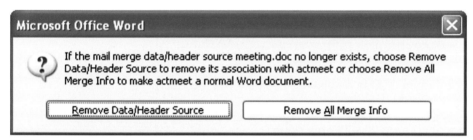

FIGURE 1.33 Remove Data/Header Source

3 Click on **Remove Data/Header Source** button.

4 Your document will now open, but you will need to reattach your data file.

5 On the **Mail Merge** toolbar, click on the **Open Data Source** icon .

6 The **Select Data Source** dialogue box will be displayed (Figure 1.34).

7 Click on the drop-down arrow next to the **Look in** box. Locate the datafile to be used.

8 Click on **Open**.

9 Your data source will now be attached and the mail merge master document will be displayed in Word.

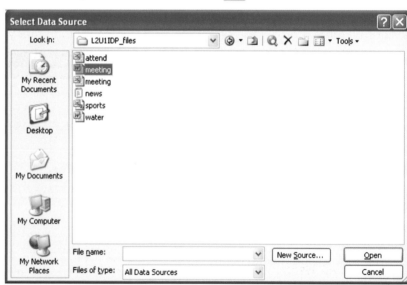

FIGURE 1.34 The Select Data Source dialogue box

▶▶ **How to...** create a mail merge query

1 Open the mail merge master document.

2 Make sure the **Mail Merge** toolbar is displayed.

3 On the **Mail Merge** toolbar, click on the **Mail Merge Recipients** icon ✏.

4 The **Mail Merge Recipients** dialogue box will be displayed (Figure 1.35).

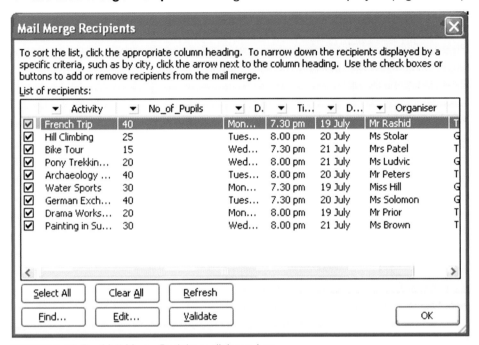

FIGURE 1.35 The Mail Merge Recipients dialogue box

To select particular records only:

1 Click on the drop-down arrow next to the column containing the data you wish to query to select it.

2 From the list shown, click on the criterion for the records that you wish to select (e.g. Monday).

3 The dialogue box will now display a list of the records that have been selected. Check that this is correct.

4 Click on **OK**.

5 The file is ready to be merged.

▶▶ **How to...** perform a mail merge

1 After performing the mail merge query, on the **Mail Merge** toolbar, click on the **Merge to New Document** icon 🔁.

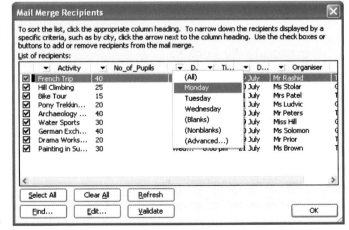

FIGURE 1.36 Selecting recipients

2 The **Merge to New Document** dialogue box will be displayed (Figure 1.37).

FIGURE 1.37 The Merge to New Document dialogue box

3 Click on **All**.

4 Click on **OK**.

5 All the merged documents will be contained in one new document.

6 Use **Print Preview** to check the layout of the merged documents before printing.

Check your understanding
File protection and perform a mail merge

1 Prepare to open the document **passmeet**.

2 Take a screen print to show evidence that password protection has been set.

3 Enter your name in the screen print document.

4 Save this screen print for printing later.

5 Enter the password **Mo7mtg19** to open the document.

6 Create a mail merge query to find all the activity meetings where the **Day** is **Monday**.

7 Merge the query to a new document.

8 Check the display of your mail merge.

9 Print the results.

10 More copies of this mail merge may need to be printed at a later date. Save this document using the filename **mergemon**.

11 Print a copy of the screen print you saved at Step 4.

ASSESS YOUR SKILLS – Create mail merge documents and protect files

By working through this chapter you will have learnt the skills listed below. Read each item to help you decide how confident you feel about each skill.

- display the Mail Merge toolbar
- create a mail merge master document
- insert merge fields
- format mail merge documents
- produce a screen print
- password protect a document
- open a previously saved mail merge master document
- find a data source
- reattach a data source
- create a mail merge query
- perform a mail merge.

If you feel that you need more practice on any of the skills in the above list, go back and work through those skills again.

If you feel confident, move on to Section 6.

6: Archive files

LEARNING OUTCOMES

In this section you will learn how to:

- archive files.

Archiving files

Archiving is the term used when you store files that must be kept safe but that will not be used on a day-to-day basis. It enables you to keep your working area tidy and, depending on the method you use, it can save disk space.

There are many methods of archiving files. In this book we will cover two. The most common method of archiving files is to compress them using file compression software such as WinZip.

If you do not have file compression software installed on your computer you can simply move the files to a different place (e.g. a CD-ROM, floppy disk, memory stick or even a folder within your working area).

▶▶ How to... *archive files to a compressed folder*

1 In your working area, locate all the files to be archived. Select the files by holding down the **Ctrl** key and clicking on each of the files to be archived. When they have all been selected, release the **Ctrl** key.

2 Position the mouse pointer over one of the selected files.

3 Right-click. From the menu, select **Send To**, select **Compressed (zipped) Folder**.

4 The files will now be in a zipped folder (the folder will have the name of one of the files).

5 The original files should still be selected. If not, re-select them. Press the **Del** key to delete the original files.

6 You may rename the compressed folder to give it a more sensible name or you may leave the filename as it is. You may wish to move the compressed folder into another area.

7 Take a screen print of your working area showing the compressed folder.

8 Double-click on the zipped folder to open it.

9 Take a screen print to show the contents of the zipped folder.

▶▶ How to... *archive files to a different area/folder*

1 In your working area, locate all the files to be archived. Take a screen print of your working area showing the files that are to be archived.

2 Select the files by holding down the **Ctrl** key and clicking on each of the files to be archived. When they have all been selected, release the **Ctrl** key.

3 Position the mouse pointer over one of the selected files.

4 Right-click. From the menu, select **Cut**.

5 Locate the area/folder where the files are to be moved. You may wish to create a new folder in the new area for the archived files.

6 Right-click. From the pop-up menu, select **Paste**. The files should now appear in the new area.

7 Take a screen print showing the files in the new location.

8 Take a screen print of your working area that shows the files are no longer there.

> **TIP!**
>
> These instructions are for Windows XP.

▶▶ How to... *archive files to a compressed folder using WinZip*

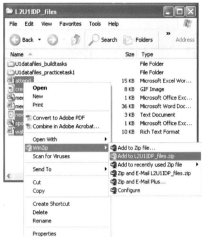

1 Follow steps 1–2 from How to... archive files to a compressed folder on page 44.

2 Right-click. From the menu, select **Add to *folder name*.zip** (the folder name will be the name of your working area) (Figure 1.38).

3 The files will now be in a zipped folder with the same folder name as your working area.

4 The original files should still be selected, if not then re-select them. Press the **Del** key to delete the original files.

5 You may rename the zipped folder to give it a more sensible name or you may leave the filename as it is.

6 Take a screen print of your working area showing the compressed folder.

7 Double-click on the zipped folder to open it.

8 Take a screen print to show the contents of the zipped folder.

FIGURE 1.38 Selecting files to archive with WinZip

Check your understanding *Archive files*

1 Archive the files **attend**, **crest**, **news**, **sports** and **water**.

2 Take screen print(s) to show they have been archived.

3 Enter your name and centre number as a header or a footer.

4 Save and print the screen print(s).

ASSESS YOUR SKILLS – Archive files

By working through this section you will have learnt the skills listed below. Read each item to help you decide how confident you feel about each skill.

◎ archive files.

If you feel that you need more practice on any of the skills in the above list, go back and work through those skills again.

If you feel confident move on to the Build-up and Practice tasks on page 52.

QUICK REFERENCE – Create an integrated document

Keep a copy of this page next to you. Refer to it when working through tasks and during any assessments.

HOW TO...	METHOD
Open a generic file	Locate the file to be opened → position the cursor over the file → right-click → Open With → Choose Program → select the program → click on OK.
Open a .txt or .rtf file in Word	Click on the Open icon → locate the folder in which the file is stored → click on the drop-down arrow at the end of the Files of type box → click on All Files → select the file → Open.
Save files in non-generic and generic formats	Click on the File menu → Save As → click on the drop-down arrow next to the Save as type box → select the format required → click on Save.
Work with several open files	From Windows Explorer or My Computer → open the folder containing the files → open the first file → on the taskbar, click on the folder containing the other files → the folder window will be displayed → open another file → on the taskbar, click on the folder containing the other files → the folder window will be displayed → open the next file → all open documents will appear in the taskbar → click on the document you want to work with → the document will be displayed on the screen → click on another document to switch between documents.
Close files from the taskbar	Position the mouse over the file to be closed → right-click → Close.
Set margins and page layout	Click on the File menu → Page Setup → Margins tab → enter the margins → click to select the orientation → check the Preview section to ensure Apply to is set to Whole document → click on the drop-down arrow to change if necessary → click on the Paper tab → check the Paper size is set to A4 → click on the drop-down arrow to change if necessary → click on the Print Options button → make sure Allow A4/Letter paper resizing is *not* ticked → click on OK → OK.
Format an entire document	Press Ctrl + A → use the Formatting toolbar to set the font, size, emphasis and alignment → click on the Format menu → Paragraph → Indents and Spacing tab → check the indentation → Left and Right will normally be set to 0 cm and Special to (none) → change if necessary → check the spacing → Before and After will normally be set to 0 pt and Line spacing to Single → change if necessary → click on the Line and Page Breaks tab → check the Widow/Orphan control is ticked → click to tick if necessary.

HOW TO...	METHOD
Format a single line of text	Select the text → use the Formatting toolbar to set the font, size, emphasis and alignment.
Change line spacing	Select the text → click on the Format menu → Paragraph → Indents and Spacing tab → under Spacing → click on the down arrow next to Line spacing → select the spacing required.
Copy formatting	Select the formatted text → double-click on the Format Painter → highlight the lines/paragraphs to be formatted in the same style → click on the Format Painter again to deselect it.
Insert headers and footers	Click on the View menu → Header and Footer → in the Header box, key in the required information → to switch to the footer → click on the Switch Between Header and Footer icon → to key in several items on the same line, press the Tab key → adjust the tab position by holding down the Tab symbol and drag it to the position required → click on the appropriate icon to insert automatic date/filename/page numbers.
Print a document	Check the document using Show/Hide and make any necessary changes → view the document using Print Preview → check the layout → close Print Preview to make any necessary changes → if changes have been made → view the document again → Click on the File menu → Print → check the printer settings page range should be All → number of copies should be 1 → pages per sheet should be 1 page → Scale to paper size should be No scaling → click on OK.
Insert a bulleted or numbered list	Select the text to be numbered or bulleted To insert bullets → click on the Bullets icon To insert numbers → click on the Numbering icon.
Insert a page break	Place the cursor in front of the first word in the line or paragraph that you want to move to the next page → hold down Ctrl and press Enter.
Insert an image	Place the cursor in the position the image is to be inserted → click on Insert menu → Picture → From File → locate the image to be inserted → click on Insert.
Format an image	Right-click on the image → Format Picture → Layout tab → select the wrapping style (usually tight) → select horizontal alignment → click on the Advanced button for more wrapping options → click on OK. Check the spacing above and below the image.
Insert a graph	Place the cursor in the position the graph is to be inserted → click on Minimise Word → open the file containing the graph → click on the outside edge of the graph (or border) → click on the Copy icon → from the taskbar switch to the Word document → click on the Paste icon. Check the spacing above and below the graph.

(continued overleaf)

HOW TO...	METHOD
Resize images and graphs maintaining proportion	Click on the object to be resized so that the handles appear → position the cursor over any corner handle → hold down the left mouse button → drag towards the centre to make the object smaller → drag away from the centre to make the object larger.
Insert a data file	Place the cursor in the position the data file is to be inserted → click on the Insert menu → File → in Files of Type select All Files → locate the data file to be inserted → click on Insert.
Display a data file as a table	Select all the imported data → click on the Table menu → Insert → Table. Check the spacing above and below the data file and amend if necessary.
Set tab stops	Click on the Format menu → Tabs → key in the position → select the alignment → click on Set → repeat until all tabs are set → click on OK.
Clear (remove) tabs	Position the cursor over the tab stop to be removed → click and hold the left mouse button → drag the tab stop away from the ruler → check the tab stop has been removed.
Adjust column widths	Position the mouse pointer over the gridline/border to be adjusted → when the symbol is displayed, hold down the left mouse button and drag the gridline or border to the desired position → release the mouse button.
Merge table cells	Select the cells to be merged → click on the Table menu → Merge Cells.
Set column/cell alignment	Select the column(s) or cell(s) to be aligned → on the Formatting toolbar, click the appropriate alignment icon.
Set tabs in a table	Select the column(s) or cell(s) in which you wish to set a tab → select the alignment of the tab to be set → click in the ruler bar to set the tab point.
Apply tab settings in a table	In the cell in which the tab has been set, click immediately in front of the data to be aligned to the tab point → hold down Ctrl + Tab → the data will move to the tab point → repeat for all cells containing data to be aligned to the tab point.
Add or remove borders	Select the table/column/row/cell to which borders need to be added or removed → on the Formatting toolbar, click on the drop-down arrow next to the Borders icon → select the border required or select No border.
Change borders	Select the table/column/row/cell to which borders need to be added or removed → click on the Format menu → Borders and Shading → select the Style, Color and Width → click on OK.
Apply shading	Select the table/column/row/cell to which borders need to be added or removed → click on the Format menu → Borders and Shading → Shading tab → click on the shading required → click on OK.

HOW TO...	METHOD
Change font size	Select the text → on the Formatting toolbar, click in the Font Size box → enter the font size required → press Enter.
Change font colour	Select the text → on the Formatting toolbar, click the drop-down arrow next to Font Color → click on the colour required.
Move text	Select all the text to be moved → right-click → Cut → position the cursor in the place where the text is to be moved to → right-click → Paste. Check punctuation has moved with the text → check spacing is correct.
Insert text	Position the cursor in place where the text is to be inserted → key in the text. Check punctuation and spacing is correct.
Delete text	Select the text to be deleted → press the Del key on the keyboard. Check punctuation and spacing is correct.
Copy text	Highlight all the text to be copied → right-click → Copy → click in the position that you want a copy of the text to be placed → right-click → Paste. Check punctuation and spacing is correct.
Insert a special symbol	Click in the position you wish to insert a symbol or highlight the letter to be replaced by a symbol → click on the Insert menu → Symbol → Symbols tab → scroll down to select the symbol required → click on the symbol → Insert → Close.
Format text as superscript or subscript	Select the character to be made superscript or subscript → click on the Format menu → Font tab → click in the Superscript or Subscript checkbox → click on OK.
Find and replace	Click on the Edit menu → Replace → More → in the box next to Find what key in the text to be replaced → in the box next to Replace with key in the replacement text → in the Search Options select how you want the replace to be performed → click on Replace All → OK → Close.
Spell check	Click on the Spelling and Grammar icon or Press F7 → select the correct word from the suggestions listed → click on Change. If there is a duplicated word, click on Delete → if the word is a 'specialist word' → click on Ignore All → click on OK.

Keep a copy of this page next to you. Refer to it when working through tasks and during any assessments.

QUICK REFERENCE – Use mail merge, protect and archive files

HOW TO...	METHOD
Display the Mail Merge toolbar	Click on the View menu → Toolbars → Mail Merge.
Create a mail merge master document	On the Mail Merge toolbar → click on the Main Document Setup icon → click on the type of document required → click on the Open Data Source icon → click on the drop-down arrow next to the Look in box → locate the data file to be used → click on Open.
Insert a merge field	Click in the position you wish to insert the merge field → on the Mail Merge toolbar, click on the Insert Merge Fields icon → in the Insert Merge Field dialogue box, click on the field to be inserted → Insert → Close.
Produce a screen print	Display the window → to take a copy of the whole screen, press the Print Screen key. To take a copy of the active window only, press Alt + Prt Sc → open a new Word document → right-click → Paste.
Password protect a document	Open the document → click on the Tools menu → Options → Security tab → if you do not want other people to access the file, in the box next to Password to open → key in the password → if you do not want other people to edit the file, in the box next to Password to modify → key in the password → click on OK → the Confirm Password window will be displayed → key in the password again → click on OK.
Open a previously saved mail merge master document	Locate and open the mail merge master document → a message displays → click on Yes.
Find the data source	From the window displaying the message that Word cannot find the data source, click on Find Data Source → click on the drop-down arrow next to the Look in box → locate the data file to be used → click on Open.
Reattach the data source	From the window displaying the message that Word cannot find the data source → click on Options → Remove Data/ Header Source → on the Mail Merge toolbar, click on the Open Data Source icon → click on the drop-down arrow next to the Look in box → locate the data file to be used → click on Open.

HOW TO...	METHOD
Create a mail merge query	Open the mail merge master document → on the Mail Merge toolbar, click on the Mail Merge Recipients icon → the Mail Merge Recipients dialogue box will be displayed → to find particular records only, click on the drop-down arrow next to the column containing the data you wish to query → from the list shown, click on the criterion for the records that you wish to select → the window will now show a list of the records that have been selected → click on OK.
Perform a mail merge	On the Mail Merge toolbar, click on the Merge to New Document icon → the Merge to New Document dialogue box will be displayed → click on All → OK. Use Print Preview to check the layout of the merged documents before printing.
Archive files to a compressed folder	Select the files to be archived by holding down the Ctrl key and clicking on each file → release the Ctrl key → position the cursor over one of the selected files → right-click → Send To → Compressed (zipped) Folder → the folder will have the name of one of the files → the original files should still be selected → if not, reselect them → press the Del key to delete the original files → you may rename the compressed folder.
Open a compressed/ zipped folder	Double-click on the compressed folder.
Archive files to a different area/folder	Take a screen print of your working area showing the files to be archived → select the files to be archived by holding down the Ctrl key and clicking on each file → release the Ctrl key → position the cursor over one of the selected files → right-click → Cut → locate the area/folder where the files are to be moved → right-click → Paste. Take a screen print showing the files in the new location → take a screen print of your working area to show that the files are no longer there.

The files for the Build-up tasks are in a folder called **U1datafiles_buildtasks**.

Before you begin this task, make sure you have the access to the files **fdoutlets**, **quick** and **popular**.

You have been asked to prepare an information leaflet about fast-food restaurants.
The text and files to be inserted have already been prepared. You will need to combine the files into one document and format the document as instructed below.

1 Load Word and, from within Word, open the text file **fdoutlets**.

2 Save this document as a Word document using the filename **restrnts**.

3 Format the entire document as follows:

Paper size	**A4 portrait**
Top margin	**2 cm** (other margins may be set to suit your document)
Alignment	**left**
Font	**Arial**
Emphasis	**none**
Font size	**12**
Line spacing	**single** (except where specified)

4 Format the heading **Popularity of Fast Food Outlets** as follows:

Alignment	**centre**
Font	**Times New Roman**
Emphasis	**bold**
Font size	**24**

5 Format the subheadings as follows:

Alignment	**left**
Font	**Times New Roman**
Emphasis	**bold, italic**
Font size	**16**

The subheadings are:

Discount Meals

Parties

Design

6 Refer to the draft document on pages 54–55 and make the following amendments.

a Insert the image **quick**.

b Centre this image between the margins of the page. The picture may be resized, but the original proportions must be maintained.

c Insert the graph contained in the file **popular**. Ensure that all the data in the graph is legible. The graph must fit on the first page of your document. You may resize the graph to achieve this.

d Ensure that there is at least one clear line space above and below the graph.

e Insert a page break in the document where shown.

f Insert bullets and double line spacing where indicated in the draft document.

g Ensure that the original alignment, font size and font style are retained.

7 Create the following headers and footers:

Header   **your name and centre number**

Footer   **automatic date and automatic filename**

8 Save the file keeping the filename **restrnts**.

9 Print one copy of the document **restrnts**.

BUILD-UP TASK ② *Insert a data file and format an integrated document*

Before you begin this task, make sure you have access to the files **staff** and **restrnts** that you created in Build-up task 1. You will need to insert a data file provided in .csv format into your integrated document as a table. You will then need to check the layout of the document before printing.

1 Using the file **restrnts**, refer to the draft document on pages 54–55 and insert the datafile **staff**. Ensure that this is displayed as a table.

2 Format all the data in the table as follows:

Font   **Arial**

Font size   **12**

Alignment   **centre** (the text may be wrapped, but words must not be split)

3 To make the table easier to read some additional formatting is required.

a Merge the four cells in the first row of the table.

b Apply dark shading to the first row of the table only.

c Format the text **AVERAGE STAFF PAY AND BENEFITS** to white.

d Embolden the data in the second row of the table only.

e Display gridlines and borders for the entire table.

f Adjust the column widths so that no entry is displayed on more than two lines.

g Ensure that the text of the table is entirely within the page margins.

h Ensure that there is at least one clear line space above the table.

(continued overleaf)

4 Check the document to ensure that:

   a All instructions have been carried out

   b All items are positioned within the margins of the page

   c The imported data file is not split across pages

   d Page breaks have been inserted where specified

   e There are no additional line spaces at the top of pages

   f Subheadings are not split from related text

   g Spacing between subheadings and related text is consistent

   h There are no widows or orphans

   i Spacing between paragraphs is consistent

   j Text, images and lines are not superimposed

   k There is at least one clear line space above and below the graph and above the table containing the imported data file.

5 Save the file using the filename **restrnts1.**

6 Print one copy of the document **restrnts1.**

Draft document

Popularity of Fast Food Outlets

Insert the image **quick** centred between each margin

Fast food outlets have become very popular with all age groups. There are several reasons for this. Meals are relatively cheap, service is very quick, prices are relatively low and these outlets can be found on almost every high street, shopping mall and city centre. A recent survey suggests the reasons why a large majority of the population in many western countries choose to eat at fast food outlets as shown in the graph below:

Insert the graph from the file **popular** here

Fast food restaurants use several methods to target customers.

Discount Meals

Regular, innovative offers of set meals at lower prices are available. Often these are linked with a current theme, e.g. a big box office film. Free gifts or souvenirs are particularly tempting to children. Marketing ploys are used to get children to buy the same meals by rewarding them with a collection of a set of toys; this increases sales since children may only buy the meal to collect the toy.

Page break

Parties

Having parties catered for is always popular with customers. Many restaurants reserve a special area for parties and often employ one or two fully trained party entertainers to organise and provide entertainment. The restaurants include food, entertainment, exclusive seating areas, party bags and the birthday cake. Their aim is to offer an all-inclusive party to save customers the time and worry of organising parties themselves.

Often, party guests can choose their meal from a wide selection or special meals at reduced rates are available. Offers such as free gifts for the birthday child are aimed at enticing younger children to persuade parents to hold their birthday parties at fast food outlets.

Design

Colourful designs and children's sections appeal to the public. In an attempt to entice the whole family, fast food restaurants often incorporate lower seating levels, high chairs and outdoor seating.

There are a number of other reasons why people find fast food restaurants convenient. Some of these are:

Drive-through

24-hour opening

Cash Points

Internet Connection

Baby Changing Facilities

> Add a bullet character to each of the five lines and set the bulleted text to double line spacing

Fast food outlets are a popular choice with those looking for employment. Jobs are relatively easy to get and many of these restaurants have schemes that employees find attractive. Different benefits and rates of pay are offered for various age groups as shown in the table below:

> Insert the data file **staff** and format as specified

Before you begin this task, make sure that you have access to the file **response**.

The information office is planning to produce a fact sheet. The text has already been prepared, but some amendments need to be made.

1 Open the text file **response.**

2 In the paragraph under the subheading **Environment**, delete the following text (ensure you delete the final comma as well):

by major chains, proven by statistics,

3 Replace the word **nutrition** with the word **nutritional** wherever it occurs.

Ensure you maintain case and that you replace whole words only.

4 In the first paragraph replace the **u** in the name **Arun Pattik** with a special character so that it becomes **Arûn Pattik**.

5 Spell check the document and correct any errors. Delete any duplicate words, but do not change the grammar of the document. Specialist words have already been checked and no changes should be made to them. Spellings must be in English (UK).

6 Insert your name, centre number, an automatic filename and an automatic date as a header or footer in this document.

7 Save your document with the filename **facts**.

8 Print one copy of the document **facts**.

BUILD-UP TASK ④ *Create a mail merge master document and protect files*

Scenario

Before you begin this task, make sure you have access to the data file **foodhall**.

You work in the information office of a large shopping complex and have been asked to create a mail merge master document. This will be used to let shoppers know the location of eating places in the shopping complex. The data file **foodhall** has already been prepared for you.

1 Create a new mail merge master document.

2 Use A4 paper in portrait orientation.

3 Key in the following text, inserting the merge fields from the **foodhall** data file. Follow the line endings and ensure there is a clear line space where shown:

Relax in the Food Mall

Come to
[clear line space]
[insert **Name** merge field]
[clear line space]
Our speciality is
[clear line space]
[insert **Type_of_Food** merge field]
[clear line space]
We are on the
[clear line space]
[insert **Situated** merge field]

We look forward to serving you!

4 Insert your name and centre number as a header or footer in the master document.

5 Format the document as follows:

Alignment   **centre**

Emphasis   **bold**

6 You may use any legible font type, font sizes and margins to suit your document.

7 Save the master document using the filename **eatnow**.

8 Print a copy of the document **eatnow** on one page, showing the merge fields.

9 Using the password **12EatN0w** protect the file **eatnow** from unauthorised access.

10 Save the file keeping the filename **eatnow**.

11 Close the document.

BUILD-UP TASK ⑤ *Create a mail merge query and perform the merge*

You will need to produce a screen print to show evidence that you protected the file using the password.

1 From your user area, prepare to open the file **eatnow** that you saved in Build-up task 4. A window will display prompting you to enter the password. Before you enter the password, take a screen print to show evidence that a password was set on the file.

2 Save this screen print in a new document using the filename **spbuild**. You will print this screen print later.

3 Open the document **eatnow**.

4 Create a mail merge query to find the eating places that are **Situated** on the **Ground Floor**.

5 Merge the query in a new document.

6 Print the results.

7 Merged documents are not normally saved. However, to show that you have carried out the mail merge correctly, you will need to save the merged file. Save this new document using the filename **groundf**.

BUILD-UP TASK ⑥ *Archive files*

Your manager has asked you to archive some of the source files used in the preparation of the documents for the information leaflet. You may use any method of archiving.

1 Archive the files **fdoutlets**, **quick**, **popular** and **staff**.

2 Take a screen print as evidence of the archiving. Paste the screen print into your document called **spbuild**.

3 Ensure that your name is displayed on the printout(s).

4 Print this updated screen print.

5 Close any programs and exit the system securely.

Scenario

You work in a school careers department. The careers teacher has asked you to prepare some materials about nursing careers and placements. You will be required to produce a placement request using mail merge, a careers information leaflet and a placement guide for students.

To produce the documentation you will need the following files:

FILENAME	FILE TYPE
wkexnurs	text file
tools	image file
hourly	spreadsheet containing a graph
schedule	datafile
depts	datafile
prepare	rich text file

You will also need to refer to the draft document.

For these tasks, you should use system and application software that will allow you to:

○ create a range of business documents

○ create mail merge documentation

○ combine text, images and datafiles

○ control page layout, columns and use of tables.

Before you begin this first task, make sure you have access to the files **wkexnurs**, **tools** and **hourly**.

You have been asked to prepare an information brief for students interested in pursuing nursing careers. The text and images have been prepared for you. You will need to combine the files into one document and format as specified in the instructions.

1 Using suitable software, open the text file **wkexnurs** as a Word document and save this as **nursebrf**.

2 Format the entire document as follows:

Paper size	**A4 portrait**
Top margin	**2.2 cm** (other margins may be set to suit your document)
Alignment	**left**
Font	**Times New Roman**
Emphasis	**none**
Font size	**11**
Line spacing	**single** (except where specified)

(continued overleaf)

3 Format the heading **Nursing Work Experience** as follows:

Alignment   **centre**

Font   **Arial**

Emphasis   **bold**

Font size   **24**

4 Format the subheadings as follows:

Alignment   **left**

Font   **Arial**

Emphasis   **bold, italic**

Font size   **16**

The three subheadings are:

A Guide for Secondary School Students

Career Opportunities

Hospital Placements

5 Referring to the draft document on pages 64–65, make the following amendments.

a Insert the image **tools**.

b Centre this between the margins of the page. The image may be resized, but the original proportions must be maintained.

c Insert the graph from the file **hourly**. Ensure that all the data in the graph is legible. The graph must fit on the second page of your document. You may resize the graph to achieve this. Ensure that there is at least one clear line space above the graph.

d Insert a page break where specified.

e Insert bullets and 1.5 line spacing where indicated in the draft document.

f Ensure that the original alignment, font size and font style are retained.

6 Create the following headers and footers:

Header   **your name and centre number**

Footer   **automatic filename and automatic date**

7 Save the file keeping the filename **nursebrf**.

8 Print one copy of the document **nursebrf**.

PRACTICE TASK ❷ *Insert a data file and format an integrated document*

Before you begin this task, make sure you have access to the files **schedule** and **nursebrf** that you created in Build-up task 1. The careers teacher has provided a datafile that you will need to insert into the information brief. You will then need to check the layout of the document before printing.

1 Using the file **nursebrf** and referring to the draft document on pages 64–65, insert the data file **schedule**. Ensure this is displayed as a table.

2 Format all the data in the table as follows:

Font	**Arial**
Font size	**10**
Alignment	**centre**

3 Text may be wrapped, but words must not be split.

4 To make the table easier to read, some additional formatting is required.

   a Merge the four cells in the first row of the table.

   b Apply dark shading to the first row of the table only.

   c Format the text **Proposed Work Experience Schedule** to white.

   d Embolden the data in the first and second rows of the table only.

   e Display gridlines and borders for the entire table.

   f Adjust the column widths so that no entry is displayed on more than two lines.

   g Ensure that the text of the table is entirely within the page margins.

   h Ensure that there is at least one clear line space above and below the table.

5 Check the document to ensure that:

   a All instructions have been carried out

   b All items are positioned within the margins of the page

   c The imported data file is not split across pages

   d Page breaks have been inserted where specified

   e There are no additional line spaces at the top of pages

   f Subheadings are not split from the related text

   g The spacing between subheadings and related text is consistent

   h There are no widows or orphans

   i The spacing between paragraphs is consistent

   j The text, pictures and lines are not superimposed

   k There is at least one clear line space above the graph and above and below the table containing the imported data file.

6 Save the file using the filename **nursebrf1**.

7 Print one copy of the document **nursebrf1**.

PRACTICE TASK **3** *Create a mail merge master document and protect files*

Before you begin this task, make sure you have access to the file **depts**.

You have been asked to create a mail merge master document to display a placement request. This will be attached to a reply received by the placement provider. The data file **depts** has already been prepared for you.

1 Using suitable software, create a new mail merge master document.

2 Use A4 paper in portrait orientation.

3 Key in the following text, inserting the merge fields from the **depts** data file. Follow the line endings and ensure there is a line space where shown:

Placement request details
[clear line space]
Thank you for your reply
[clear line space]
The department is:
[clear line space]
[insert **Department** merge field]
[clear line space]
The dates are from [insert **From** merge field] **to** [insert **To** merge field]
[clear line space]
I look forward to hearing from you.

4 Insert your name and centre number as a header or footer in the master document.

5 Format the document as follows:

Alignment **left**

Emphasis **bold**

6 You may use any legible font type, font size and margins to suit your document.

7 Save the master document using the filename **request**.

8 Print a copy of the document **request** on one page, showing the merge fields.

9 Using the password **Nur53Cd** protect the file **request** from unauthorised modification.

10 Save the file keeping the filename **request**.

11 Close the document.

PRACTICE TASK ④ *Create a mail merge query and perform the merge*

You have been asked to print the requests for placements. To save disk space, normal company policy states that merged documents should not be saved. On this occasion you will be required to save the merged file. You will need to produce a screen print to evidence file protection.

1 Prepare to open the document **request** that you saved in Task 3.

2 Take a screen print to show evidence that password protection has been set. Save this screen print for printing later.

3 Open the document **request**.

4 Create a mail merge query to find the records where the number of **Weeks** is **2**.

5 Merge the query in a new document.

6 Print the results.

7 More copies of the mail merge may need to be printed at a later date. As an exception to normal policy, save this document as **2weeks**.

PRACTICE TASK ⑤ *Amend a document*

Before you begin this task, make sure you have access to the file **prepare**.

A guide for placement students needs to be updated. The text has already been prepared, but some amendments need to be made.

1 Open the text file **prepare**.

2 In the second paragraph delete the words **Seek help if you need it**.

3 Replace all instances of the word **place** with the word **location** wherever it occurs. Ensure that you maintain case and that you replace whole words only.

4 In the final sentence, replace the **e** in the name **Jean Augut** with a special character so that it becomes **Jéan Augut**.

5 Spell check the document and correct any errors. Delete any duplicate words, but do not change the grammar of the document. Specialist words have already been checked and no changes should be made to them. Spellings must be in English (UK).

6 Insert your name and centre number as a header or footer in this document.

7 Save your document with the filename **placement**.

8 Print one copy of the document **placement**.

9 Close all open files and exit the software securely.

PRACTICE TASK 6 *Archive files*

Your manager has asked you to archive the source files used in the preparation of the documents for work experience. You may use any method of archiving.

1 Archive the files **wkexnurs**, **prepare**, **hourly**, **schedule** and **tools**.

2 Take a screen print as evidence of the archiving.

3 Print both this screen print and the screen print saved at Task 4, step 2. Ensure that your name is printed on the printout(s).

4 Close any programs and exit the system securely.

Draft document

Nursing Work Experience

Insert the image **tools** centred between each margin

A Guide for Secondary School Students

This information brief has been prepared by the Careers Department to help any students that are considering a career in nursing. It aims to provide an insight into the role of nurses working in a health care setting.

Nursing placements can be arranged through the school for a duration of two, three or four weeks after students complete their summer examinations. Students are rotated within a hospital through areas of interest. Where students have no particular preference, a general rotation of various specialties can also be arranged. Students on work placement are attached to staff who are trained health care professionals as well as experienced placement supervisors.

Students will be supervised at all times during the period of work experience. The table below is a typical example of a two-week placement:

Insert the data file **schedule** and format as specified in Task 2

Career Opportunities

Nursing offers a challenging, diverse and rewarding career with ample opportunities for professional advancement. Exciting employment opportunities exist in many clinical areas for motivated, enthusiastic nurses.

These are some of the benefits of a nursing career:

Job satisfaction

Flexible hours

Long service leave

Generous maternity leave.

Add a bullet character to each of the four lines and set the bulleted text to 1.5 line spacing

Hospital Placements

A number of local hospitals and clinics are committed to accepting up to three students per month during June and July. The school will make the initial request directly to the hospital Staff Development Officer on behalf of the students. Students will then be asked to complete an information form and to provide further details as required.

All hospital placements arranged through the school can provide clinical opportunities for sixth form students who wish to enhance their career prospects and expand their knowledge base in order to improve their employment prospects.

Clinical placements can be provided throughout many specialties. The placement duration is dependent on the individual. As a general rule, students are rotated through a number of departments in order to provide a varied experience. The graph below shows the average number of hours allocated to each specialty during a typical fortnight placement.

Insert the graph from the file **hourly** here

UNIT 1: Integrated e-document production

Active window	The window in which the current task is being performed.
Automatic fields	A code that can be inserted, by the click of an icon, to instruct Word to insert items into the document automatically (e.g. the date and time, filename, page numbers).
Criterion	A selection condition used to find specific records.
.csv	Comma separated value. Tabular data saved in a format that can be read by a number of applications. A comma usually separates the data in each column. Only the text is preserved – formatting will be lost.
Customised	Changes made to the 'default' settings to suit the individual user.
Data file	Any file that contains data. This data can be in any format.
Default	The setting that a computer program (or system) will use unless it is changed or 'customised'. For example, the default font on your Word package may be Times New Roman. Unless you change this, documents will always be produced in this font.
Drag	A term used to describe the action of clicking and holding a selected item and sliding it to a new position by moving the mouse.
Find and replace	A method of searching for a particular word or phrase and replacing it with a specified alternative wherever it appears.
Formatting	Changing the layout and appearance of text.
Generic file type/ format	A file saved in a format that can be read by most systems and in a large number of software applications.
Headers and footers	The area in the top and bottom margins of the page. Items placed in headers and footers will appear at the top and bottom of every page (unless you specify otherwise). See also automatic fields.
Mail merge	A facility that allows text from a master document to be combined with information from a data source so that personalised documents can be produced quickly and easily.
Mail merge data source	A set of records (data) that is linked to a mail merge master document. Information from this data source will be inserted into the document when the mail merge is performed.

Mail merge field	A code that is inserted into the mail merge master document to specify which information from the data source will be included in the merged document. A merge field is sometimes called a placeholder.
Mail merge master document	A document containing the information that will remain the same in each copy, together with the merge field(s) from the data source.
Mail merge query	A method of selecting only certain records from the data source to be merged with the mail merge master document (e.g. only those people who live in Birmingham).
Menu	A list of items.
Multitasking	Working with more than one open file and/or program at the same time.
My Computer	A folder created in all versions of Windows. File management tasks can be performed through My Computer.
Native file type/ format	The default format that files will be saved in, unless an alternative format is selected. For example, the native file format for a file saved in Microsoft Word would be .doc.
Non-generic file type	Also referred to as a 'native' or 'normal' file type. The file type in which the file will be saved by 'default' (unless you change it).
Normal file type	The file type in which documents will be saved, unless the user specifies an alternative format. The 'normal' file type for a Word document is a .doc.
Orientation	The term used to describe how the pages of a document will be displayed. Portrait orientation will have the shortest edge of the paper at the top of the page. Landscape orientation will have the longest edge of the paper at the top of the page.
Placeholder	Another name for a merge field.
Proofread	Carefully reading through a document to ensure that no errors have been made.
Read only	A file that can be opened and read but no changes can be made to the original file.
.rtf	A text file saved in a format that can be read by most systems and a range of applications (rtf stands for rich text file or format). The text and some basic formatting (e.g. font size, alignment and emphasis) will be preserved. Other formatting will be lost.
Special symbol	A character not generally found on a keyboard (e.g. à é ê © ®).
Submenu	A further list of choices available from some menu items.
Subscript	Text that is slightly lower on the line than other text. Normally displayed in a slightly smaller size.
Superscript	Text that is slightly higher on the line than other text. Normally displayed in a slightly smaller size.

Tab	A marker that indicates where and how data in columns will line up when the tab key on the keyboard is pressed.
Tab (in a window)	A marker (like a file marker) to indicate that more options are available by clicking on the tab.
Tab stop	The position that is set to align the data when the tab key is pressed. Often used for data that is to be displayed in columns.
Taskbar	A bar, usually at the bottom of the screen, that runs the length of the Desktop. It shows which tasks the computer is performing.
.txt	A text file saved in a format that can be read by most systems and a wide range of applications. Only the text is preserved – all formatting will be lost.

Assessment guidelines for Unit 1

1   Your tutor will provide you with all the files you need for the assessment.

2   Before an assessment you should create a new folder just for the assessment.

3   You will usually be provided with 6 files:

> a data file for the mailmerge task
>
> a text file, an image file, a graph and a data file for the integrated document
>
> a text file to be updated.

The order of tasks will vary from paper to paper. In some assignments, you will carry out the mail merge tasks at the beginning of the assessment, in others the first task may be to produce the integrated document.

TIP!

Before you start, **COPY** the folder containing the files into another folder in case you need to open an original file again.

DURING THE ASSESSMENT, YOU WILL NEED TO COMPLETE ABOUT 6 TASKS

General assessment tips

- Follow each instruction in the correct sequence. Do not leave an instruction intending to do it later.

- Your line endings will probably be different to those on the assessment paper, this is expected. Do not press Enter at the end of lines within paragraphs.

- Do not enter any text in bold unless instructed, the text is presented in bold to help you to identify filenames, text to be entered and instructions.

- When asked to insert an automatic date and an automatic filename, do not type the date or the filename – you must use the automatic date and automatic filename option in Word.

- Remember the saving tip. Read through the whole of a task and save a file with the new filename before you start working through the task to prevent accidental overwriting of a file.

Mail merge tasks

This will usually be over two tasks. To carry out the mail merge task, you will be provided with a datafile containing approximately 10 records. Your tutor will provide this datafile in either .csv or .doc file format.

You will need to:

1   Create a mail merge master document, e.g. a menu, a poster, a notice, or leaflet. This document will require some minimal formatting, e.g. align text, format as bold. You will need to insert a number of merge codes into this master document, save it with a specified filename, and print this master document.

2 Use a password to protect a document, save it again and close it.

3 Open the password protected document, take a screen print of the window that displays prompting you to enter the password, paste this screen print into a Word document, then save the Word document for printing later.

4 Create a mail merge query, merge the query results, save this document with a specified filename and print the results.

Mail merge assessment tips

- Ensure you insert only the specified merge fields.
- Use a font size and font type that is suitable for the document.
- Check your printout to ensure that the merge fields are clearly displayed on the first printout.
- Ensure that your screen print is clearly readable and clearly displays the name of the protected document.
- Make sure you carry out the mail merge query correctly. Open the original datafile to check that the number of records you found in your query is correct.

Create an integrated document

This will usually be over two tasks. To produce the integrated document, you will be provided with the following files:

- a text file
- a graph
- an image
- a datafile.

You will need to:

- open the text file in Word and save it as a Word file
- apply some formatting, e.g. to headings, subheadings, body text; set the margins, set the orientation.

As part of the assignment, you will be provided with a hard copy of the text file, this will show the amendments that you need to make. You will usually be required to:

- insert the image and apply alignment
- insert the graph
- insert the datafile as a table and apply some formatting, e.g. merge some cells, use shading for at least one cell, change the text colour, emphasise text (e.g. use bold), set and apply tabs in the table, insert a page break.
- save the document with a specified filename and print it.

Integrated document assessment tips

- Make absolutely sure that you save the text file from within Word as a Word document.
  - In the **Save As** window, click the drop-down arrow next to **Save As type**, scroll up to the top of the list, and select **Word document**.
  - If you do not save it as a Word document, you will lose all the formatting you applied, the image will not be saved, all headers and footers will not be saved and all the formatting in the data file will be lost.
- Ensure that you insert the image in the correct place in your document, so that the image is displayed within the margins and you apply the alignment specified. It is easy to forget to align the image once you have inserted it.
- There are many ways to insert the graph. Whichever method you use, ensure that all parts of the graph are clearly readable and that the chart fits within the margins. If there is no specific instruction to apply a border, you have a choice whether or not to insert one.
- In many assignments, you will be instructed to apply bullets to specified text and to the change the linespacing for the same text. Ensure that you carry out both instructions. Candidates often forget to apply the specified linespacing once they have applied the bullets. You can use any style of bullet character. In Word, when you apply bullets the text may automatically indent, make sure you apply the correct alignment if this is specified.
- Check to ensure that you have applied the correct font style and font size to the bulleted text.
- There will usually be several instructions relating to the formatting of the table. To ensure that you follow every instruction, tick each sub-bullet as you complete it. Ensure that the text in the table does not extend into the left or the right margin. Unless otherwise instructed, it is acceptable if the table borders extend into the margin area, reducing the table borders is optional. Ensure that no words are split. Use black borders and use Print Preview to ensure that all borders and gridlines will be clearly displayed when printed.

Update a document

This will usually be one task. To update the document, you will be provided with an .rtf file (rich text format). You may need to:

- edit some text (move, copy, insert delete)
- insert a special character (in some assignments)
- use find and replace to find whole words only and/or match the use of case
- save the document with a specified filename and print it.

Update a document assessment tips

- You may save the document in the same file format as the original document (rtf) or save it as a Word document (.doc).

- When you replace a word, ensure that you use **Match Case** if specified and/or that you replace Whole **Words only** and that you **Replace All** (not Replace).
- Insert the special character correctly, ensuring that you select the option to insert the correct letter as well as the special character.

Archive files

This will usually be one task. You will usually be required to archive some or all of the files that you were provided with for the assessment. You may use any suitable method of archiving. For example:

- compress the files then delete the original files
- move the files to another folder.

You will be instructed to take screen print evidence that you have archived the specified files.

Archive files assessment tips

- Ensure that you archive only the files specified.
- When you take the screen print(s), you should paste it/them into the document containing the screen print that you took earlier of the protected file. Ensure that the screen print clearly displays evidence that the files were archived.
- Make sure that all the files you archived are clearly displayed on the screen print(s).
- Ensure that your name is on the screen print(s).

Good luck!

Contents

In Unit 2, you need to use spreadsheet software to open existing datafiles, enter, edit and manipulate data, use formulae and common functions to calculate results, link live data from one spreadsheet to another, sort spreadsheet data and use filters to select data. You will also need to present data using graphs and charts, select and control data sources, and use formatting and alignment in both spreadsheets and graphs.

You will use a software program called Microsoft Office Excel 2003 which is part of Microsoft Office 2003. Excel is a program that allows you to perform calculations, manipulate, analyse and present data. We will refer to it as Excel from now on.

This book is divided into two chapters:

Chapter 1
- in Section 1 you will learn to open datafiles, save files in Excel and apply formatting
- in Section 2 you will learn to identify, input and amend data
- in Section 3 you will learn to use formulae and functions
- in Section 4 you will learn to change the page setup and print spreadsheets
- in Section 5 you will learn to link spreadsheets and sort data using AutoFilter.

Chapter 2
- in Section 1 you will learn how to select data for charts and how to create exploded pie charts
- in Section 2 you will learn how to create comparative charts and how to define the data series
- in Section 3 you will learn how to create line-column graphs
- in Section 4 you will learn how to create xy scatter graphs.

Files for this book

To work through the tasks in this book, you will need the files from the folder called **L2U2SG_files**, which you will find on the CD-ROM provided with this book. Copy this folder into your user area before you begin.

 **How to...** *copy the folder L2U2SG_files from the CD-ROM*

1 Insert the CD-ROM into the CD-ROM drive of your computer.

2 Close any windows that may open.

3 From the desktop, double-click the **My Computer** icon to display the **My Computer** window.

4 Under **Devices with Removable Storage**, double-click on the CD-ROM drive icon to view the contents of the CD-ROM.

5 Click once on the folder **L2U2SG_files**.

6 The folder will be highlighted (usually blue).

7 In the **File and Folder Tasks** box, click **Copy this folder**.

8 A **Copy Items** dialogue box will display.

9 Click on the user area to which you want to copy the folder **L2U2SG_files**.

10 Click on **Copy**.

11 The folder **L2U2SG_files** is copied to your user area.

TIP!

It is advisable to copy and paste a second copy to another folder in your user area as backup.

Preparing your work area

You are advised to prepare your user area in order to keep your files organised. An example of a well organised folder structure is listed below:

○ create a folder for your CLAiT Plus work

○ in this folder, create subfolders for all your CLAiT Plus units

○ in each unit subfolder, create further subfolders, for example:

- **U2 working** Your working folder in which all working files will be saved

- **L2U2SG_files** The source files folder copied from the CD-ROM

- **L2U2SG_worked** The worked copies folder copied from the CD-ROM.

Terms and symbols used in this book

TERM	METHOD
Click	Press and release the **left** mouse button once.
Double-click	Quickly press and release the left mouse button **twice**.
Drag	Press and hold down the left mouse button while moving the mouse.
Select	Click on an item, or highlight text.
Right-click	Press the **right** mouse button once.
+	Used to indicate that two keys should be held down together, e.g. Alt + Enter – hold down the **Alt** key then press the **Enter** key.
➔	Indicates that a new instruction follows.

LEARNING OUTCOMES

In this section you will learn how to:

- ○ *open a .csv file*
- ○ *save a .csv file as an Excel workbook*
- ○ *select adjacent and non-adjacent cells*
- ○ *apply formatting to multiple cells*
- ○ *locate a cell containing specific data*
- ○ *wrap cell contents*
- ○ *apply vertical and horizontal alignment*
- ○ *set text orientation*
- ○ *merge cells*
- ○ *add a border*
- ○ *format numeric data to integer*
- ○ *format numeric data to 2 decimal places*
- ○ *format numeric data as currency*
- ○ *format numeric data as percentages.*

Understanding .csv files

A .csv file is a generic datafile saved in a format that can be read by most systems and in a large number of software applications. Some formatting may be lost, but the data can be read.

A spreadsheet that has been saved in a .csv format will retain any figures generated by formulae, but the underlying formulae will be lost. If any of the figures in the cells used to generate the formulae are amended the figures in the formulae column will not update to reflect the change.

Figures 2.1 and 2.2 show examples of the same spreadsheet saved as an Excel file and as a .csv file. Both files have been reopened in Excel. The spreadsheet view is the same, but the formula view shows that the underlying formula has been lost in the .csv file (Figure 2.2).

Numeric formatting (e.g. a number formatted to two decimal places) will be retained in a .csv file, but any 'hidden' figures after the decimal place will be lost. If, for example, in the original spreadsheet the figure 2.3333 had been formatted to two decimal places, when this is saved in .csv format only 2.33 would be retained. Only significant figures after the decimal

Spreadsheet view | Formula view

	A	B	C
1	2	2	4
2	4	4	8
3	6	6	12

	A	B	C
1	2	2	=SUM(A1:B1)
2	4	4	=SUM(A2:B2)
3	6	6	=SUM(A3:B3)

FIGURE 2.1 Data in an Excel file

Spreadsheet view | Formula view

	A	B	C
1	2	2	4
2	4	4	8
3	6	6	12

	A	B	C
1	2	2	4
2	4	4	8
3	6	6	12

FIGURE 2.2 The same data imported into Excel from a .csv file

point will be retained in a .csv file (e.g. a figure is shown as 234.00 in the spreadsheet, only 234 will be retained in the .csv file).

A .csv file is only able to save one worksheet. If multiple worksheets are contained in a workbook each worksheet must be saved individually with a different name. A graph cannot be saved in .csv format.

▶▶ How to... *open a .csv file in Excel*

1 Load Excel, either from the Start menu or by double-clicking on the desktop icon.

2 On the Standard toolbar, click on the **Open** icon.

3 The Open dialogue box will display (Figure 2.3). Locate the folder in which your file is stored.

4 Click on the drop-down arrow on the right-hand side of the **Files of type** box.

5 Click on **All Files**.

6 Select the file that you want to open by clicking on it.

7 Click **Open**.

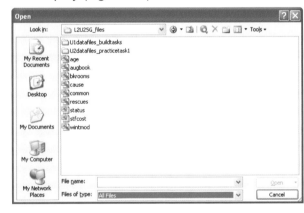

FIGURE 2.3 The Open dialogue box

▶▶ How to... *save a .csv file as an Excel file*

1 In the Menu bar, click on **File**.

2 In the drop-down menu, click on **Save As**.

3 The **Save As** dialogue box will display (Figure 2.4).

4 Click on the drop-down arrow on the right-hand side of the **Save as type** box.

5 From the list of file types, select **Microsoft Office Excel Workbook**.

TIP!

After opening a .csv file widen all columns to familiarise yourself with the data (you may also wish to print) then close the file **without** saving. Reopen the file to begin a task.

To widen all columns, click in an *empty* cell in the first row of the spreadsheet, press **Ctrl + A**, click **format** in the Menu bar, click **Column** from the drop-down menu and select **Autofit Selection**.

TIP!

Microsoft Office Excel Workbook will be at the top of the list.

TIP!

A workbook can consist of many worksheets. When you open a .csv file in Excel the program will automatically rename the worksheet with the name of the .csv file.

6 Click the drop-down arrow next to **Save in**.

7 Locate the folder in which you want to save the file.

8 In the **File name** box, enter the required filename.

9 Click on **Save**.

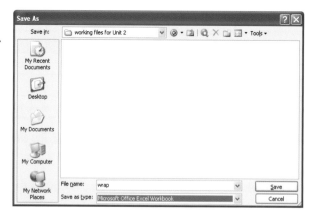

FIGURE 2.4 The Save As dialogue box

Check your understanding *Open and save a .csv as an Excel workbook*

1 Open Excel.

2 From within Excel, open the .csv file **augbook**.

3 Widen all columns to display all data in full.

4 Study the data contained in the spreadsheet (you may wish to print).

5 Close the file without saving.

6 Reopen the .csv file **augbook**.

7 Save the file in your working area as an Excel workbook using the filename **wedaug**.

8 Close the spreadsheet file.

Formatting text in a spreadsheet

To allow you to work more efficiently and to make the spreadsheet easier to read it will be necessary to format your spreadsheet. You will need to locate the cell(s) that contains the data you wish to format. It is generally quicker to use the Find facility in Excel (see page 88).

Basic formatting

Use the Formatting toolbar to apply basic formatting, such as bold, italic and to change font size.

In OCR assignments you may be asked to format data to be large, medium and small.

○ Large should be the largest size.

○ Medium should be a size in-between large and small.

○ Small should be the smallest size.

The following sizes are given as a guide:

DESCRIPTION	FONT SIZE
Small	10–12
Medium	14–16
Large	18+

Formatting multiple cells

If you wish to apply the same formatting to multiple cells this can be done in one action by selecting all the cells then applying the formatting.

Selecting cells

To make the application of formatting more efficient, you can select all cells that are to have the same format and then apply the formatting. The following table describes how to select the required cells.

When you have selected a range of cells do not click in the spreadsheet with your mouse or you will deselect all cells.

SELECTION	ACTION
A single cell	Click in the cell, or use the cursor (arrow) keys to move to the cell.
A range of adjacent cells (two or more cells that are next to each other on a sheet)	Click the first cell in the range then: when the white cross appears, drag to the last cell, **or** hold down **Shift** then click in the last cell in the range, **or** press **F8** and use the arrow keys to highlight the cells to be selected. (You can scroll to make the last cell visible.)
A range of non-adjacent cells	Click in the first cell, hold down the **Ctrl** key, click in each cell to be included. When all cells have been selected, release the **Ctrl** key.
All cells in the worksheet	Click in the **Select All** button, **or** click in any *empty* cell in the first row of the spreadsheet then press **Ctrl+A**. A ← Select All button
All cells in a section (area)	Click in any cell in the section then press **Ctrl+A**.
Non-adjacent cells or cell ranges	Click on the first cell (or highlight the first range), then hold down **Ctrl** while you select the other cell(s) or ranges, **or** select the first cell or range of cells and then press **Shift + F8** to add another non-adjacent cell or range to the selection. Note: If you make a mistake when selecting non-adjacent cells you will need to cancel the selection and start again as you cannot deselect individual cells or ranges.

 **How to...** *format multiple cells using the Format Painter*

1 Click in one of the cells to be formatted.

2 Apply the required formatting.

3 Double-click on the Format Painter icon 🖌 in the toolbar.

4 Select (highlight) all cells to apply the same formatting.

5 When all cells have been formatted click on the Format Painter icon again (or press **Esc**) to deselect it.

TIP!

To copy formatting to a single cell you only need to single-click the format painter.

How to... *locate a cell containing specific data*

1 In the Menu bar, click on **Edit.**

2 In the drop-down menu, click on **Find**.

3 The **Find and Replace** dialogue box will display.

4 In the box next to **Find what** enter the text contained in the cell that you wish to locate.

5 Click on the **Find Next** button.

6 Click on **Close** to exit the Find and Replace dialogue box. The cell containing the specified data will be selected.

TIP!

You do not need to match case when keying text in the **Find what** box.

How to... *wrap cell contents*

1 Select the cell(s) that contain the data you wish to wrap.

2 In the Menu bar, click on **Format.**

3 In the drop-down menu, click on **Cells**.

4 Click on the **Alignment** tab in the **Format Cells** dialogue box.

5 In the **Text control** section, click to insert a tick in the box next to **Wrap text** (Figure 2.5).

6 Click on **OK.**

7 The cell contents will now be wrapped.

8 If necessary, adjust the column width and/or row height to ensure words are not split and/or data is displayed on the specified number of lines.

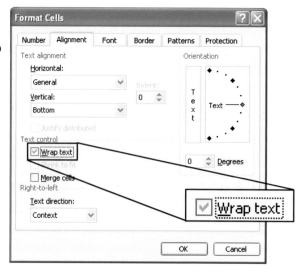

FIGURE 2.5 Wrap text in the Format Cells dialogue box

TIP!

If a column is wide enough to display the data on one line, text wrap will have no effect. If you cannot reduce the column width without hiding data you can force the text to wrap.

To force text to wrap, or to choose where to wrap, click in front of the text to be displayed on the next line then press **Alt + Enter**.

1 Reopen your saved file **wedaug**.

2 Format the cells containing the following data with a bold font and wrap the cell contents on to two lines:

ROOM PER NIGHT

WEDDING PLAN

COST PER HEAD

FLOWERS PER HEAD

WEDDING COST

ROOMS REQUIRED

3 Locate the cell containing **CHARGE PER ROOM** and wrap the cell contents on to three lines.

4 Adjust column widths to ensure that words in the wrapped cells are not split and that all data is displayed in full.

5 Save the file in your working area as an Excel workbook using the filename **wrap**.

6 Close the spreadsheet file.

▶▶ How to... *apply vertical and horizontal alignment*

1 Open the spreadsheet file in Excel.

2 Select the cell(s) to be formatted.

3 Click on **Format** in the Menu bar.

4 Click on **Cells** in the drop-down menu.

5 In the **Format Cells** dialogue box, click on the **Alignment** tab.

6 In the Text alignment section, click on the drop-down arrow in the box under **Horizontal** (Figure 2.6).

7 Select the required horizontal alignment.

8 Click on the down arrow in the box under **Vertical** (Figure 2.6).

9 Select the required vertical alignment.

10 Click **OK** (unless you want to apply other formatting).

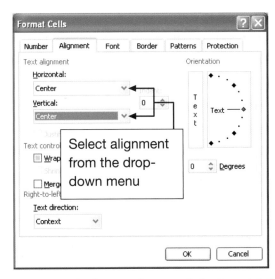

FIGURE 2.6 Setting text alignments in the Format Cells dialogue box

1 Select the cell(s) containing the text to be orientated.

2 In the Menu bar, click on **Format**.

3 In the drop-down menu, click on **Cells**.

4 Click on the **Alignment** tab in the **Format Cells** dialogue box.

5 In the **Orientation** section, either:

   a Click and drag the text marker up or down until the required number appears in the box next to **Degrees**, or

   b Enter the required number in the box to the left of **Degrees** (or use the up/down arrows).

6 Click **OK**.

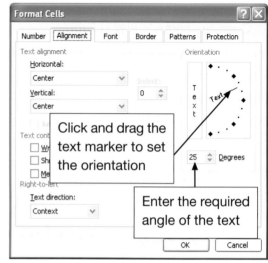

FIGURE 2.7 Setting the text orientation in the Format Cells dialogue box

TIP!

If text orientation is set to a minus figure (e.g. –25 degrees) the text will start at the top of the cell and flow down (this is sometimes referred to as clockwise because the hands of a clock move around the clock in this direction).

If the direction is a plus figure (e.g. 25 degrees) then the text will start at the bottom of the column and flow up (this is sometimes referred to as anti-clockwise because the text will flow in the opposite direction to the hands of a clock).

Check your understanding *Set horizontal and vertical alignment and text orientation*

1 Open your saved file **wrap**.

2 Format the data as listed in the table below.

COLUMN LABELS	HORIZONTAL ALIGNMENT	VERTICAL ALIGNMENT	TEXT ORIENTATION
WEDDING PLAN and **COST PER HEAD**	Left	Bottom	
CUSTOMER – INVOICE (Columns A–I)	Centre	Centre	
PLAN: BRONZE(A15) **PLAN: SILVER (A21)** **PLAN: GOLD (A26)**	Centre	Centre	25 degrees

3 Save the file as an Excel workbook using the filename **align**.

4 Close the spreadsheet file.

▶▶ *How to...* *merge cells*

1 Open the spreadsheet in Excel.

2 Select the cells to be merged.

3 Click on **Format** in the Menu bar.

4 In the drop-down menu, click on **Cells**.

5 In the **Format Cells** dialogue box, click on the **Alignment** tab.

6 In the **Text control** section, click to insert a tick in the box next to **Merge cells** (Figure 2.8).

7 Click on **OK**.

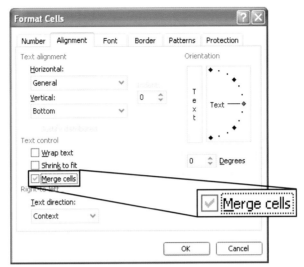

FIGURE 2.8 Merge cells in the Format Cells dialogue box

▶▶ *How to...* *add a border*

1 Select the cells to be framed with a border.

2 On the **Standard Toolbar**, click the drop-down arrow to the right of the Borders icon.

3 Select the **Outside Borders** or **Thick Box Border** option (Figure 2.9).

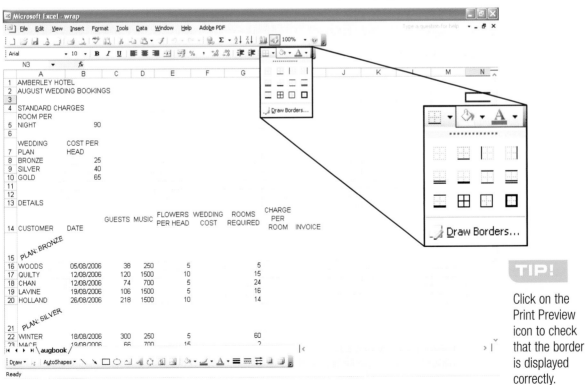

FIGURE 2.9 The drop-down borders menu

1   Open your saved file **align**.

2   Format the data listed in the table below.

LABELS	SIZE AND STYLE	COLUMNS
AMBERLEY HOTEL	Large	Centred across all columns containing data: Columns A–I Framed by a border
AUGUST WEDDING BOOKINGS	Medium	Centred across all columns containing data: Columns A–I
STANDARD CHARGES	Small, bold	Centred across all columns A–B Framed by a border
WEDDING PLAN	Small, bold	A
COST PER HEAD	Small, bold	B
DETAILS	Small, bold	Centred across all columns containing data: Columns A–I Framed by a border
CUSTOMER – INVOICE	Small, bold	A–I
PLAN: BRONZE PLAN: SILVER PLAN: GOLD	Small, bold	A

3   Check the formatting in **Print Preview**.

4   Save the file as an Excel workbook using the filename **merge**.

5   Close the spreadsheet file.

Formatting numeric data in a spreadsheet

The 'default' format in Excel is 'general'. When you enter numeric data, this format will allow you to see all the figures exactly as you enter them (e.g. with the exception of zeros, all numbers after the decimal point will be visible). The results generated by formulae will also show the appropriate number of figures after the decimal point. Whilst it is useful to show the 'true' value, it does not always make the figures easy to read and you will probably want to apply a numeric format to give a more consistent display.

There are many formats for numeric data. The most common formats are integer (0 decimal places) and 2 decimal places. However, you can select to display as many decimal places as you wish. Changing the formatting of the numeric data does not change the underlying figure – just the way it looks on the spreadsheet.

In the spreadsheet that follows, the formula **A2*B2** has been entered in cell **C2**.

Note that the result generated by the formula in C2 does not change when the formatting of cell **A2** is changed.

Decimal places in an Excel worksheet:

	A	B	C
1	FIGURE 1	FIGURE 2	TOTAL
2	1.4	10	14

Column A formatted to 1 decimal place

	A	B	C
1	FIGURE 1	FIGURE 2	TOTAL
2	1	10	14

Column A formatted to Integer

▶▶ How to... *format numeric data to integer or 2 decimal places*

1 Select the cell(s) to be formatted.

2 Click on **Format** in the Menu bar.

3 In the **Format Cells** dialogue box, click on **Cells**.

4 Click on the **Number** tab.

5 In the **Category** section, select **Number**.

6 Click on the up/down arrows to the right of the **Decimal places** box to select the required number of decimal places.

7 In the box under **Negative numbers** click on the required format (Figure 2.10).

8 Click on **OK**.

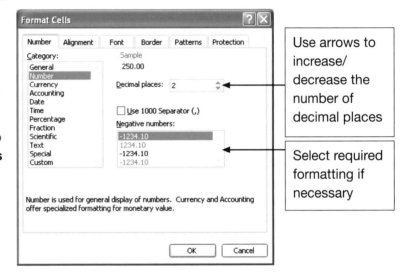

Use arrows to increase/decrease the number of decimal places

Select required formatting if necessary

FIGURE 2.10 The number formatting options

Monetary amounts can be formatted to currency. When currency format is selected you can choose to display the figures with or without the currency symbol and may also display the figures to integer or select any number of decimal place(s).

Negative numbers may be displayed in black or red with the minus sign in front of the number (e.g. –4.30). They may also be displayed in red without the minus sign. If you are printing in black and white you should avoid this option as the printed sheet may not clearly show that the numbers are negative!

Care must be taken when entering figures that will be formatted to percentage, date and time.

FORMAT	CORRECT DATA ENTRY	RESULT OF CORRECT ENTRY WHEN FORMATTED	INCORRECT DATA ENTRY	RESULT OF INCORRECT ENTRY WHEN FORMATTED
Percentage	Either 4% or 0.04	4%	4	400%
Date	12/6/05 (/ separates day/ month/year)	12/06/2005	12.6.05	12.6.05 (this is treated as text and therefore cannot be calculated)
Time	10:15 (: separates hours from minutes)	10:15	10.5	03:36:00

▶▶ How to... *format numeric data to currency*

1 Select the cell(s) to be formatted.

2 Click on **Format** in the Menu bar.

3 In the drop-down menu, click on **Cells**.

4 In the **Format Cells** dialogue box, click on the **Number** tab (Figure 2.11).

5 In the Category section, select **Currency**.

6 Click on the up/down arrows to the right of the **Decimal places** box to select the required number of decimal places.

7 In the box under **Symbol** click on the drop-down arrow then click on the required currency symbol (may be none).

8 In the box under **Negative numbers** click on the required format.

9 Click on **OK**.

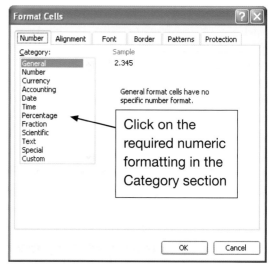

FIGURE 2.11 The Number tab in the Format Cells dialogue box

▶▶ How to... *format numeric data to percentage*

1 Select the cell(s) to be formatted.

2 Click on **Format** in the Menu bar.

3 In the drop-down menu, click on **Cells**.

4 In the **Format Cells** dialogue box, click on the **Number** tab.

5 In the **Category** section, select **Percentage**.

6 Click on the up/down arrows to the right of the **Decimal places** box to select the required number of decimal places.

7 Click on **OK**.

1   Open your saved file **merge**.

2   In the **DETAILS** section format the figures under the column labels **GUESTS** and **ROOMS REQUIRED** to number and integer (0 decimal places).

3   Format the figures under the column labels **MUSIC** and **FLOWERS PER HEAD** to currency and integer (0 decimal places) with a currency symbol.

4   Format **all** the figures in the **STANDARD CHARGES** section to currency and 2 decimal places with a currency symbol.

5   In the **DETAILS** section check that all figures under the **DATE** column are formatted to English date format (day/month/year).

6   Save the file in your working area as an Excel workbook using the filename **numcur**.

7   Close the spreadsheet file.

ASSESS YOUR SKILLS – Open a datafile, save as an Excel file and apply formatting

By working through Section 1 you will have learnt the skills listed below. Read each item to help you decide how confident you feel about each skill:.

○ open a .csv file

○ save a .csv file as an Excel workbook

○ select adjacent and non-adjacent cells

○ apply formatting to multiple cells

○ locate a cell containing specific data

○ wrap cell contents

○ apply vertical and horizontal alignment

○ set text orientation

○ merge cells

○ add a border

○ format numeric data to integer

○ format numeric data to 2 decimal places

○ format numeric data as currency

○ format numeric data as percentages.

If you think that you need more practice on any of the skills in the above list, go back and work through the skill(s) again.

If you feel confident, move on to Section 2.

LEARNING OUTCOMES

In this section you will learn how to:

- ○ use Find and Replace
- ○ insert text and numeric data
- ○ amend text and numeric data
- ○ insert a row/column
- ○ delete a row/column
- ○ clear the contents of a cell/row/column
- ○ move text and numeric data.

Inputting and amending data

When you input and amend data in a spreadsheet it is very important that you enter the data accurately. Numeric data must be entered with 100 per cent accuracy.

If you are editing an existing spreadsheet, look carefully at how the original data has been entered. Make amendments/additions in the same case as the original data and ensure that the data entered is formatted in the same way as the existing data in the spreadsheet.

Using Find and Replace to edit data

In Section 1 you used the Find facility to locate data. On some occasions you may need to replace data that appears in several places on the spreadsheet. Although this could be done manually, it is far more efficient to use Excel's Find and Replace facility. Using the Find and Replace facility will ensure that all occurrences of the data are found and will reduce the risk of error because the data will only need to be entered once.

▶▶ How to... *use Find and Replace*

1 In the Menu bar click on **Edit**.

2 Click on **Find** in the drop-down menu.

3 In the **Find and Replace** dialogue box click on the **Replace** tab.

4 In the box next to **Find what** enter the text to be replaced.

TIP!

If you want to move between cells in Excel without using the mouse:

- ○ pressing the **Tab** key moves to the cell to the right
- ○ pressing **Enter** usually moves to the cell below
- ○ pressing an arrow key moves one cell in the direction of the arrow.

FIGURE 2.12 The Find and Replace dialogue box

5 In the box next to **Replace with** enter the replacement text.

6 Check to ensure that you have not made any mistakes.

7 Click on the **Replace All** button.

8 Click on **Close**.

9 All instances of the original data will have been replaced.

Check your understanding Use Find and Replace

1 Open the datafile **wintmod**.

2 Ensure that all data is displayed in full.

3 Replace all instances of the word **September** with the word **October**

4 Save the file in your working area as an Excel workbook using the filename **replaced**

5 Close the file.

▶▶ How to... insert text and numeric data

1 Click in the cell in which you want to enter data.

2 Enter the data.

3 Move to the next cell in which you wish to enter data or move to any other cell.

4 Check to ensure that the additions are correct and that numbers are 100 per cent accurate.

5 Check that the formatting of the inserted data is correct.

▶▶ How to... amend text and numeric data

1 Click in the cell containing the data that you wish to edit.

2 Enter the new data.

3 Move to the next cell you wish to edit or move to any other cell.

4 Check to ensure that the amendments are correct and that numbers are 100 per cent accurate.

5 Check that the formatting of the amended data is correct.

Inserting and deleting rows and columns

When you insert or delete rows or columns in your spreadsheet, Excel will update formulas by adjusting both relative and absolute cell references to reflect their new locations.

For example, if the formula in a cell was =A3+B3+$G$10 and a new column was inserted between columns A and B, Excel would automatically adjust the formula to become =A3+C3+$H$10.

Any values added in the new column B would **not** be included. If you wanted the values in the new column to be inserted you would have to adjust the formula manually.

If the formula had been =SUM(A3:B3,$G$10) Excel would adjust the formula to become =SUM(A3:C3,$H$10).

The values in column B would automatically be included.

If you want references to adjust automatically, it's a good idea to use range references (whenever appropriate) in your formulas, rather than specifying individual cells.

Note: only formulae within the range will be updated – if you add a row/column that was not included in the original formula you wil need to adjust the formula to reflect the change.

If a formula refers to a deleted cell the message #REF! will appear in the affected cell. You will need to amend the formula to reflect the changes in your spreadsheet.

Inserting rows and columns

You may need to add rows and columns to an existing spreadsheet. When a new row is inserted it will be placed *above* the active cell. When a new column is inserted it will be placed *to the right* of the active cell.

▶▶ **How to...** *insert a row*

1 Click in any cell in the row immediately *below* the position in which you want the new row to be inserted.

2 Click on **Insert** in the Menu bar.

3 In the drop-down menu, click on **Rows**.

4 The new row will be inserted.

▶▶ **How to...** *insert a column*

1 In your spreadsheet, click in any cell in the column *to the right* of the position that you want the new column to be inserted.

2 In the Menu bar click on **Insert**.

3 In the drop-down menu, click on **Columns**.

4 The new column will be inserted.

1   Open your saved file **replaced**.

2   Insert a new row between the rows containing the data for **Room 211 and Room 215**.

3   Under the appropriate column labels enter the following data in the new row:

AREA	MONTH	CONTRACTOR	DAYS	SUPERVISOR
Room 212	October	Perkins	7	Verity

4   Insert a new column to the left of the column containing the data for Area (the first column).

5   Enter the label **Completed** as a label for the new column. Make sure this label is displayed in the same row as the column label **Area**.

6   Save the file in your working area as an Excel workbook using the filename **insert**.

7   Close the file.

Deleting rows and columns

When a row or column is deleted from the spreadsheet, the data contained in the deleted row or column is permanently removed from the spreadsheet.

If you make a mistake, you can click on the **Undo** icon but once you have re-saved the spreadsheet all data in the deleted column will be permanently lost.

▶▶ How to... *delete a column*

1   Click on the letter of the column you wish to delete so that the entire column is highlighted.

2   Right-click the mouse anywhere in the highlighted column.

3   In the menu, click on **Delete**.

4   The column will be deleted.

▶▶ How to... *delete a row*

1   Click on the number of the row you wish to delete so that the entire row is highlighted.

2   Right-click anywhere in the highlighted row.

3   In the menu, click on **Delete**.

4   The row will be deleted.

1   Open your saved file **insert**.

2   Delete the entire column containing the data for **Contractor**.

3   Delete the entire row containing the data for **Beauty Salon**.

4   Save the file in your working area as an Excel workbook using the filename **delete**.

5   Close the file.

1   Open your saved file **delete**.

2   In the **Days** column amend the figure for Pool to be **10**.

3   In the **Area** column amend Pool to be **Swimming Pool**.

4   Save the file in your working area as an Excel workbook using the filename **edit**.

5   Close the spreadsheet file.

Clearing rows and columns

On some occasions you may wish to clear the contents of a row or column without actually deleting that row or column. Once the contents have been cleared the row or column will still be present on the spreadsheet but it will contain no data.

You can also clear the contents of part of a row or column by selecting the cells containing the data to be cleared. The advantage of clearing the contents of cells, rather than deleting the cell contents, is that when cells are cleared any formatting is also removed. When the contents of cells are deleted the data is deleted but the formatting remains.

Clearing rows and columns will have no effect on cell references in existing formulae as the row and/or column are still present.

▶▶ How to... *clear the contents of a column*

1   Click on the letter of the column in which you wish to clear the contents.

2   The column will be selected.

3   Check it is the correct column.

4   Right-click anywhere in the selected column.

5   In the menu, click on **Clear Contents**.

6   All data in the column will be removed but the column will remain.

TIP!

To clear the cell contents of part of a column or row, select only the cells to be cleared and follow the instructions for How to… clear the contents of a column/row.

1 Click on the number of the row in which you wish to clear the contents.

2 The entire row will be selected.

3 Check it is the correct row.

4 Right-click anywhere in the selected area.

5 In the menu, click on **Clear Contents**.

6 All data in the row will be removed but the row will remain.

Check your understanding *Clear the contents of a column or row*

1 Open the datafile **bkrooms**.

2 Ensure all data is displayed in full.

3 Clear the entire contents of the 3 rows containing the following data:

   ○ STANDARD

   ○ LUXURY

   ○ PREMIER

4 Clear the cell containing the label **OTHER BOOKINGS** and all the data below this label.

5 Save the file in your working area as an Excel workbook using the filename **clear**.

6 Close the file.

Moving data

Data can be moved from one cell to another by cutting and pasting or by dragging and dropping.

▶▶ **How to...** move data using Cut and Paste

1 Select the data to be moved.

2 Right-click anywhere in the selected area.

3 In the menu, click on **Cut**.

4 Click on the cell that is to be the new location (if you are moving a range of cells click on the cell that is to contain the data in the first cell).

5 Right-click on the selected cell.

6 In the menu, click on **Paste**.

TIP!

Take great care when pasting, any existing data in the target cell(s) will be overwritten when you paste the new data.

If you make a mistake, click on the **Undo** icon .

1   Select the cell(s) containing the data to be moved.

2   Hover the mouse over an outside edge of the selected cell(s).

3   A black cross with 4-way arrows will appear ⊹.

4   Hold on the edge of the selection and drag it to the new location.

5   Release the mouse button.

6   Press a cursor key or click in a different cell to confirm the new location.

> If you have difficulty using the mouse, or are not confident when dragging and dropping use the cut and paste method.

Check your understanding *Move data*

1   Open your saved file **edit**.

2   Move the label **Winter Refurbishment Programme** to the first column of the first row.

3   Save the file in your working area as an Excel workbook using the filename **move**.

4   Close the spreadsheet file.

ASSESS YOUR SKILLS – Identify, input and amend data

By working through Section 2 you will have learnt the skills listed below. Read each item to help you decide how confident you feel about each skill:

- ○   use Find and Replace
- ○   insert text and numeric data
- ○   amend text and numeric data
- ○   insert a row/column
- ○   delete a row/column
- ○   clear the contents of a cell/row/column
- ○   move text and numeric data.

If you think that you need more practice on any of the skills in the above list, go back and work through the skill(s) again.

If you feel confident, move on to Section 3.

3: Use formulae and functions

LEARNING OUTCOMES

In this section you will learn how to:

- ○ *enter formulae*
- ○ *use mathematical operators in formulae*
- ○ *use brackets appropriately*
- ○ *use relative cell references*
- ○ *use absolute cell references*
- ○ *use mixed cell references*
- ○ *replicate formulae*
- ○ *name a cell*
- ○ *use a named cell reference in formulae*
- ○ *use comparison operators*
- ○ *replicate formulae using a variety of cell references*
- ○ *use functions in formulae*
- ○ *use the IF function*
- ○ *use the SUMIF function*
- ○ *use the COUNTIF function*
- ○ *use the COUNT and COUNTA functions*
- ○ *use the MAX and MIN functions.*

Entering formula

A formula is a set of instructions that tells Excel to take data (the value) from a specified location (the reference) and perform a calculation. Cell (or range) references are used in formulae to enable Excel to find the data that needs to be calculated.

Understanding cell references

A cell reference tells Excel where to find the data to be used in a formula. The type of reference (e.g. relative, absolute, named, etc.) gives further instructions about what to do if the formula is replicated (copied) or if the cell is moved.

CELL REFERENCE	EXAMPLE	
Relative	=A1+B1	When copied to the row below, the formula will become =A2+B2.
		Because the copied formula is now in row 2, Excel will now use the values in row 2 to make the calculation.
		The cell reference is *relative* to the position of the formula (the cell reference is changed in relation to the position of the formula).
Absolute	=$A$1+$B$1	When copied to the row below, the formula will still be =$A$1+$B$1.
		If this formula is copied anywhere in the spreadsheet it will still use the values from cells A1 and B1.
Mixed	=$A1+$B1	When copied to the row below, the formula will be =$A2+$B2.
	=A$1+B$1	If this formula is copied anywhere in the spreadsheet the values in the A and B column will always be used, the row values used will be relative to the position of the formula.
		In a mixed cell reference either the row is absolute and the column is relative or the row is relative and the column absolute.
Named	overheads	Any cell (or any range of cells) in a spreadsheet can be given a name. This name can then be used in formula.
		If a formula containing a named cell reference is copied it will always use the value in the named cell (or range) when calculating results.
		The named cell (or named range) can be moved anywhere in the spreadsheet. Excel will still use the value of the named cell (or range) in the calculation.

Mathematical operators

Mathematical operators are used between cell references to instruct Excel how to perform the calculation. For example, A1+B1 instructs Excel to take the value in the cell A1 and add it to the value in the cell B1.

The table opposite shows the operators that you will need to use.

OPERATOR	ACTION
+	Add
–	Subtract
* (asterisk)	Multiply
/	Divide
%	Per cent

Understanding brackets

When entering a formula to perform a calculation, remember the order in which any calculation will be carried out. Calculations in **brackets** are always carried out first then **divide** and/or **multiply** then **add** and/or **subtract**.

For example:

5+2*2 will give the answer **9** because **2*2=4** then **4+5=9**.

Whereas:

(5+2)*2 will give the answer **14** because **5+2=7** then **7*2=14**.

When you are entering a formula you must think very carefully about how you are entering it. You must include brackets around the part(s) of the formula that you want to be calculated first. Remember that a formula in a spreadsheet must always begin with = (equal sign).

Look at the spreadsheet below.

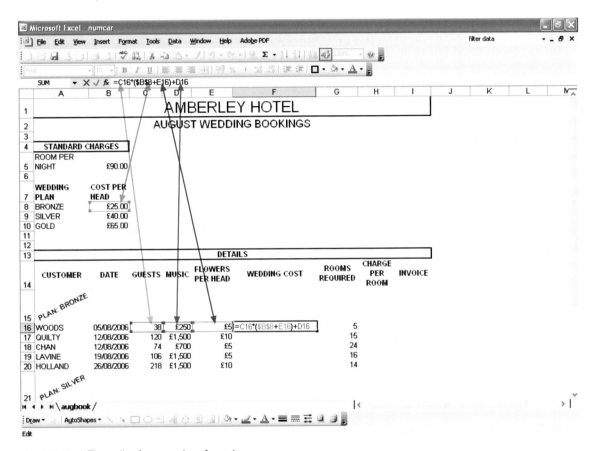

FIGURE 2.13 The cell references in a formula

The number of GUESTS has been multiplied by the (COST PER HEAD added to the FLOWERS PER HEAD) then MUSIC has been added.

The COST PER HEAD and the FLOWERS PER HEAD have been enclosed in brackets because these figures need to be added together *before* they are multiplied by the GUESTS. The figure for MUSIC has then been added.

38*(25+5) + 250

Result of calculation with and without brackets

	FIRST PART OF CALCULATION	SECOND PART OF CALCULATION	THIRD PART OF CALCULATION	RESULT
With brackets Add then multiply	(25+5)=30	30*38 =1140	1140+250=1390	Correct
Without brackets Multiply then add	38*25=950	950+5=955	955+250=1205	Incorrect

▶▶ How to... enter a formula

1 Click in the cell in which the result of the formula is to be displayed.

2 Enter the = sign.

3 Click in the cell (or select the range) that contains the first value (set of values).

4 Enter the mathematical operator.

5 Click in the cell (or select the range) that contains the second value (set of values).

If the formula is to be a multi-stage calculation, continue entering the mathematical operator and clicking in the cell (or selecting the range) until all stages of the calculation have been entered.

6 Check the formula, inserting brackets and absolute cell references if required.

7 Press **Enter** to complete the formula. The answer to the calculation will now appear in the cell in which you entered the formula.

TIP!

You can also use the keyboard to enter the required formula. If you choose to use this method, check your work very carefully to make sure you have been 100 per cent accurate.

Using absolute, relative and mixed cell references

If a formula is to be replicated to other cells you will need to think about whether the cell references need to be relative, absolute or mixed.

Look at the spreadsheet shown in Figure 2.14. In the **WEDDING COST** column, the formula =C16*($B$8+E16)+D16 has been entered for the first customer (WOODS).

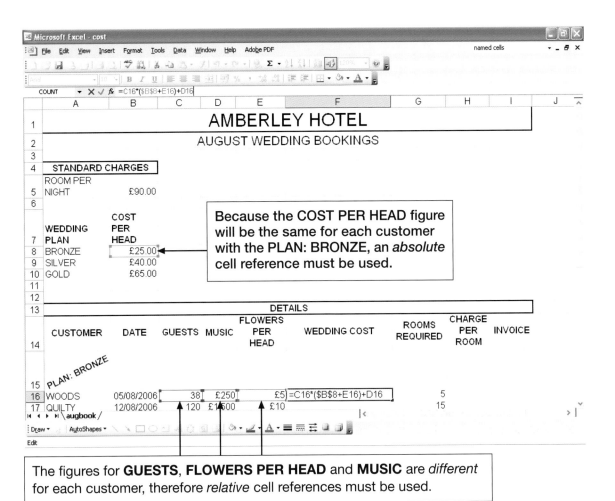

The figures for **GUESTS**, **FLOWERS PER HEAD** and **MUSIC** are *different* for each customer, therefore *relative* cell references must be used.

FIGURE 2.14 Absolute and relative cell references in a formula

When the formula is replicated the value in the cell B8 (£25.00) will always be used in the calculation.

▶▶ How to... *replicate formula*

1 Click in the cell containing the formula to be replicated.

2 Position the mouse over the bottom right corner of the cell until the cursor turns into a black plus sign.

3 Hold down the mouse button and drag across the cells into which the formula is to be copied.

4 Release the mouse button.

5 The formula will be replicated into the selected cells.

TIP!

If there are empty rows in your spreadsheet you should not display the results of the formula (or zero values) in the blank rows. You should delete (or clear) any formula contained in blank rows.

In some calculations (such as AVERAGE and COUNT) all data (including zero values) would be included in the calculation and would result in incorrect figures! If cells are blank they are ignored.

TIP!

You can change between relative, absolute and mixed cell references by highlighting the cell reference you want to change then clicking on **F4** until the reference you require is displayed.

The **STAFF BONUS** and the **SECURITY** figures must be multiplied by the **NO OF GUESTS** to generate the bonus to be given to staff and the security cost from each wedding.

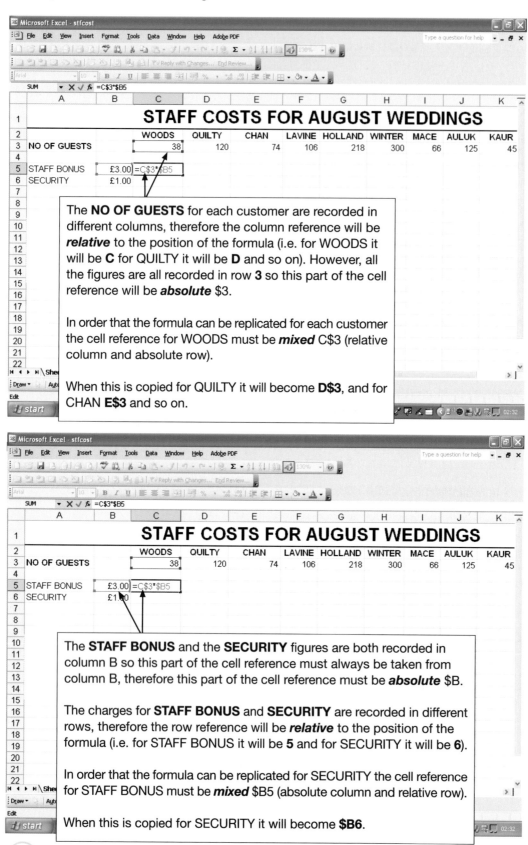

1   Open file **stfcost**.

2   In the **STAFF BONUS** row, in the **WOODS** column calculate the bonus generated for **WOODS** by multiplying the figure in the cell next to **STAFF BONUS** (£3.00) by the **NUMBER OF GUESTS** for **WOODS**.

You will need to use mixed cell references in this formula.

3   Replicate this formula to generate the figure for **SECURITY** for **WOODS**.

4   Replicate the formula to generate the figures for **STAFF BONUS** and **SECURITY** for all other customers (QUILTY to SMYTHE).

5   Save the file in your working area as an Excel workbook using the filename **bonus**.

1   Open your saved file **numcur**.

2   In the **DETAILS** section, in the **WEDDING COST** column, enter a formula to calculate the WEDDING COST for the first customer (WOODS):

Multiply the figure for **GUESTS** by the result of **COST PER HEAD** (BRONZE) plus **FLOWERS PER HEAD** then add the figure for **MUSIC**.

You will need to use relative and absolute cell references.

3   Replicate the formula for all **PLAN: BRONZE** customers.

4   Calculate the **WEDDING COST** for the first **PLAN: SILVER** customer (WINTER):

Multiply the figure for **GUESTS** by the result of **COST PER HEAD** (SILVER) plus **FLOWERS PER HEAD** then add the figure for **MUSIC**.

You will need to use relative and absolute cell references.

5   Calculate the **WEDDING COST** for the first **PLAN: GOLD** customer (PATEL):

Multiply the figure for **GUESTS** by the result of **COST PER HEAD** (GOLD) plus **FLOWERS PER HEAD** then add the figure for **MUSIC**.

You will need to use relative and absolute cell references.

6   Save the file in your working area as an Excel workbook using the filename **abref**.

7   Close the spreadsheet file.

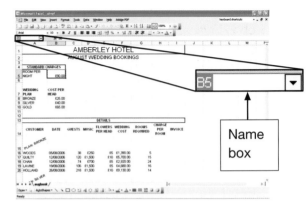

▶▶ *How to...* *name a cell*

1 Click in the cell to be named.

2 Click in the **name box** (Figure 2.16).

3 Enter the name for the cell.

4 Press **Enter**.

FIGURE 2.16 Naming a cell

Check your understanding *Name a cell*

1 Open your saved file **abref**.

2 In the **STANDARD CHARGES** section, name the cell containing the value £90.00 overnight.

3 Save the file in your working area as an Excel workbook using the filename **named**.

Using a named cell in a formula

When you include a named cell in a formula, the cell name is displayed instead of the cell reference. The named cell does not have a row and column reference so it can be moved anywhere in the spreadsheet. Whenever a named cell is used in a formula Excel will locate the named cell and will use the values from the named cell in the calculation.

Understanding functions

A function is a pre-written set of instructions that tells Excel what to do. For example, the SUM function will tell Excel to add up all the numbers in the specified cells. Some functions perform common calculations (e.g. SUM, COUNT, etc.), others allow you to create a conditional formula, for example the IF function.

An IF statement will return one value if a condition is met and another value if a condition is not met. For example, IF A1=200, return the value 'FULL' otherwise return the value 'BOOK NOW'. Excel will look at the data in cell A1. If the value is 200, the value in the cell containing the formula will be 'FULL'. If the data in cell A1 is not 200, then the value in the cell containing the formula will be 'BOOK NOW'. If you don't specify the results to be displayed if the criterion is not met, Excel will return the value

'FALSE'. To display a blank cell if the condition is not met you can press the spacebar. This will show in the formula as ' '.

Excel has numerous available functions, but you will only need to understand and use a few of these. The following table gives a brief explanation of the functions that you will need to be able to use.

FUNCTION	WHAT IT DOES
SUM	Adds the values in a range of cells.
SUMIF	Adds the values of cells that meet a specified condition.
AVERAGE	Calculates the average of a range of cells.
COUNT	Counts the number of cells containing numeric data.
COUNTA	Counts the number of cells that contain data (numeric or alphabetic).
COUNTIF	Counts the number of cells that meet a specified condition.
MIN	Returns the smallest value from a range of cells.
MAX	Returns the largest value from a range of cells.
IF	Returns one value if a condition is met and another value if the condition is not met.

Comparison operators

When you use IF functions (e.g. SUMIF, COUNTIF, IF) you will need to use a comparison operator so that Excel can compare the values in the cells to see whether or not the condition is met.

OPERATOR	ACTION
=	Equal to
>	Greater than
<	Less than
>=	Greater than or equal to
<=	Less than or equal to
<>	Not equal to

TIP!

If the function you wish to use is not listed, enter the function, or a description of what you want to do, in the box under **Search for a function** in the Insert Function dialogue box. Excel will list the functions that best match your description.

▶▶ How to... *enter formulae containing a function*

1 Click in the cell in which the result of the formula is to be displayed.

2 Click on the **Insert Function** button *fx* .

3 The **Insert Function** dialogue box appears.

4 In the **Select a Function** section, click on the required function.

5 Click on **OK**.

6 Follow the instructions below for the function you wish to enter.

FIGURE 2.17 The Insert Function dialogue box

1 Follow the instructions in How to... enter a formula.

2 In the **Function Arguments** dialogue box, click in the **Logical_test** box.

In the Logical_test box:

3 Click on the spreadsheet cell that contains the data that you wish to compare (e.g. F16) (or key in the cell reference).

4 Enter the comparison operator (e.g. >).

5 Enter the comparison data (a cell reference or data).

In the Value_if_true box:

6 Enter the result to be displayed in the cell if the condition is met (a cell reference or data).

In the Value_if_false box:

7 Enter the result to be displayed in the cell if the condition is NOT met (a cell reference or data).

8 Click on **OK**.

TIP!

To select cells to compare, click 🔲 to minimise the dialogue box. Click again to return to the full-size dialogue box.

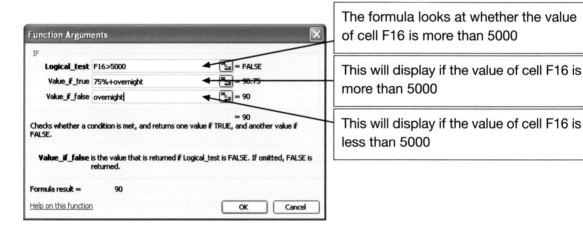

The formula looks at whether the value of cell F16 is more than 5000

This will display if the value of cell F16 is more than 5000

This will display if the value of cell F16 is less than 5000

FIGURE 2.18 The IF Function Arguments dialogue box

1 Open your saved file named **named**.

2 In the **CHARGE PER ROOM** column, use a function to calculate the figure for the first customer (WOODS):

> If the **WEDDING COST** is greater than **5000** then return 75% of the value of the named cell **room per night**, otherwise return the value of the named cell **room per night**.

3 Replicate this formula for all other customers.

4 Delete any values that are displayed in blank cells.

5 In the **INVOICE** column, use a formula to calculate the charge for the first customer:

> Multiply the **ROOMS REQUIRED** by the **CHARGE PER ROOM**, then add the figure for **WEDDING COST**.

6 Delete any values that are displayed over blank cells.

7 Format the figures in the **CHARGE PER ROOM** and the **INVOICE** columns to currency with a currency symbol and 2 decimal places.

8 Save the file in your working area as an Excel workbook using the filename **wedcomp**.

9 Close the file.

▶▶ How to... use the SUMIF function

1 Follow the instructions in How to... enter a formula.

2 In the **Function Arguments** dialogue box click in the **Range** box.

In the Range box:

3 Select the spreadsheet cells that contain the data to be compared (IF).

In the Criteria box:

4 Enter the comparison criteria (or click in a cell that contains the criteria).

In the **Range** box:
- select the spreadsheet cells that contain the data to be compared (IF).

In the **Criteria** box:
- enter the comparison criteria (or click in a cell that contains the criteria).

In the **Sum_range** box:
- select the spreadsheet cells that contain the data to be totalled if the criteria is met
- click on OK.

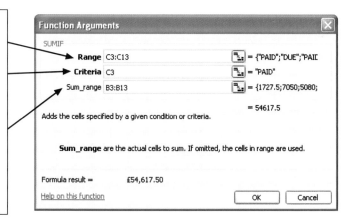

FIGURE 2.19 The SUMIF Function Arguments dialogue box

In the Sum_range box:

5   Select the spreadsheet cells that contain the data to be totalled if the criteria is met.

6   Click on **OK**.

Check your understanding *Use the SUMIF function*

1   Open the file **status**.

2   In the cell to the right of **AMOUNT RECEIVED** use a function to **TOTAL** the figures in the **AMOUNT** column **IF** the value in the **STATUS** column is **PAID**.

3   In the cell to the right of **AMOUNT DUE** use a function to **TOTAL** the figures in the **AMOUNT** column **IF** the value in the **STATUS** column is **DUE**.

4   Save the file in your working area as an Excel workbook using the filename **sumif**.

5   Close the file.

▶▶ **How to...** *use the COUNTIF function*

1   Follow the instructions in How to... enter a formula.

2   In the **Function Arguments** dialogue box, click in the **Range** box.

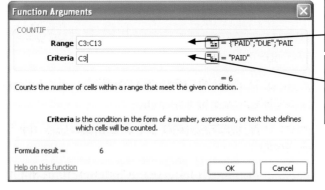

The selected range of data is cell C3 to cell C13

The comparison criteria is contained in cell C3

In the Range box:

3   Select the spreadsheet cells that contain the data to be compared (IF).

FIGURE 2.20 The COUNTIF Function Arguments dialogue box

In the Criteria box:

4   Enter the comparison criteria (or click in a cell that contains the criteria).

5   Click on **OK**.

▶▶ **How to...** *use the COUNT and COUNTA function*

The **COUNT** and the **COUNTA** functions both operate in the same way, the difference is that **COUNT** will only count numeric data and **COUNTA** will count cells that contain any data (numeric or text).

1   Follow the instructions in How to... enter a formula.

2   In the **Function Arguments** dialogue box, click in the **Value1** box.

In the Value1 box:

3 Select the spreadsheet cells that contain the data to be counted. (Note: empty/blank cells will not be included in the count.)

In the Value2 box:

4 You may add another range of cells to be included in the count or it may be left blank.

5 Click on **OK**.

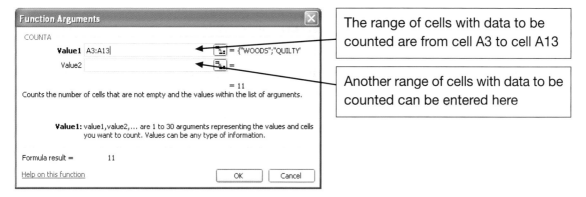

The range of cells with data to be counted are from cell A3 to cell A13

Another range of cells with data to be counted can be entered here

FIGURE 2.21 The COUNTA Function Arguments dialogue box

Check your understanding *Using the COUNT, COUNTA and COUNTIF function*

1 Open the file named **sumif**.

2 In the cell to the right of **NUMBER OF CUSTOMERS** use a function to count the number of **CUSTOMERS** (row 3 to row 13).

3 In the cell to the right of **NUMBER PAID** use a function to count if the value in the **STATUS** column is **PAID**.

4 In the cell to the right of **NUMBER DUE** use a function to count if the value in the **STATUS** column is **DUE**.

5 Save the file with the filename **count**

▶▶ How to... *use the MAX and MIN function*

The **MIN** and **MAX** functions operate in the same way.

1 Follow the instructions in How to... enter a formula.

2 In the **Function Arguments** dialogue box, click in the **Number1** box.

In the NUMBER1 box:

3 Select the spreadsheet cells that contain the data from which you want to return the MIN or MAX.

In the NUMBER2 box:

4 You may add another range of cells or it may be left blank.

5 Click on **OK**.

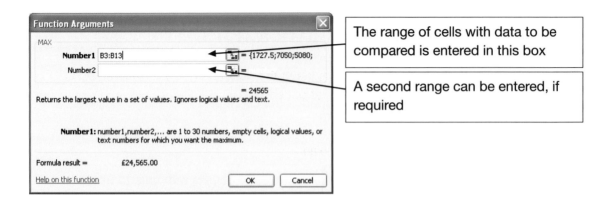

Function Arguments

MAX

Number1 B3:B13 = {1727.5;7050;5080;

Number2 =

= 24565

Returns the largest value in a set of values. Ignores logical values and text.

Number1: number1,number2,... are 1 to 30 numbers, empty cells, logical values, or text numbers for which you want the maximum.

Formula result = £24,565.00

Help on this function [OK] [Cancel]

The range of cells with data to be compared is entered in this box

A second range can be entered, if required

FIGURE 2.22 The Max Function Arguments dialogue box

Using the MAX function

Check your understanding

1 Open the file **count**.

2 In the cell to the right of **MAXIMUM ORDER VALUE** use a function to return the figure for the **MAXIMUM** from the AMOUNT column for the CUSTOMERS (row 3 to row 13).

3 Save the file in your working area as an Excel workbook using the filename **max**

4 Save and close any open spreadsheet files.

By working through Section 3 you will have learnt the skills listed below. Read each item to help you decide how confident you feel about each skill:

- ○ enter formulae
- ○ use mathematical operators in formulae
- ○ use brackets appropriately
- ○ use relative cell references
- ○ use absolute cell references
- ○ use mixed cell references
- ○ replicate formulae
- ○ name a cell
- ○ use a named cell reference in a formula
- ○ use comparison operators
- ○ replicate formulae using a variety of cell references
- ○ use functions in formulae
- ○ use the IF function
- ○ use the SUMIF function
- ○ use the COUNTIF function
- ○ use the COUNT and COUNTA functions
- ○ use the MAX and MIN functions.

If you think that you need more practice on any of the skills in the above list, go back and work through the skill(s) again.

If you feel confident, move on to Section 4.

LEARNING OUTCOMES

In this section you will learn how to:

- change the page setup
- set the page orientation
- fit to one page
- adjust margins
- insert headers and footers
- use automatic fields in headers and footers
- display gridlines and row and column headings
- print a document selection
- set and clear a print area
- hide rows and/or columns
- display formulae
- print formulae.

Changing the page setup

A spreadsheet is easier to read if related information is printed on the same page. Although this is not always possible, amending the page setup can often improve the display.

Excel has an option to fit the spreadsheet to a specified number of pages. This is a useful option, but it can result in the size of the text being very small. Care should be taken to ensure that the spreadsheet is still readable if this option is used.

Always check the layout of the spreadsheet in Print Preview to see what, if any, adjustments need to be made.

Automatic fields can be inserted into headers and/or footers. This ensures that the date and filename will always be displayed on the document when printed.

The How to… guidelines that follow will use the Print Preview method of accessing the Page Setup window so that you can view the changes you have made.

TIP!

You can access the **Page Setup** window either by clicking on Page Setup within the drop-down **File** menu, or by clicking on the **Print Preview** icon and clicking on the **Setup** button.

Using the **Print Preview** method allows you to view the changes you have made before printing.

▶▶ **How to...**   *change the page orientation and fit to one page*

1 On the Standard Toolbar, click on the **Print Preview** icon .

2 From Print Preview click on the **Setup** button.

3 In the **Page Setup** dialogue box, click on the **Page** tab.

4 In the **Paper size** section check that the paper size is set to **A4**, if not click on the drop-down arrow to the right of the box and select A4 from the list.

5 In the **Orientation** section, click in the radio button next to the required orientation.

6 If required, in the **Scaling** section click in the radio button next to **Fit to**.

7 Use the up and down arrows to the right of the **Fit to** boxes to specify the number of pages to fit to.

8 Make any other changes, then click on **OK**.

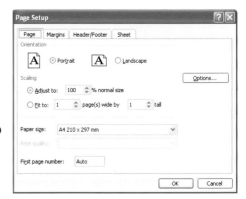

FIGURE 2.23 The Page Setup dialogue box

▶▶ How to... adjust margins

1 On the Standard toolbar, click on the **Print Preview** icon.

2 From Print Preview click on the **Setup** button.

3 In the **Page Setup** dialogue box, click on the **Margins** tab.

4 In the boxes under Top, Left, Right, and Bottom click on the up or down arrows to adjust the margins.

5 Make any other changes, then click on **OK**.

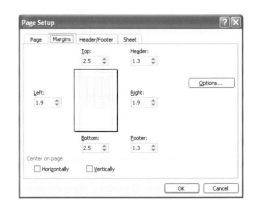

FIGURE 2.24 The Margins tab in the Page Setup dialogue box

▶▶ How to... insert headers and footers and use automatic fields

1 On the Standard toolbar, click on the **Print Preview** icon.

2 From Print Preview click on the **Setup** button.

3 In the Page Setup dialogue box, click on the **Header/Footer** tab.

4 Click on the **Custom Header** or **Custom Footer** button.

5 In the Header/Footer dialogue box, click in a section (Left, Center or Right).

6 Enter any text (e.g. your name and centre number).

7 Click in another section.

8 Click on the icon(s) for the automatic fields to be displayed.

9 Click on **OK**.

10 The **Page Setup** dialogue box will be displayed.

11 Make any other changes then click **OK**.

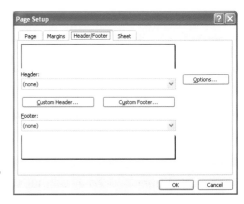

FIGURE 2.25 The Header/Footer tab in the Page Setup dialogue box

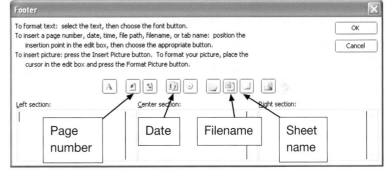

FIGURE 2.26 The Footer dialogue box

▶▶ How to... *display gridlines and row and column headings*

1 In the Standard toolbar, click on the **Print Preview** icon.

2 From Print Preview click on the **Setup** button.

3 In the **Page Setup** dialogue box, click on the **Sheet** tab (Figure 2.27).

4 Click in the box next to **Gridlines**.

5 Click in the box next to **Row and column headings** to display a tick.

6 To remove, click in the box again to remove the tick.

7 Click on **OK**.

FIGURE 2.27 The Sheet tab in the Page Setup dialogue box

TIP!

Row and column headings are the column letters, A, B, C, etc. and the row numbers 1, 2, 3, etc. Do not confuse row and column headings with the row and column labels (titles) that you enter in the cells of the spreadsheet. Displaying row and column headings is normally required on a formula printout.

Check your understanding **Set the page layout**

1 Open your saved file **wedcomp**.

2 Set the page orientation to **landscape**.

3 Adjust the margins and/or page settings to ensure that the spreadsheet will be displayed **on one page**.

TIP!

Look at the spreadsheet display (in Print Preview) before entering headers and footers – try to enter headers and footers in a position that will not interfere with the spreadsheet (e.g. if you have an empty area to the right or bottom of the spreadsheet use this area).

4 Enter the following as a header or footer:

 ○ **your name and centre number**
 ○ **an automatic file name**
 ○ **an automatic date**
 ○ **automatic page numbers**.

5 Display gridlines.

6 View the spreadsheet in Print Preview.

7 Check that all data is displayed in full and will be clearly legible when printed.

8 Print the spreadsheet **wedcomp** showing the figures, on one page.

9 Save the file, in your working area, as an Excel workbook with the filename **setup**

10 Close the spreadsheet file.

Printing a document selection

You can print part of a spreadsheet either by hiding the rows and/or columns that you do not want to print, or by selecting the data and then printing the selection. Printing a document selection is a temporary print setting – when the file is saved the print selection is lost.

In some circumstances you may only ever wish to print a particular section of the spreadsheet. In these circumstances you can set a print area. When you save the file the print area is also saved. When the document is reopened and printed only the cells in the print selection will print. If you wanted to print areas of the spreadsheet not in the print selection, the print area would need to be cleared.

Printing a document selection by selecting the cells to print will only print adjacent rows/columns on one page. For example, if you wished to print three non-adjacent columns each column would be printed on a separate page. If you wish to print non-adjacent rows/columns on one page you must hide the rows/columns that are not to be printed. When the spreadsheet is saved the rows/columns remain hidden. To print the hidden rows and columns you would need to unhide them.

▶▶ How to... *print a document selection*

1 Select the cells to be printed.

2 In the Menu bar, click on **File**.

3 In the drop-down menu, click on **Print**.

4 Click in the box next to **Selection** (Figure 2.28).

5 Only the selected cells will print.

FIGURE 2.28 The Selection box in the Print dialogue box

TIP!

Remember non-adjacent cells will be printed on separate pages.

Check your understanding *Print a document selection*

1 Open your saved file **setup**.

2 Select only the **DETAILS** section of the spreadsheet (columns A to I, rows 13 to 28 inclusive).

3 Print only the **DETAILS** section of the spreadsheet.

4 Close the file.

1 Select the cells to be included in the print area.

2 In the Menu bar, click on **File**.

3 In the drop-down menu, click on **Print Area**.

4 Click on **Set Print Area**.

Whenever the spreadsheet is printed only the selected area will print.

Remember: non-adjacent cells will be printed on separate pages.

1 In the Menu bar, click on **File**.

2 In the drop-down menu, click on **Print Area**.

3 Click on **Clear Print Area**.

Check your understanding **Set and clear a print area**

1 Open your saved file **setup**.

2 Set a print area to print only the **STANDARD CHARGES** section of the spreadsheet (columns A and B, rows 4 to 10 inclusive).

3 Print the spreadsheet showing the figures on one page.

4 Save the file in your working area as an Excel workbook with the filename **charges**

5 Clear the print area.

6 Print the entire spreadsheet showing the figures on one page.

7 Save the file in your working area as an Excel workbook with the filename **full**

1 Select the entire column(s) or row(s) to be hidden.

2 Position the mouse over the selected area.

3 Right-click anywhere in the selected area.

4 In the menu, click on **Hide**.

5 The column(s) or row(s) will be hidden.

1 Select the entire spreadsheet. This can be done by either clicking the **Select All** button or pressing **Ctrl + A**.

2 Right-click the mouse over the row number or column letter divider where the rows or columns have been hidden.

3 Select **Unhide** from the menu.

4 The column(s) or row(s) will be revealed.

Displaying formulae

When you display formulae, Excel will automatically widen all the columns. However, the formulae will not necessarily be displayed in full.

You can autofit the columns (select the entire spreadsheet, click **Format** in the Menu bar, select **Column** followed by **Autofit Selection**). However, this option unhides any hidden columns so they will need to be hidden again.

▶▶ How to... *display formulae*

1 In the Menu bar, click on **Tools**.

2 Select **Options** from the drop-down menu.

3 In the **Options** dialogue box, click on the **View** tab.

4 In the Window options section click to insert a tick in the box next to **Formulas**.

5 To return to spreadsheet view, remove the tick.

Printing formulae

Formulae can be printed by following the steps in How to… print a document selection on page 113. When making a formula print in formula view you must ensure that all formulae are displayed in full – check first in Print Preview, but also check your print carefully to ensure that the formulae has been printed as you expected.

TIP!

In formula view some of the formatting will not be displayed, e.g. numeric formatting (dates in the spreadsheet will display as numbers). Also, wrapped cells may not wrap. This is normal and will not affect the display in spreadsheet view.

What does it mean?

Spreadsheet view: the standard presentation of a spreadsheet, all formulas are hidden and results of formulas are presented as data.

TIP!

To switch from the spreadsheet view to formula view and vice versa, press the **Ctrl +`** key (the accent is key usually above the Tab key or next to the spacebar).

Check your understanding *Print formulae*

1 Open your saved file **setup**.

2 Display the formulae.

3 Hide the entire **STANDARD CHARGES** section and the two rows that follow (rows 4 to 12).

4 Display row and column headings.

5 Ensure that all data and all formulae will be displayed in full and will be clearly legible when printed.

6 Save the file with the filename **wedform**

7 Print the formula **wedform** showing the formulae in full, on one page.

8 In your working area, save the file keeping the name **wedform**

9 Close the file.

1   Open your saved file **max**.

2   Enter your name and centre number, an automatic filename and an automatic date as footer.

3   Display gridlines.

4   Print a copy of the entire spreadsheet on one page.

5   Ensure all data is fully visible on your printout.

6   Save your file using the filename **max1**

7   Display the formulae.

8   Display gridlines and row and column headings.

9   Ensure that all formulae will be fully displayed and clearly legible when printed.

10 Save the file with the filename **maxform**

11 Save and close any open spreadsheet files.

1   Open your saved file **bonus**.

2   Set the page orientation as landscape.

3   Display gridlines.

4   Display row and column headings.

5   Enter your name and centre number as a header.

6   Enter an automatic filename and an automatic date as a footer.

7   Ensure that all data is shown in full.

8   Save the file in your working area as an Excel workbook using the filename **bonus1**

9   Print a copy of the spreadsheet showing all the figures in landscape orientation.

10 Display the formulae.

11 Print one copy of the spreadsheet showing all formulae in full.

12 Save the file in your working area as an Excel workbook using the filename **bonform**

13 Save and close any open spreadsheet files.

ASSESS YOUR SKILLS – Change the page setup and print spreadsheets

By working through Section 4 you will have learnt the skills listed below. Read each item to help you decide how confident you feel about each skill.

- ○ change the page setup
- ○ set the page orientation
- ○ fit to one page
- ○ adjust margins
- ○ insert headers and footers
- ○ use automatic fields in headers and footers
- ○ display gridlines and row and column headings
- ○ print a document selection
- ○ set and clear a print area
- ○ hide rows and/or columns
- ○ display formulae
- ○ print formulae.

If you think that you need more practice on any of the skills in the above list, go back and work through the skill(s) again.

If you feel confident, move on to Section 5.

5: Link spreadsheets, sort data and use AutoFilter

LEARNING OUTCOMES

In this section you will learn how to:

- ○ *create a reference to a cell in another spreadsheet*
- ○ *replicate a formula containing a reference to a cell in another spreadsheet*
- ○ *use tools to sort data*
- ○ *use tools to filter data (AutoFilter).*

Linking spreadsheets

Spreadsheets can be linked so that the values from one spreadsheet are recorded or used in the linked spreadsheet. The advantage of linking a spreadsheet, rather than copying the values into a second spreadsheet, is that a linked spreadsheet will update when changes are made to the original spreadsheet. If the data is simply copied to a new spreadsheet the values will not update.

Links can be made either to separate workbooks (a different file) or to a different sheet within the same workbook (the same file). You may use either method to link your spreadsheets.

One of the advantages of linking worksheets within the same workbook is that all related spreadsheets are kept together in one file. If the file is moved then all the related worksheets will remain together. As a result, when formulae are displayed, the reference to the linked spreadsheet will be short because it will only need to show the reference to the worksheet within the file. When separate workbooks are used, if only the file containing the linked data is open, Excel needs to show the exact location of the linked file from which it is getting the data.

Below is an example of how the formula showing the linked cell reference might look:

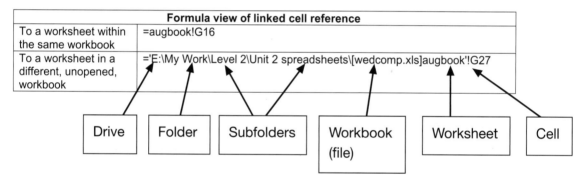

Formula view of linked cell reference	
To a worksheet within the same workbook	=augbook!G16
To a worksheet in a different, unopened, workbook	='E:\My Work\Level 2\Unit 2 spreadsheets\[wedcomp.xls]augbook'!G27

Drive   Folder   Subfolders   Workbook (file)   Worksheet   Cell

You can avoid having a long linked cell reference by opening the source file before opening the file containing the link.

A link can be made to a single cell, or to a range of cells. Formulae can be entered that will enable calculations from one spreadsheet to be recorded in the other spreadsheet.

If you want to replicate the link so that the values in the adjacent cells of the original spreadsheet are also recorded in the linked spreadsheet you **must** make sure that the cell reference is **relative** (e.g. G27) before you replicate. If the link is **absolute** (e.g. $G$7) the value of the original cell in the source spreadsheet will be recorded in all cells of the linked spreadsheet. Always check the cell references before replicating.

TIP!

You can use **F4** to change the cell reference. Select the cell that contains the formula, in the formula bar highlight the cell reference that you want to change, press **F4**. Every time you press **F4** Excel will move through each of the possible cell references (i.e. A1, $A$1, A$1, $A1).

1   Open the source spreadsheet (the spreadsheet that contains the data that you are going to link to).

2   Open the spreadsheet that will contain the link.

3   Click in the cell in which you want the value from the source spreadsheet to be recorded.

4   Enter =.

5   Click on the source spreadsheet in the taskbar.

6   Click in the cell (or select the range of cells) that contains the data you wish to link the active cell to.

7   Press **Enter**.

8   You will be returned to the linked spreadsheet.

9   The value of the link will be recorded.

Check your understanding *Create a reference to a cell in another spreadsheet*

1   Open your saved file **setup**.

2   Open your saved file **clear**.

3   In the **clear** spreadsheet in the **ROOMS BOOKED** column, create a link for the first HOST (cell C7) to the cell containing the figure for the **ROOMS REQUIRED** for **WOODS** (cell G16) in the setup spreadsheet. You will need to use a relative cell reference.

4   Replicate this formula for the other HOSTS.

5   In the **clear** spreadsheet in the **ROOM CHARGE** column, create a link for the first HOST (cell D7) to the cell containing the figure for the **CHARGE PER ROOM** for **WOODS** (cell H16) in the setup spreadsheet. You will need to use a relative cell reference.

6   Replicate this formula for the other HOSTS.

7   Clear any zero values (0) displayed in blank cells.

8   Format the figures in the **ROOM CHARGE** column to 2 decimal places. Do not display a currency symbol.

9   In the **clear** spreadsheet in the **NO OF ROOMS** column in the cell next to 05/08/2006 use a function to calculate the bookings for 05/08/2006 (i.e. cell B23).

    If the value in the **WED DAY** column (absolute cell reference) is 05/08/2006 (**A23** relative cell reference), total the values in the **ROOMS BOOKED** column (absolute cell reference).

10 Replicate this formula for the other dates:

    12/08/2006 (**A24**), 18/08/2006 (**A25**), 19/08/2006 (**A26**) and 26/08/2006 (**A27**).

11 Save the file in your working area using the filename **link**

12 Close any open spreadsheet files.

Use tools to sort and filter data

Sorting a spreadsheet

The data in the spreadsheet can be sorted in ascending or descending order by any of the columns in the spreadsheet. Be very careful to ensure that all the data relating to the sorted data also moves when the data is sorted. This is referred to as 'maintaining the integrity of data'.

▶▶ How to... *sort data*

1 Click in the column label containing the data to be sorted. Do **not** select the entire column unless you want to sort only the data in the selected column and not the related data.

2 In the Menu bar, click on **Data**.

3 In the drop-down menu, click on **Sort** to display the **Sort** dialogue box (Figure 2.29).

4 Check that the correct column label is shown in the **Sort by** section of the dialogue box.

5 Click in the relevant button to select the order (Ascending or Descending).

6 In the **My data range has** section check that the correct selection has been made (Header row or No header row).

7 Click **OK**.

8 The data will be sorted.

FIGURE 2.29 The Sort dialogue box

Check your understanding *Sort data*

1 Open your saved file **move**.

2 Sort the data in ascending order of **Supervisor**.

3 Insert your name, centre number and an automatic filename as a header or footer.

4 Display gridlines and row and column headings.

5 Set the page orientation to **Portrait**.

6 Save the file using the filename **super**.

7 Print the spreadsheet showing values on one page.

8 Close the spreadsheet.

Filtering data using AutoFilter

Using AutoFilter allows you to find records that meet specified criteria (conditions). Filtering *temporarily* hides rows. The filtered data will show only those rows that meet the criteria. Unlike sorting it will not re-arrange the data. Once the filter has been turned off, all the data in the spreadsheet will be revealed.

▶▶ How to... *filter data using AutoFilter*

1   Click in the column label containing the data (or highlight the column) to be filtered.

2   In the Menu bar, click on **Data**.

3   In the drop-down menu, click on **Filter**.

4   Click on **AutoFilter**.

5   Arrow buttons will appear to the right of the column label cell (Figure 2.30).

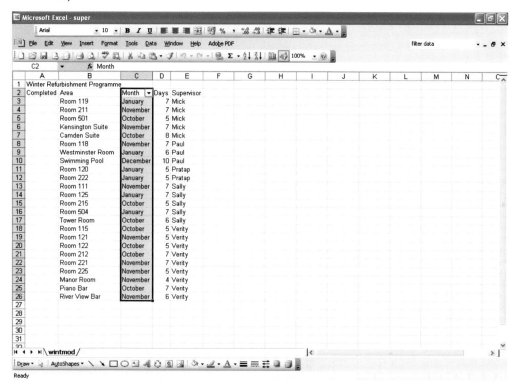

FIGURE 2.30 A drop-down button in a column to be filtered

6   Click on the drop-down arrow of the column to be filtered.

7   If the filter criterion is listed, click on it to filter the data, otherwise move on to step 8.

8   Click on **Custom** to display the **Custom AutoFilter** dialogue box (Figure 2.31).

9   Click on the drop-down arrow to the right of the **Show rows where** box.

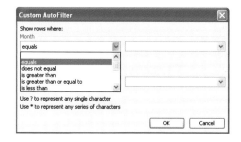

FIGURE 2.31 The Custom AutoFilter dialogue box

10 Select the required criterion (e.g. **is greater than**).

11 In the box on the top right-hand side click on the drop-down arrow and select the comparison to be made (e.g. 5).

12 Click on **OK**.

FIGURE 2.32 The criteria in the Custom AutoFilter dialogue box

TIP!

To filter on just one column, highlight the data to be filtered before clicking on the **Data** menu and selecting **AutoFilter**. Only one filter button (down arrow) will appear.

▶▶ How to... *turn off the filter*

1 In the Menu bar, click on **Data**.

2 In the drop-down menu, click on **Filter**.

3 Click on AutoFilter.

Check your understanding *Sort data*

1 Open your saved file **super**.

2 Filter the data to find all refurbishments where the **month** is **November**.

3 Check that your name, centre number and an automatic filename will be displayed as a header or footer.

4 Check that gridlines and row and column headings will be displayed.

5 Save the file using the filename **nov**

6 Print the filtered spreadsheet showing all the filtered data in full.

7 Turn off the AutoFilter.

8 Filter the data to find all refurbishments where the **day** is **greater than 5**.

9 Check that your name, centre number and an automatic filename will be displayed as a header or footer.

10 Check that gridlines and row and column headings will be displayed.

11 Save the file using the filename **5day**

12 Close the spreadsheet.

1   Open your saved files **setup** and **link**.

2   Using the file **link** in the column **WEDDING PARTIES** use a function to:

Count the number of weddings where the **WED DATE** is the value of the first **DATE** in the **BLOCK BOOKINGS** section (cell **A23**). You will need to use the COUNTIF function and absolute and relative cell references.

TIP!

If you are printing the formulae of a file containing links, open the source file (the spreadsheet that you linked to) first. This will prevent the linked formulae from being too long.

3   Replicate the formula for the other dates.

4   Enter your name, centre number, an automatic date and an automatic filename.

5   Display gridlines and row and column headings.

6   Save the spreadsheet using the filename **finish**

7   Print a copy of the spreadsheet showing values. Ensure all data is displayed in full.

8   Display the formulae.

9   Set the page orientation to **landscape**.

10 Check that row and column headings, your name and centre number will be displayed when printed.

11 Ensure that all formulae will be displayed on one page and will be legible when printed.

12 Print the formulae on one page.

13 Save the file with the filename **finform**

14 Close any open files and exit the software.

ASSESS YOUR SKILLS – Link spreadsheets, sort data and use AutoFilter

By working through Section 5 you will have learnt the skills listed below. Read each item to help you decide how confident you feel about each skill.

- ○ create a reference to a cell in another spreadsheet
- ○ replicate a formula containing a reference to a cell in another spreadsheet
- ○ use tools to sort data
- ○ use tools to filter data (AutoFilter).

If you think that you need more practice on any of the skills in the above list, go back and work through the skill(s) again.

If you feel confident, move on to Chapter 2.

UNIT 2: Manipulating Spreadsheets and Graphs

For the second part of Unit 2, you need to know how to create various types of graphs: exploded pie charts, comparative charts (bar/line), line-column graphs and xy scatter graphs.

1: Create exploded pie charts

LEARNING OUTCOMES

In this section you will learn how to:

- understand the types and purpose of graphs
- view a datafile and identify data for a chart
- select contiguous and non-contiguous data for a pie chart
- identify the parts of a pie chart
- create an exploded pie chart
- set the chart orientation
- format numeric data on a pie chart
- emphasise one sector of a chart
- understand legends and the importance of distinctive data
- use fill effects for pie chart sectors
- set the chart to print in black and white.

What are graphs?

Graphs (also referred to as charts) are an effective way of presenting numeric data in a visual (graphical) form. Graphs can be used to identify particular trends or patterns, sales of products, differences in performances, etc. Sometimes it can be difficult to identify important information from a spreadsheet – a visual picture of the numbers makes it easier to identify trends or changes in data.

Excel offers a wide range of graph styles and options to present data for different types of information. The chart types that you will need to create for this unit are:

Exploded pie charts	Data is displayed as slices of a round pie. Each piece of the pie shows the proportion of each slice as a part of the total.
Comparative graphs	Used to show comparisons between categories.

	Bar graphs	Data is displayed as vertical or horizontal bars.
	Line graphs	Data is displayed as lines to show trends in data.

Line-column graphs	Data is displayed as a line with one or two columns. These show a comparison of related data against a benchmark (displayed as the line).
xy scatter graphs	An xy (scatter) chart either shows the relationships among the numeric values in several data series, or plots two groups of numbers as one series of xy coordinates. This chart shows uneven intervals or clusters of data.
Live data modelling	When the data in a spreadsheet is changed, the graph automatically updates, this is referred to as live data modelling.

Viewing a provided datafile

Before you create any chart, you should look at the data in the datafile. Check to see:

- if the data is presented in columns or rows
- if the data to be plotted on the x-axis is numeric
- which cells you will need to select for the chart. At level 2 you will be expected to select non-contiguous data.

Understanding the selection of data for creating a chart (pie chart, bar and line graphs, line-column graphs and xy scatter graphs)

The datafile on page 126 (Figure 2.32) lists various categories of common injuries over a period of years.

To create a pie chart to show the common injuries for the 6 subtotals for the year 2003, you would need to select the cells shown i.e. non-contiguous data.

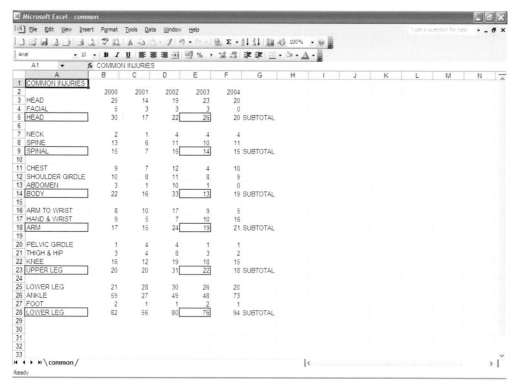

FIGURE 2.32 Non-contiguous data in a datafile (worksheet) selected to create a chart

▶▶ How to... *select non-contiguous data (cells that are not next to each other)*

1 Click in the first cell containing data that you wish to use.

2 Press the **Ctrl** key down, keep it held down and click in all the remaining cells to be selected. After you have selected all the cells release the **Ctrl** key.

3 Once you have selected the data, do **not** click in any part of the datasheet, if you do, you will deselect the data.

▶▶ How to... *select contiguous data (cells that are next to each other)*

Method 1

1 Click in the first cell to be selected and drag the mouse across the range (block) of cells to the last cell to be selected.

2 A block of cells will be highlighted.

Method 2

1 Click with the mouse in the first cell to be selected.

2 Hold the **Shift** key down.

3 Click in the last cell to be selected.

4 A range (block) of cells will be highlighted.

Reminder: In Chapter 1 of this unit, you learnt how to:

○ open a csv file, display data in full and save it as an Excel file

○ insert headers and footers including automatic fields.

Refer to pages 77 and 111 if you need to recap on these skills.

Check your understanding Select non-contiguous data for the creation of a chart

1   Start Excel and open the file named **common**.

2   Save the file as an Excel file using the filename **injuries**

3   Display all the data in full.

4   In your file called **injuries** select the data to display the location of injuries for the **six different subtotals** (HEAD, SPINAL, BODY, ARM, UPPER LEG, LOWER LEG) for **2003**. Do not include the text SUBTOTAL.

   Check your selection of data, you should have selected the following cells:

   A5, E5, A9, E9, A14, E14, A18, E18, A23, E23, A28, E28

Chart Wizard

Using the Chart Wizard makes creating graphs simple because it guides you step-by-step and presents a preview of the chart at each step. Once the chart has been created, changes can still be made to any part of it.

The Chart Wizard steps

Step 1 Select the chart type and sub-type.

Step 2 Check the selection of cells, preview the chart and define the data series, if required.

Step 3 Select and enter, or display, the chart options e.g. Titles, Legends, Data labels.

Step 4 Select the chart location and name the chart tab (optional).

Pie charts

A pie chart shows data as slices of a pie. The size of each slice represents the value (number) from the data on which the chart is based. A slice shows each item of data in proportion to the whole set of data. Pie charts always show only one data series and are useful to emphasise a significant element. Each slice is called a **sector**.

In Excel there are many different pie chart sub-types. You are advised to avoid selecting 3-D charts, as these can sometimes be difficult to read.

Understanding an exploded pie chart

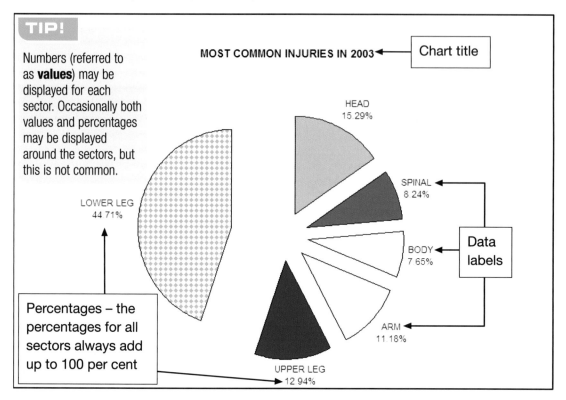

FIGURE 2.33 An exploded pie chart

▶▶ How to... *create an exploded pie chart*

1 In the datafile, select only the range of cells that contain data to be used in the pie chart.

2 Click the **Chart Wizard** 📊 icon.

3 The Chart Wizard **Step 1 of 4** dialogue box will open (Figure 2.34).

4 In the **Standard Types** tab, in the Chart type section, click on **Pie**.

5 In the Chart sub-type section, click on **Exploded Pie**.

6 Click **Next**.

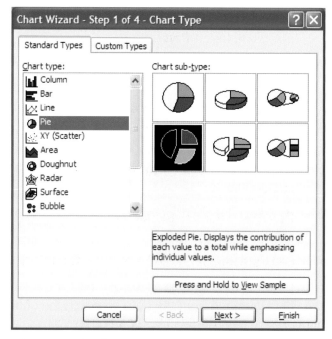

FIGURE 2.34 The Chart Wizard Step 1 of 4 dialogue box

7   The Chart Wizard **Step 2 of 4** dialogue box will open (Figure 2.35).

8   A preview of the chart displays.

9   The data range displays the selected range with the sheet name and a $ sign before the column letter and row number.

10   Check that the preview is correct. If the preview of the chart is incorrect, click **Cancel** and start again.

11   If the preview is correct click **Next**.

12   The Chart Wizard **Step 3 of 4** dialogue box will open (Figure 2.36).

You will need to set options in each of the 3 tabs.

13   Click the **Titles** tab.

14   In the **Chart Title** box, enter the title.

15   Click the **Legend** tab.

16   Click to remove or place a tick in the **Show legend** box (as required).

17   Click the **Data Labels** tab.

18   Click to place a tick in **Category name** (if data labels are required).

19   Click in **Value** or **Percentage** (as required).

20   Click **Next**.

21   The Chart Wizard **Step 4 of 4** dialogue box will open (Figure 2.37).

22   Click in the button for **As new sheet**.

23   Optional: enter a name for the sheet.

24   Click the **Finish** button.

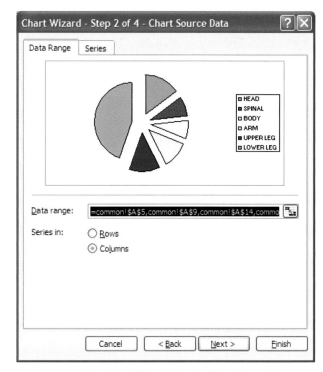

FIGURE 2.35 The Chart Wizard Step 2 of 4 dialogue box

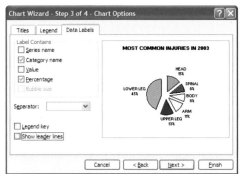

FIGURE 2.36 The Chart Wizard Step 3 of 4 dialogue box

FIGURE 2.37 The Chart Wizard Step 4 of 4 dialogue box

TIP!

Notice how the chart preview updates as you make changes.

TIP!

Click to remove the tick for Show leader lines (optional).

TIP!

If you are creating more than one chart in the same file, it is helpful to enter a name for the sheet. Click in the box next to **As new sheet**, delete the existing text and enter an appropriate name (Figure 2.37).

TIP!

If you have mistakenly created the chart on the worksheet, you can move it to a separate sheet. Right-click within the chart, a menu displays, select **Location**. A **Chart Location** dialogue box displays, click the button for **As new sheet**, click **OK**.

1 In the Menu bar, click on **File**.

2 Click on **Page Setup**. The **Page Setup** dialogue box displays.

3 In the **Page** tab, click the button for **Portrait** or **Landscape**.

4 Click **OK**.

Check your understanding *Create an exploded pie chart*

1 In your saved file **injuries**, check that the cells you selected earlier are still selected (Check your understanding: select non-contiguous data for the creation of a chart, page 127).

2 Create an exploded pie chart to display the location of injuries using the six subtotals for 2003 that you selected.

3 Title the chart: **MOST COMMON INJURIES IN 2003**

4 Ensure that **data labels** and **percentages** are displayed for each sector.

5 Do not display a legend.

6 Create the chart on a sheet that is separate from the data source.

7 Set the chart orientation to **landscape**.

8 Save the file keeping the filename **injuries**

How to... *format numeric data on a pie chart*

1 In your pie chart, click once on any of the numbers or percentages.

2 Black, square handles display around the numbers/percentages for all the sectors.

3 Right-click on any number.

4 A menu displays.

5 Select **Format Data Labels**.

6 A **Format Data Labels** dialogue box displays (Figure 2.38).

7 Click the **Number** tab.

8 In the Category section, click on the required category e.g. Number, Percentage, etc.

9 In the **Decimal Places** section, enter the required number of decimal places or use the up/down arrows.

10 Click **OK**.

FIGURE 2.38 The Number tab in the Format Data Labels dialogue box

In your pie chart titled MOST COMMON INJURIES IN 2003.

1   Format the percentages to **2 decimal places**.

2   Save the updated file keeping the filename **injuries**

▶▶ How to... *emphasise a sector*

1   Click once on a sector, all the sectors will be selected (black, square handles are displayed around all the sectors).

2   Click again to select only the required sector (black, square handles will display on the selected sector only).

3   Click and drag the sector outwards so that it is further away from the rest of the chart.

In your pie chart titled MOST COMMON INJURIES IN 2003.

1   Emphasise the pie chart sector with the largest percentage of injuries by pulling it further away from the rest of the chart.

2   Insert your **name** and **centre number** as a header or footer.

3   Save the updated file keeping the filename **injuries**.

Understanding legends

A **legend** acts as a key for the data on a chart. It is a box that identifies the colours or patterns for each item of data. Legends are mainly used on comparative charts. A legend should only be displayed on a pie chart if the data labels are not displayed next to each sector. Legends should be distinctive in order to ensure that the chart is interpreted correctly.

What is distinctive data?

If a chart displays a legend, it is very important that the legend identifies the data clearly. On the screen all the sectors are different colours, so by referring to the different colour squares in the legend, the label of each sector can be identified.

If the chart is printed in colour, the legend will still identify each sector clearly. However, if it is printed in black and white, then the sector shades will be grey and the corresponding shades in the legend will be shades of grey. This can often mean that not all of the grey shades are clearly

TIP!

For comparative charts, to create a legend automatically, select the row/column labels.

different on the printout, therefore it is not possible to identify the label for each sector by referring to the legend. Such a chart is unusable as it does not identify the data clearly.

There are 2 ways to make the data distinctive:

○ to fill each of the sectors on a pie chart or bars on a bar chart with a different fill effect (e.g. a pattern or texture)
○ to set the chart option to print in pure black and white.

▶▶ How to... *fill pie chart sectors with patterns*

1 Click once on a sector (all the sectors are selected), click again to select one sector (square handles will display on the selected sector only).

2 Right-click on the selected sector. A menu displays.

3 Click on **Format Data Point** in the menu.

4 A **Format Data Point** dialogue box displays.

5 Click the **Fill Effects** button.

6 A **Fill Effects** dialogue box opens.

7 Click the **Pattern** tab and select a pattern from the options.

8 To change the colour, click the drop-down arrow for **foreground** and choose a colour from the list.

9 Click **OK**. Click **OK** to close the **Format Data Point** dialogue box.

▶▶ How to... *set the option to print in black and white*

1 From the chart view, click the **Print Preview** icon.

2 From Print Preview click the **Setup** button Setup... .

3 A **Page Setup** dialogue box will open.

4 Click the **Chart** tab (Figure 2.39).

5 Click the button for **Print in black and white**.

6 Click **OK**.

7 The sectors will be filled with different fill effects.

8 Click **Close** to close the Print Preview.

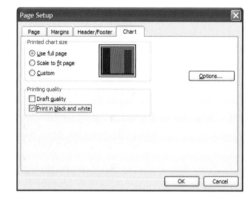

FIGURE 2.39 The Chart tab in the Page Setup dialogue box

TIP!

In the chart view, the different fill effects will not display, but they will usually show on the printout. Remember to check that each shade is clearly distinctive on the printout. If not, you will need to fill any indistinctive sectors/bars with a pattern.

In your pie chart titled MOST COMMON INJURIES IN 2003.

1 Set the option to print the chart in black and white.

2 Do not save the chart.

3 Print one copy of the chart.

In your pie chart titled MOST COMMON INJURIES IN 2003.

1 Fill the largest sector (LOWER LEG) with a pattern.

2 Save the updated file keeping the filename **injuries**

3 Print one copy of the chart.

4 Compare this printout with the previous printout of the pie chart.

ASSESS YOUR SKILLS – Create exploded pie charts

By working through Section 1 you will have learnt the skills listed below. Read each item to help you decide how confident you feel about each skill.

- ○ understand the types and purpose of graphs
- ○ view a datafile and identify data for a chart
- ○ select contiguous and non-contiguous data for a pie chart
- ○ identify the parts of a pie chart
- ○ create an exploded pie chart
- ○ set the chart orientation
- ○ format numeric data on a pie chart
- ○ emphasise one sector of a chart
- ○ understand legends and the importance of distinctive data
- ○ use fill effects for pie chart sectors
- ○ set the chart to print in black and white.

If you think that you need more practice on any of the skills in the above list, go back and work through the skill(s) again.

If you feel confident, move on to Section 2.

LEARNING OUTCOMES

In this section you will learn how to:

- understand comparative charts
- identify the parts of a comparative chart
- understand the selection of data for comparative charts
- create a comparative chart
- enter the chart title, x-axis and y-axis titles
- define the data series for a chart (remove an unwanted series, select the data to be plotted on the x- and y- axis, select the name for legend items)
- format the axis values (scale, intervals, numbers)
- format text
- remove the fill from the plot area
- use a pattern fill for the bars
- set the text orientation.

Bar charts

A bar chart is used to show data changes over a period of time, comparisons between individual items, or comparisons between data. A comparative bar chart displays comparisons for two or more sets of data. Data can be displayed as vertical or horizontal bars. Excel refers to a horizontal bar chart as a bar chart and a vertical (upright) bar chart as a column chart. In the UK, bar charts are usually vertical (upright bars) – therefore the column chart option in Excel should always be selected.

In Excel, there are many different bar chart sub-types. You are advised to use 2-dimensional vertical bar charts (choose the option for column chart).

Line graphs

Line graphs are used to show trends in data at intervals, they display a set of related values plotted as a line. A marker is usually displayed for each value (data point). Comparative line graphs show trends for more than one data series.

Understanding comparative charts

Comparative charts are a simple and effective way to show a direct comparison between data in visual form.

x-axis labels   are the category labels, they describe what the bars or lines represent.

y-axis   is the value axis, it shows the numeric value (quantity).

Legend   is a key to interpreting the data on the chart. The small boxes in the legend are used to identify each set of bars or lines.

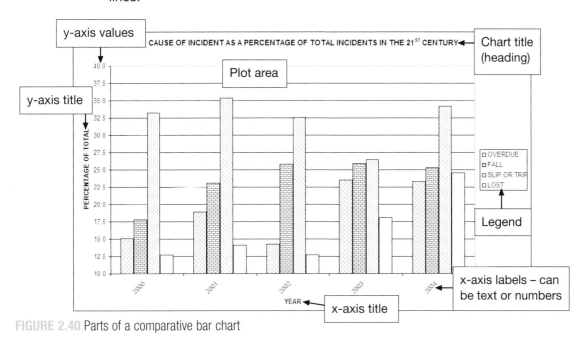

FIGURE 2.40 Parts of a comparative bar chart

Selecting data for comparative charts

Comparative bar charts are created in exactly the same way as simple bar charts, except that more than one data series is selected. When selecting the data for a comparative chart, you should also select the cells that need to be displayed as the axis titles and the legend. Refer to How to... select contiguous data and How to... select non-contiguous data on page 126.

Legends in comparative charts

Any comparative chart **must** display a legend. This must identify the data clearly on a printout. The small boxes in the legend are used to identify each set of bars by colour or pattern.

▶▶ How to... *create a comparative bar chart*

1   In the datafile, select only the relevant range of cells.

2   Click the **Chart Wizard** 📊 icon.

3   The Chart Wizard **Step 1 of 4** dialogue box will open (Figure 2.41).

4   In the **Standard Types** tab, in the **Chart type** section, click on **Column** (do not click on **Bar**).

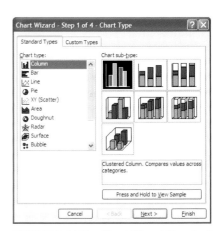

FIGURE 2.41 The Chart Wizard Step 1 of 4 dialogue box

5   In the Chart sub-type section, check that **Clustered Column** is selected.

6   Click **Next**.

7   The Chart Wizard **Step 2 of 4** dialogue box will open.

8   Check that the preview of the chart in this box is correct. If the preview is incorrect, you *must* define the data series before continuing. Refer to Defining data series on pages 137–139.

9   If the preview is correct, click **Next**.

10 The Chart Wizard **Step 3 of 4** dialogue box will open.

11 Click the **Titles** tab.

12 In the **Chart Title** box, enter the title.

13 In the **Category (X) axis** box, enter the x-axis title.

14 In the **Value (Y) axis** box, enter the y-axis title.

15 Click the **Legend** tab.

16 Check that there is a tick in the **Show legend** box.

17 Click **Next**.

18 The Chart Wizard **Step 4 of 4** dialogue box will open.

19 Click the button for **As new sheet**.

20 Optional: enter a name for the sheet.

21 Click **Finish**.

▶▶ How to... *create a comparative line graph*

1   In the datafile, select only the relevant range of cells.

2   Click the **Chart Wizard** 📊 icon.

3   The Chart Wizard **Step 1 of 4** dialogue box will open (Figure 2.42).

4   In the **Standard Types** tab, in the **Chart type** section, click on **Line**.

5   In the Chart sub-type section, check that **Line with markers...** is selected.

6   Click **Next**.

7   Follow steps 7 to 21 as described in How to... create a comparative bar chart.

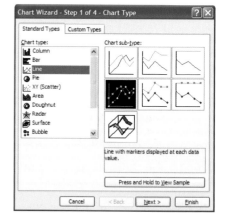

FIGURE 2.42 The Chart Wizard Step 1 of 4 dialogue box

1   Open the file called **cause**.

2   Save the file as an Excel file using the filename **incidents**

3   View the data in the datafile. Note that using AutoFit to display all data in full is not appropriate for all datafiles (such as this one). Widen the columns so that all data is visible.

4   Select the data for the most common causes of rescue incidents for the five years from **2000 to 2004 inclusive**. The most common causes were **OVERDUE, FALL, SLIP OR TRIP** and **LOST**.

Check your selection of data: you should have selected the cells shown below (Figure 2.43).

	A	B	C	D	E	F	G	H	I	J	K
1	CAUSE OF INCIDENT AS A PERCENTAGE OF TOTAL INCIDENTS										
2		1995	1996	1997	1998	1999	2000	2001	2002	2003	2004
3	OVERDUE	13.32	13.23	14.79	16.26	15.21	15.11	18.87	14.29	23.56	23.28
4	COLLAPSE	9.05	5.85	6.85	10.43	8.09	4.53	6.13	4.35	7.18	8.9
5	IN DIFFICULTY	4.27	4.58	3.84	1.84	4.21	6.34	4.72	5.9	6.32	10.34
6	FALL	19.6	24.94	24.38	21.78	24.27	17.82	23.11	25.78	25.86	25.29
7	SLIP OR TRIP	27.89	28.5	34.25	30.98	31.72	33.23	35.38	32.61	26.44	34.19
8	SHOUTS OR LIGHTS	2.76	3.31	8.22	5.21	4.85	1.51	4.25	2.17	2.01	3.44
9	LOST	6.78	7.12	10.41	9.51	11.97	12.69	14.15	12.73	18.1	24.57
10											

FIGURE 2.43 Selected data in the **incidents** datafile

5   Create a **comparative vertical bar chart**.

6   Title the chart: **CAUSE OF INCIDENT AS A PERCENTAGE OF TOTAL INCIDENTS IN THE 21ST CENTURY**

7   Title the x-axis: **YEAR**

8   Title the y-axis: **PERCENTAGE OF TOTAL**

9   Ensure that the legend clearly displays the following causes:

    OVERDUE   FALL   SLIP OR TRIP   LOST

10 Create the chart on a sheet that is separate from the data source.

11 Set the chart orientation to **landscape**.

12 Insert your **name**, **centre number**, an **automatic date** and an **automatic filename** as a header or footer.

13 Save the chart.

Defining data series

You may need to define the data series for comparative bar and line graphs, line-column graphs and xy scatter graphs.

When creating a chart using the Chart Wizard, you must check the preview of the chart in the Chart Wizard Step 2 of 4 (Figure 2.44). You may need to define each data series so that Excel knows which row/column of data is to be used for the x-axis, the y-axis and which data should be displayed as a legend. You may also need to remove unwanted data series at this stage.

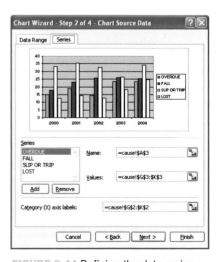

FIGURE 2.44 Defining the data series

▶▶ How to... *remove an unwanted series*

1   In the Chart Wizard **Step 2 of 4** dialogue box, click the **Series** tab.

2   In the **Series** section below the chart preview, click on the name of the unwanted series.

3   Click the **Remove** button.

4   The chart preview will change – the incorrect data set will be removed from the preview.

▶▶ How to... *select the correct data to be plotted on the x-axis*

1   In the Chart Wizard **Step 2 of 4** dialogue box, click the **Series** tab.

2   Click on the **Collapse Dialog** button next to the **Category (X) axis labels**.

3   You will see the worksheet and a small (collapsed) window (Figure 2.45).

TIP!

Click and drag the title bar (usually blue) of this window to move it out of the way, if required.

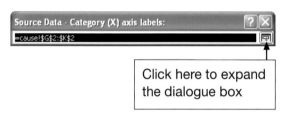

Click here to expand the dialogue box

FIGURE 2.45 The collapsed Chart Source Data dialogue box

4   In the worksheet, select only the cells that should display as the x-axis labels. Do not include the row/column label.

5   A marquee (dotted line) will display around the selected cells.

6   The range of cells will display in the **Category (X) axis labels box**.

7   In the collapsed window, click the **Expand Dialog** button .

8   You will return to the **Source Data** dialogue box.

▶▶ How to... *select the correct data to be plotted on the y-axis*

1   In the Chart Wizard step 2 of 4 dialogue box, click the **Series** tab.

2   In the **Series** section below the chart preview, click on the name of the incorrect series so that it is selected (highlighted).

3   Click the **Collapse Dialog** button next to **Values**.

4   In the worksheet, select the correct range of cells to be plotted on the y-axis for that series (do not include the row/column label).

5   A marquee (dotted line) will display around the selected cells.

6   The range of cells will display in the **Values** box.

7   In the collapsed window, click the **Expand Dialog** button.

8   You will return to the **Source Data** dialogue box.

 *select the data for the remaining data series to be plotted on the y-axis*

1   In the Chart Wizard **Step 2 of 4** dialogue box, click the **Series** tab.

2   Click on the name on the second data series.

3   Repeat steps 2 to 8 in How to… select the correct data to be plotted on the y-axis.

 *select the name for a legend item*

1   In the Chart Wizard **Step 2 of 4** dialogue box, click the **Series** tab.

2   In the **Series** section below the chart preview, click on the name displayed (e.g. this may be displayed as Series1).

3   In the **Name** section, delete any existing text. Click on the **Collapse Dialog** button. You will see the worksheet and a small (collapsed) window.

4   In the worksheet (datafile) click in the cell to be used as the name of the legend item.

5   Click the **Expand Dialog** button.

6   Repeat this process for the remaining items to be displayed in the legend.

When you have selected all the data series and checked the name of the items to be displayed in the legend:

○   check that the chart preview is correct in the Source Data window

○   click **Next**

○   continue setting the options in the Chart Wizard steps 3 and 4.

 *format the axis values (scale, intervals, numbers)*

1   In your chart, hover the mouse pointer over any of the y-axis values (numbers).

2   A **Value Axis** Tool tip displays. If numeric data is plotted on both the x- and the y-axis, then the Tool tip will display as **Value (X) Axis** or **Value (Y) Axis**.

3   Double-click on the axis value. A **Format Axis** dialogue box opens.

Changes to the axis are made once the chart is created.

What does it mean?

Axis scale: the scale is the minimum (lowest) value and the maximum (largest) value displayed on the x- or y-axis.

Interval: the 'gap' between the numbers (values) on the x- or y-axis. Excel refers to the interval as **major unit**.

Negative number: a number below zero, usually preceded with a minus sign.

4   In the dialogue box, click the **Scale** tab.

5   Click in the **Minimum** box, delete the existing number and enter the required minimum value. To display a negative number, type a minus sign before the number e.g. –75.

6   Click in the **Maximum** box, delete the existing number and enter the required maximum value.

7   Click in the **Major unit** box, delete the existing number and enter the required interval.

When you enter minimum, maximum values and intervals (major unit), the tick in the box is removed. This ensures that the values remain set. If the values you are required to set are already displayed, you must click in the check box to remove the tick otherwise Excel may change the minimum or maximum value (Figure 2.46).

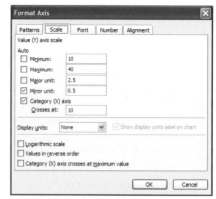

FIGURE 2.46 Setting the intervals and values in the Format Axis dialogue box

8   Click the **Number** tab (Figure 2.47).

9   In the **Category** section, check that **Number** is selected. In the **Decimal Places** section, enter the required number of decimal places or use the up/down arrows.

10   Click **OK**.

 **How to...** *format text on a chart (chart title, x- and y-axis titles, legend, text box)*

1   Click on the relevant text box in the chart to select it.

2   Square handles appear around the text box.

3   If you need to format only some of the text, highlight the relevant text within the text box.

4   In the Menu bar, click on **Format**.

If the selected text is in the title, the first item in the Format menu will display as **Selected Chart Title**. Similarly, if the selected text is in a text box, the first item will display as **Selected Object**.

5   In the drop-down menu, click **Selected Chart Title/Object**. A **Format Chart Title/Object** dialogue box displays.

6   Select the required formatting (Figure 2.48).

Note that some formatting options can be selected from the Formatting toolbar, e.g. bold, font size, font type.

7   Click **OK**.

FIGURE 2.47 The Number tab in the Format Axis dialogue box

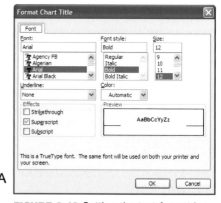

FIGURE 2.48 Setting the text formatting in the Format Chart Title dialogue box

In the file **incidents**, apply the following formatting to your bar chart titled **CAUSE OF INCIDENT AS A PERCENTAGE OF TOTAL INCIDENTS IN THE 21ST CENTURY**.

1 Format the **y-axis** as follows:

- minimum value: **10**
- maximum value: **40**
- interval: **2.5**
- numbers set to **1 decimal place.**

2 Format the ST in **21ST** in the title to be **superscript**.

3 Save the updated chart.

▶▶ How to... *remove the fill from the plot area (optional)*

Excel usually displays the plot area as grey. To make the chart clearer and to save printer ink the fill can be removed.

1 Hover your mouse pointer anywhere in the grey plot area, a **Plot Area** Tool tip displays.

2 Double-click in the plot area.

3 A **Format Plot Area** dialogue box opens (Figure 2.49).

4 In the **Area** section, click **None**.

5 Click **OK**.

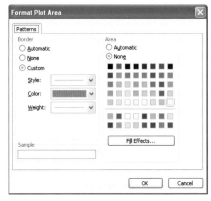

FIGURE 2.49 The Format Plot Area dialogue box

TIP!

You may select white instead of None.

In your file **incidents**, make the following changes to your bar chart titled **CAUSE OF INCIDENT AS A PERCENTAGE OF TOTAL INCIDENTS IN THE 21ST CENTURY**.

1 Remove the fill of the plot area.

2 Save the updated file keeping the same filename.

3 Set the chart option to Print in black and white (refer to How to... set the option to print in black and white on page 132 if you need to recap on these skills).

4 Print the chart.

5 Do not save the updated file.

1　In your chart, click on one of the bars. A square dot displays in all the bars for that series.

2　Double-click on one of the selected bars.

3　A **Format Data Series** dialogue box opens (Figure 2.50).

4　In the dialogue box, click the **Patterns** tab.

5　Click the **Fill Effects** button.

6　A **Fill Effects** dialogue box will open (Figure 2.51).

7　In the dialogue box, click the **Pattern** tab.

8　Click on one of the patterns to select it.

9　The pattern sample will display.

10　Click **OK** to close the **Fill Effects** dialogue box.

11　Click **OK** to close the **Format Data Series** dialogue box.

12　Repeat for the remaining sets of bars.

Fill effects are applied after the chart is created.

FIGURE 2.50 The Patterns tab in the Format Data Series dialogue box

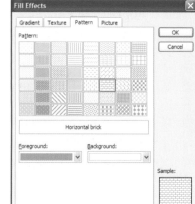

FIGURE 2.51 The Fill Effects dialogue box

In the Fill Effects dialogue box, click the drop-down arrow next to Foreground and/or Background to choose a different colour (Figure 2.51).

1　Hover the mouse pointer over any of the x-axis labels.

2　A **Category Axis** Tool tip will display. Double-click on the label.

3　A **Format Axis** dialogue box displays.

4　Click on the **Alignment** tab (Figure 2.52).

5　Click in the **Degrees** box and enter the required number.

6　Check the preview.

7　Click **OK**.

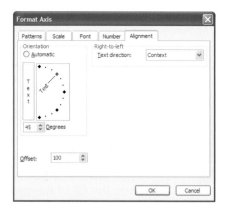

FIGURE 2.52 The Alignment tab in the Format Axis dialogue box

In your saved file **incidents**, make the following changes to your bar chart titled **CAUSE OF INCIDENT AS A PERCENTAGE OF TOTAL INCIDENTS IN THE 21ST CENTURY**.

1   Apply a different fill effect to each of the four series so that the legend and the bars will be clearly distinguishable when printed.

2   Set the orientation of the x-axis labels to **45°**.

3   Save the updated chart keeping the same filename.

4   Print the chart.

5   Close the file.

Check your printout against the solution on the CD-ROM.

ASSESS YOUR SKILLS – Create comparative charts and define the data series

By working through Section 2 you will have learnt the skills listed below. Read each item to help you decide how confident you feel about each skill.

○ understand comparative charts

○ identify the parts of a comparative chart

○ understand the selection of data for comparative charts

○ use the Chart Wizard to create a comparative chart

○ enter the chart title, x-axis and y-axis titles

○ define the data series for a chart (remove unwanted series, select the data to be plotted on the x- and y- axis, select the name for legend items)

○ enter the chart title, x-axis and y-axis titles

○ format the axis values (scale, intervals, numbers)

○ format text

○ remove the fill from the plot area

○ use a pattern fill for the bars

○ set the text orientation.

If you think that you need more practice on any of the skills in the above list, go back and work through the skill(s) again.

If you feel confident, move on to Section 3.

In this section you will learn how to:

- understand line-column graphs
- identify the parts of a line-column graph
- create a line-column graph
- enter the chart title, x-axis and y-axis titles
- display the legend
- select the chart location
- format the line(s)
- format the markers.

Line-column graphs

Line-column graphs are used to show a comparison of related data. One or more sets of data can be displayed as column(s) and another set as a line. Line-column graphs are usually used to show a comparison of data displayed as bar(s) against a benchmark, displayed as a line.

Parts of a line-column graph

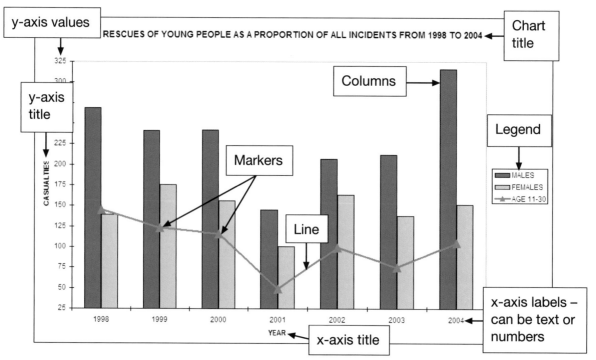

FIGURE 2.54 The parts of a line-column graph

1 In the datafile, select only the relevant range of cells.

2 Click the **Chart Wizard** icon 📊 .

3 The Chart Wizard **Step 1 of 4** dialogue box will open.

4 Click the **Custom Types** tab, scroll down the list and select **Line-Column** (Figure 2.54).

5 Click **Next**.

6 The Chart Wizard **Step 2 of 4** dialogue box will open.

7 A preview of the chart displays, check that the preview is correct.

If the preview is incorrect, you *must* define the data series before continuing. Refer to Defining data series on pages 137–139 before proceeding to the Chart Wizard Step 3 of 4.

8 If the preview is correct, click **Next**.

9 The Chart Wizard **Step 3 of 4** dialogue box will display.

10 In the **Titles** tab, enter the Chart title, x-axis title and y-axis title.

11 Click the **Legend** tab, ensure there is a tick in the **Show Legend** box.

12 Click **Next**.

13 The Chart Wizard **Step 4 of 4** dialogue box will display.

14 Click the button for **As new sheet**.

15 Optional: name the chart.

16 Click **Finish**.

FIGURE 2.54 Line - Column selected in the Custom Types tab of the Chart Wizard dialogue box

Check your understanding: Create a line-column graph

1 Open the file called **age** and save it as an Excel file using the filename **young**

2 Ensure that all data is displayed in full.

3 Create a **line-column graph** to plot the number of **MALES** and **FEMALES** (as columns) with the numbers of people **AGE 11–30** (as a line) from **1998** to **2004**

Check your data selection. The range selected should be **A3:H5** and **A10:H10**.

4 Title the chart: **RESCUES OF YOUNG PEOPLE AS A PROPORTION OF ALL INCIDENTS FROM 1998 TO 2004**

5 Title the x-axis: **YEAR**

6 Title the y-axis: **CASUALTIES**

7 Display a legend showing: **MALES   FEMALES   AGE 11–30**.

8 Format the **y-axis** as follows:

- ○ minimum value: **25**
- ○ interval: **25**
- ○ maximum value: **325**
- ○ numbers set to **0** decimal places.

9 Set the chart orientation to **landscape**.

10 Enter your **name** and an **automatic filename** as a footer.

11 Save the file keeping the filename **young**

Formatting lines and markers on a line-column graph

It is important that the data will be clearly distinctive on the printout – especially if it is printed on a black and white printer. To make the data distinctive, the line and/or marker style can be changed.

What does it mean?

Markers are the symbols (e.g. diamonds, squares, etc.) that show on each data point.

▶▶ How to... *format a line on a line-column graph*

1 Hover your mouse pointer over the line on the graph.

2 Double-click on the line.

3 A **Format Data Series** dialogue box will open (Figure 2.55).

4 Click the **Patterns** tab.

5 In the **Line** section, click the **Custom** button.

6 Click the drop-down arrow next to **Style**. Choose a line style.

7 Click the drop-down arrow next to **Weight**. Choose a thick line.

8 Optional: click the drop-down arrow next to **Color** to change the line colour.

9 To format the markers see below, or click **OK**.

FIGURE 2.55 The Patterns tab in the Format Data Series dialogue box

TIP!

If Format Data Point displays instead of Format Data Series, you have clicked on a marker. Click Cancel. Left-click in the plot area to deselect the marker, then hover the mouse pointer over the line and double-click to display the correct dialogue box.

▶▶ How to... *format the markers on a line-column graph*

1 Hover your mouse pointer over the line on the graph.

2 Double-click on the line to display a menu.

3 In the **Format Data Series** dialogue box, in the **Marker** section, click the **Custom** button.

4 Click the drop-down arrow next to **Style**. Choose one of the marker styles.

5 To change the marker colour, click the drop-down arrow next to **Foreground** and/or **Background**.

6 To change the marker size, click in the **Size** box and enter the required size or use the up/down arrows.

7 Click **OK**.

In your saved file **young**, format your chart titled **RESCUES OF YOUNG PEOPLE AS A PROPORTION OF ALL INCIDENTS FROM 1998 TO 2004** as follows.

1   Format the line so it appears as a solid, dark line with thick line weighting.

2   Format the markers as large triangles (e.g. size 12) in a dark shade. The line and markers must be clearly visible across the bars.

3   Make sure that the legend clearly identifies the three data sets.

4   Save the files keeping the same filename.

5   Close the file.

6   Check your printout against the solution on the CD-ROM.

ASSESS YOUR SKILLS – Create line-column graphs

By working through Section 3 you will have learnt the skills listed below. Read each item to help you decide how confident you feel about each skill.

○   understand line-column graphs

○   identify the parts of a line-column graph

○   create a line-column graph

○   enter the chart title, x-axis and y-axis titles

○   display the legend

○   select the chart location

○   format the line(s)

○   format the markers.

If you feel that you need more practice on any of the skills in the above list, go back and work through the skill(s) again.

If you feel confident, move on to Section 4.

In this section you will learn how to:

- understand xy scatter graphs
- identify the parts of an xy scatter graph
- understand the selection of data for xy scatter graphs
- use the Chart Wizard to create an xy scatter graph
- enter the chart title, x-axis and y-axis titles
- join the data points on an xy scatter graph
- add a text box to a graph.

xy scatter graphs

xy scatter graphs are used to plot **pairs** of co-ordinates. On an xy scatter graph, a point (shown by a marker) is plotted where the x value meets the y value. xy scatter graphs are usually plotted using two sets of numeric data (i.e. numeric data is displayed on the y-axis and the x-axis). On other charts (e.g. line graphs, etc.), the data on the x-axis is usually descriptive (i.e. text).

xy scatter graphs can be used for two purposes:

- to plot a definite relationship between two *variables* (e.g. the cost of chocolate in relation to sales)
- to determine if there is any relationship between the two variables.

What does it mean?

Co-ordinate: a co-ordinate is made up of an x value and a y value.

Variable: an item that can have many different values (e.g. each person has a different height and weight).

Parts of an xy scatter graph

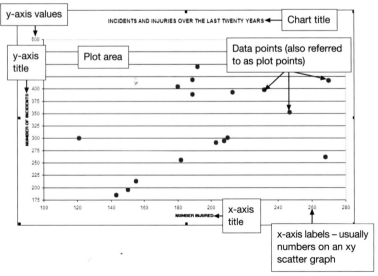

FIGURE 2.56 Parts of an xy scatter graph

 **How to...** *create an xy scatter graph*

1. In the datafile, select only the relevant range of cells.

2. Click the **Chart Wizard** icon .

3. The Chart Wizard **Step 1 of 4** dialogue box will open.

4. In the **Standard Types** tab, in the Chart type section, click on **XY (Scatter)** (Figure 2.57).

5. In the Chart sub-type section, check that **Scatter** is selected.

6. Click **Next**.

7. The Chart Wizard **Step 2 of 4** dialogue box will open.

8. A preview of the chart displays, check the preview.

If the preview is incorrect, you **must** define the data series before continuing. Refer to Defining data series on pages 137–139 before proceeding to the Chart Wizard Step 3 of 4.

9. If the preview is correct, click **Next**.

10. The Chart Wizard **Step 3 of 4** dialogue box will open.

11. Click the **Titles** tab.

12. In the **Chart Title** box, enter the title.

13. In the **Category (X) axis** box, enter the x-axis title.

14. In the **Value (Y) axis** box, enter the y-axis title.

15. Click the **Legend** tab.

16. Click to place or remove the tick in the **Show legend** box as required for the chart.

17. Click **Next**.

18. The Chart Wizard **Step 4 of 4** dialogue box will open.

19. Click the button for **As new sheet**.

20. Optional: enter a name for the sheet.

21. Click **Finish**.

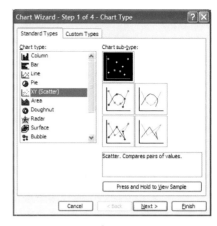

FIGURE 2.57 XY (Scatter) in the Chart Wizard dialogue box

TIP!

Look at the figures in the original datafile to make sure the data points plotted on the chart have been plotted correctly.

1   Open the file called **rescues**.

2   Save the file as an Excel file using the filename **20years**

3   Select the data to create a chart to show the number of **INCIDENTS** against the numbers **INJURED** from **1985 to 2004**.

Check your selection of data. You should have selected the following range of cells:
From C2 to V3

4   Create an **xy scatter graph**.

5   Title the chart: **INCIDENTS AND INJURIES OVER THE LAST TWENTY YEARS**

6   Title the x-axis: **NUMBER INJURED**

7   Title the y-axis: **NUMBER OF INCIDENTS**

8   Do not display a legend.

9   Create the chart on a sheet that is separate from the data source.

10 Set the chart orientation to **landscape**.

11 Format the **x-axis** as follows:

   ○ minimum value: **100**
   ○ maximum value: **280**
   ○ interval: **20**

   numbers set to **0** decimal places.

12 Format the **y-axis** as follows:

   ○ minimum value: **175**
   ○ maximum value: **550**
   ○ interval: **25**

   numbers set to **0 decimal places**.

13 Ensure that the markers on the graph are clearly visible as **circles**.

14 Optional: remove the fill of the plot area.

15 In the footer enter **your name**, **your centre number**, an **automatic date** and an **automatic filename**.

16 Save the chart.

17 Print the chart.

Check your printout against the solution on the CD-ROM.

 **How to...** *join the data points on an xy scatter graph*

1 Hover the mouse pointer over one of the data points and double-click.

2 **Format Data Series** dialogue box displays.

3 Select the **Patterns** tab (Figure 2.58).

4 In the **Line** section, click the **Custom** button.

5 Click the drop-down arrow next to **Style** box and select the required line style.

6 Click the drop-down arrow next to **Weight** and select the required thickness of the line.

7 If you need to remove the markers, see below, otherwise click **OK**.

FIGURE 2.58 The Patterns tab in the Format Data Series dialogue box

TIP!

Select a thick line weighting.

 **How to...** *remove the markers*

1 In the **Format Data Series** dialogue box, in the **Marker** section, click **None**.

2 Click **OK**.

TIP!

To display the Drawing toolbar click **View** in the Menu bar, select **Toolbars** from the drop-down menu and select **Drawing**.

 **How to...** *add a text box to a graph*

1 Ensure that the **Drawing toolbar** is displayed.

2 From the Drawing toolbar, select the **Text Box** icon ▲ (Figure 2.59).

FIGURE 2.59 The Drawing toolbar

3 Move the mouse pointer into the plot area and draw a frame for the text box. Ensure that the text box is not drawn in a position where it will touch or overlap any existing lines on the graph.

4 A cursor will display in the text box, enter the required text.

5 To change the size of the text box, click and drag one of the round handles on the side of the text box.

6 To move the text box, click and drag the frame of the text box.

TIP!

Displaying a border around a text box is optional. To remove a border, select the text box, click the drop-down arrow next the Line Color icon on the Drawing toolbar ▲ and select **No Line**. To select a line colour for the border, click on a colour square.

1   Open your saved file named **incidents**. You are going to create a second chart in this file.

2   Select the worksheet named **cause**. (Click on the tab named **cause** at the bottom left of the screen.)

3   Select the data to create a chart to show the **CHANGE FROM PREVIOUS YEAR** against the YEARS from **1998–2004**.

   Check your selection of data. You should have selected the cells shown in Figure 2.60.

4   Create an **xy scatter graph**.

5   Title the chart: **CHANGE IN THE NUMBER OF INJURIES FROM PREVIOUS YEAR**

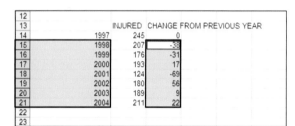

12			
13		INJURED	CHANGE FROM PREVIOUS YEAR
14	1997	245	0
15	1998	207	-38
16	1999	176	-31
17	2000	193	17
18	2001	124	-69
19	2002	180	56
20	2003	189	9
21	2004	211	22
22			
23			

6   Title the x-axis: **YEAR**

7   Title the y-axis: **CHANGE**

8   Do not display a legend.

FIGURE 2.60 Selected cells in the cause worksheet

9   Create the chart on a sheet that is separate from the data source.

10 Set the chart orientation to **portrait**.

11 Join the points on the scatter graph together to produce a solid line with no markers.

12 Format the **x-axis** as follows:

   ○ minimum value: **1998**
   ○ maximum value: **2004**

13 Format the **y-axis** as follows:

   ○ minimum value: **-75**
   ○ maximum value: **75**
   ○ interval: **10**

   numbers set to **0 decimal places**.

14 In the plot area, insert a text box with the words: **EFFECT OF FOOT AND MOUTH DISEASE**

   Ensure that the text box does not overlap/touch the line.

15 Optional: remove the fill of the plot area.

16 Insert **your name** as a header or footer.

17 Save the chart.

18 Print the chart.

Check your printout against the solution on the CD-ROM.

TIP!

Selecting the option for **Smoothed line** is optional.

ASSESS YOUR SKILLS – Create xy scatter graphs

By working through Section 4 you will have learnt the skills listed below. Read each item to help you decide how confident you feel about each skill.

- understand xy scatter graphs
- identify the parts of an xy scatter graph
- understand the selection of data for xy scatter graphs
- use the Chart Wizard to create an xy scatter graph
- enter the chart title, x-axis and y-axis titles
- join the data points on an xy scatter graph
- add a text box to a graph.

If you think that you need more practice on any of the skills in the above list, go back and work through the skill(s) again.

If you feel confident, do the Build-up and Practice tasks on pages 163–172.

QUICK REFERENCE – *Manipulating spreadsheets*

Keep a copy of this page next to you.
Refer to it when working through
tasks and during any assessments.

HOW TO...	METHOD
Open a .csv file in Excel	Load **Excel** → click on the **Open** icon → locate the folder in which your file is stored → click on the drop-down arrow at the end of the **Files of type** box → click on **All Files** → select the file → click **Open.**
Save a .csv file as an Excel File	Click on the **File** menu → click on **Save As** → click on the drop-down arrow next to **Save as type** box → from the list of file types, select **Microsoft Office Excel Workbook** → click on the drop-down arrow next to **Save in** → locate the folder in which you want to save the file → in the **File name box**, enter the required filename → click on **Save.**
Select text size	A guide to sizes: Small – 10–12pt Medium – 14–16pt Large – 18pt+
Formatting multiple cells using the Format Painter	Click in a cell to be formatted → apply the required formatting → **double-click** on the **Format Painter** icon → select (highlight) all cells to apply the same formatting → when all cells have been formatted click on the Format Painter icon again (or press **Esc**) to deselect it.
Locate a cell containing specific data	Click on the **Edit** menu → click on **Find** → the **Find and Replace** dialogue box will display → in the box next to **Find what** enter the text contained in the cell you wish to locate → click on the **Find Next** button → click on **Close**, the cell containing the specified data will be selected.
Wrap cell contents	Select the cell(s) that contain the data you wish to wrap → click on the **Format** menu → click on **Cells** → click on the **Alignment** tab → in the **Text control** section → click to insert a tick in the box next to **Wrap text** → click on **OK** → the cell contents will be wrapped → if necessary, adjust the column and/or row width to ensure words are not split and/or data is displayed on the specified number of lines.
Apply vertical and horizontal alignment	Select the cell(s) to be formatted → click on the **Format** menu → click on **Cells** → click on the **Alignment** tab → in the **Text alignment** section, click on the drop-down arrow in the box under **Horizontal** → select the required horizontal alignment → click on the drop-down arrow in the box under **Vertical** → select the required vertical alignment → click **OK** (unless you need to apply other formatting).

HOW TO...	METHOD
Set text orientation	Select the cell(s) containing the text to be orientated → click on the **Format** menu → click on **Cells** → click on the **Alignment** tab → in the **Orientation** section → **EITHER** hold on the red marker and slide the bar up or down until the required number appears in the box next to **Degrees OR** enter the required number in the box to the left of **Degrees** (or use the up/down arrows) → click **OK**.
Merge cells	Select the cells to be merged → click on the **Format** menu → click on **Cells** → click on the **Alignment** tab → in the **Text control** section → click to insert a tick in the box next to **Merge cells** → click on **OK**.
Add a border	Select the cells to be framed with a border → on the toolbar, click on the drop-down arrow to the right of the **Borders** icon → select the **Outside Borders** or **Thick Box Border** option.
Format numeric data to integer or 2 decimal places	Select the cell(s) to be formatted → click on the **Format** menu → click on **Cells** click on the **Number** tab → in the **Category** section, select **Number** → click on the up/down arrows to the right of the **Decimal places** box to select the required number of decimal places → in the box under **Negative numbers** click on the required format → click on **OK**.
Format numeric data to currency	Select the cell(s) to be formatted → click on the **Format** menu → click on **Cells** → click on the **Number** tab → in the **Category** section, select **Currency** → click on the up/down arrows to the right of the **Decimal places** box to select the required number of decimal places → in the box under **Symbol** click on the drop-down arrow click on the required currency symbol (may be none) → in the box under **Negative numbers** click on the required format → click on **OK**.
Format numeric data to percentage	Select the cell(s) to be formatted → click on the **Format** menu → click on **Cells** → click on the **Number** tab → in the **Category** section, select **Percentage** → click on the up/down arrows to the right of the **Decimal places** box to select the required number of decimal places → click on **OK**.
Use Find and Replace	Click on the **Edit** menu → click on **Find** → click on the **Replace** tab → in the box next to **Find what** enter the text to be replaced → in the box next to **Replace with** enter the replacement text → check to ensure you have not made any mistakes → click on the **Replace All** button → click on **Close** → all instances of the original data will have been replaced.
Insert text and numeric data	Click in the cell in which you want to enter data → enter the data → move to the next cell in which you wish to enter data or move to any other cell → check to ensure that the additions are correct and that numbers are 100 per cent accurate → check that the formatting of the inserted data is correct.
Amend text and numeric data	Click in the cell containing the data you wish to edit → enter the new data → move to the next cell you wish to edit or move to any other cell → check to ensure that the amendments are correct and that numbers are 100 per cent accurate → check that the formatting of the amended data is correct.

(continued overleaf)

HOW TO…	METHOD
Insert a column	Click in any cell in the column **to the right** of the position you want the new column to be inserted → click on the **Insert** menu → click on **Columns** → the new column will be inserted.
Insert a row	Click in any cell in the row immediately **below** the position in which you want the new row to be inserted → click on the **Insert** menu → click on **Rows** → the new column will be inserted.
Delete a column	Click on the column letter of the column you wish to delete → right-click → the column will be selected → check it is the correct column → click on **Delete** → the column will be deleted.
Delete a row	Click on the row number of the row you wish to delete → right-click → the row will be selected → check it is the correct row → click on **Delete** → the row will be deleted.
Clear the contents of a column	Click on the column letter of the column in which you wish to clear the contents → right-click → the column will be selected → check it is the correct column → click on **Clear Contents** → all data in the column will be removed but the column will remain.
Clear the contents of a row	Click on the row number of the row in which you wish to clear the contents → right-click → the row will be selected → check it is the correct row → click on **Clear Contents** → all data in the row will be removed but the row will remain.
Move data using Copy and Paste	Select the data to be moved → right-click → click on **Cut** → click on the cell that is to be the new location (if you are moving a range of cells click on the cell that is to contain the data in the first cell) → right-click → click on **Paste.**
Move data using drag and drop	Select the data to be moved → with the mouse, hover over an outside edge of the cell(s) to be moved → a black cross with 4-way arrows will appear → click and hold on the edge of the selection and drag it to the new location → release the mouse button → press an Arrow key or click in a different cell to confirm the new location.
Insert mathematical operators	

Operator	Action
+	Add
–	Subtract
* (asterisk)	Multiply
/	Divide
%	Per cent

| --- | --- |
Enter a formula	Click in the cell in which the result of the formula is to be displayed → enter the = sign → click in the cell (or select the range) that contains the first value (set of values) → enter the mathematical operator → click in the cell (or select the range) that contains the second value (set of values) → if the formula is to be a multi-stage calculation, continue entering the mathematical operator and clicking in the cell (or selecting the range) until all stages of the calculation have been entered → check the formula and insert brackets and absolute cell reference if required → press **Enter**.
Replicate a formula	Click in the cell containing the formula to be replicated → position the mouse over the bottom right corner of the cell until a black plus sign appears → hold down the mouse button and drag across the cells into which the formula is to be copied → release the mouse button → the formula will be replicated into the selected cells → remember to delete any zero values or values in blank cells.
Name a cell	Click in the cell to be named → click in the **name box** → enter the name for the cell → press **Enter**.
Comparison operators	

Operator	Action
=	Equal to
>	Greater than
<	Less than
>=	Greater than or equal to
<=	Less than or equal to
<>	Not equal to

HOW TO...	METHOD
Enter formula containing a function	Click in the cell in which the result of the formula is to be displayed → click on the **Insert Function** button → an **Insert Function** dialogue box appears → in the **Select a function** section click on the required function → click on **OK** → follow the instructions below for the function you wish to enter.
Use the IF function	Follow the instructions for **enter a formula containing a function** → in the **Function Arguments** window click in the **Logical_test** box → in the **Logical_test** box click on the spreadsheet cell that contains the data that you wish to compare (e.g. F16) (or key in the cell reference) → enter the comparison operator (e.g. >) → enter the comparison data (a cell reference or data) → in the **Value_if_true** box enter the result to be displayed in the cell if the condition is met (a cell reference or data) → in the **Value_if_false** box enter the result to be displayed in the cell if the condition is NOT met (a cell reference or data) → click on **OK**.

(continued overleaf)

HOW TO...	METHOD
Use the SUMIF function	Follow the instructions for **enter a formula containing a function** → in the **Function Arguments** window click in the **Range** box → in the **Range** box select the spreadsheet cells that contain the comparison criteria (or click in a cell that contains the criteria) → in the **Criteria** box enter the comparison criteria (or click in a cell that contains the criteria) → in the **Sum_range** box select the spreadsheet cells that contain the data to be totalled if the criteria is met → click on **OK.**
Use the COUNTIF function	Follow the instructions for **enter a formula containing a function** → in the **Function Arguments** window click in the **Range** box → in the **Range** box select the spreadsheet cells that contain the comparison criteria (or click in a cell that contains the criteria) → in the **Criteria** box enter the comparison criteria (or click in a cell that contains the criteria) → click on **OK.**
Use the COUNT and COUNTA function	The **COUNT** and the **COUNTA** function operate in the same way – **COUNT** will only count numeric data, **COUNTA** will count cells that contain any data (numeric or text). Follow the instructions for **enter a formula containing a function** → in the **Function Arguments** window click in the Value1 box → in the **Value1** box select the spreadsheet cells that contain the data to be counted (note: empty/blank cells will not be included in the count) → in the **Value2** box you may add another range of cells to be included in the count or it may be left blank → click on **OK.**
Use the MAX and MIN function	Follow the instructions for **enter a formula containing a function** → in the **Function Arguments** window click in the Number1 box → in the **Number1** box select the spreadsheet cells that contain the data from which you want to return the MIN or MAX → in the **Number2** box you may add another range of cells or it may be left blank → click on **OK.**
Change the page orientation and fit to one page	Click on the **Print Preview** icon → from Print Preview click on the **Setup** button → click on the **Page** tab → in the **Paper size** section check that the paper size is set to **A4**, if not click on the drop-down arrow to the right of the box and select A4 from the list → in the **Orientation** section, click in the button next to the required orientation → if required: in the **Scaling** section, click in the button next to **Fit to** → use the up and down arrows to the right of the **Fit to** boxes to specify the number of pages to fit to → make any other changes, then click on **OK.**
Adjust margins	Click on the **Print Preview** icon → from Print Preview click on the **Setup** button → click on the **Margins** tab → in the boxes under Top, Left, Right and Bottom click on the up or down arrows to adjust the margins → make any other changes, then click on **OK.**
Insert headers and footers and use automatic fields	Click on the **Print Preview** icon → from Print Preview click on the **Setup** button → click on the **Header/Footer** tab → click on the **Custom Header** or **Custom Footer** button → click in one section → enter any text (e.g. your name and centre number) → click in another section → click on the icon(s) for the automatic field(s) to be displayed → click on **OK** → the **Page Setup** window will be displayed → make any other changes, then click **OK.**

HOW TO...	METHOD
Display gridlines and row and column headings	Click on the **Print Preview** icon → from Print Preview click on the **Setup** button → click on the tab **Sheet** → click in the box next to **Gridlines** → click in the box next to **Row and column headings** to display a tick → to remove, click in the box again to remove the tick → click on **OK**.
Print a document selection	Select the cells to be printed → click on **File** menu → click on **Print** → click in the box next to **Selection** → only the selected cells will print → remember, non-adjacent cells will be printed on separate pages.
Clear the selected print area	Click on the **File** menu → click on **Print Area** → click on **Clear Print Area**.
Hide rows and/or columns	Select the entire column(s) or row(s) to be hidden → position the mouse over the selected area → right-click → click on **Hide** → the column(s) or row(s) will be hidden.
Unhide rows and/or columns	Select the entire spreadsheet → position the mouse over the row number or column letter divider where the rows or columns have been hidden → right-click → click on **Unhide** → the column(s) or row(s) will be revealed.
Display formulae	Click on the **Tools** menu → select **Options** → click on the **View** tab → in the **Window options** section click to insert a tick in the box next to **Formulas** → to return to spreadsheet view, remove the tick.
How to create a reference to a cell in another spreadsheet	Open the source spreadsheet (the spreadsheet that contains the data that you are going to link to) → open the spreadsheet that will contain the link → click in the cell in which you want the value from the source spreadsheet to be recorded → enter = → click on the source spreadsheet in the taskbar → click in the cell (or select the range of cells) that contains the data you wish to record → press **Enter** → you will be returned to the linked spreadsheet → the value of the link will be recorded.
Sort data	Click in the column label containing the data to be sorted (do **NOT** select the entire column unless you want to sort only the data in the selected column and not the related data) → click on the **Data** menu → click on **Sort** → check that the correct column label is shown in the **Sort by** section of the window → click in the button to select the order (Ascending or Descending) → in the **My data range has** section check that the correct selection has been made (Header row or No header row) → click **OK** → the data will be sorted.
Filter data using AutoFilter	Click in the column label containing the data (or highlight the column) to be filtered → click on the **Data** menu → click on **Filter** → click on **AutoFilter** → drop-down arrow buttons will appear to the right of the column label cell → click on the drop-down arrow of the column to be filtered → if the filter criterion is listed, click on it → the data will be filtered, otherwise → click on **Custom** → in the box under **Show rows where** click on the drop-down arrow to the right of the box → select the required criterion (e.g. **is greater than**) → in the top blank box on the right-hand side click on the down arrow comparison to be made (e.g. **7**) → click on **OK**. To turn off the filter click on the **Data** menu → click on **Filter** → click on AutoFilter.

Click means click with the left mouse button

QUICK REFERENCE – Creating graphs

HOW TO...	METHOD
Open a .csv file in Excel	Load **Excel** → click on the **Open** icon → locate the folder in which your file is stored → click on the drop-down arrow at the end of the **Files of type** box → click on **All Files** → select the file → click **Open.**
Save a .csv file as an Excel File	Click on the **File** menu → click on **Save As** → click on the drop-down arrow next to **Save as type** box → from the list of file types, select **Microsoft Office Excel Workbook** → click on the drop-down arrow next to **Save in** → locate the folder in which you want to save the file → in the **File name** box, enter the required filename → click on **Save.**
Select contiguous data	**Method 1:** Click in the first cell and drag the mouse across the range (block) of cells to be highlighted. **Method 2:** Click with the mouse in the first cell, hold down the **Shift** key, click in the last cell.
Select non-contiguous data	Click in the first cell, hold down the **Ctrl** key and click in the remaining cells (or drag the mouse over a block of cells).
Create an exploded pie chart	Select only the relevant range of cells → click the **Chart Wizard** icon → in **Step 1 of 4,** in the **Standard Types** tab, in the **Chart types** section, click on **Pie** → in **Chart sub-type** section, click on **Exploded Pie** → click **Next** → in **Step 2 of 4** check the chart preview → if preview is correct click **Next,** if incorrect, click **Cancel** and start again → in **Step 3 of 4** click the **Titles** tab → in the **Chart Title** box, enter the title → click the **Legend** tab → click to remove tick in **Show legend** box (unless required) → click the **Data Labels** tab → click in **Category name** (for data labels) → click in **Value** or **Percentage** → click to deselect **Show leader lines** → click **Next** → in **Step 4 of 4,** click button for **As new sheet** → click **Finish.**
Set the chart orientation	Click the **File** menu → click **Page Setup** → select **Portrait** or **Landscape.**
Format numeric data on a pie chart	Double-click once on any of the numbers → a **Format Data Labels** dialogue box displays → click the **Number** tab → set the required formatting → click **OK.**
Emphasise a sector by pulling it away	Click once on a sector, then click again to select one sector only → click and drag the sector further away.
Set a chart to print in black and white	From the chart view, click the **Print Preview** icon → click **Setup** button → in **Page Setup** dialogue box → click **Chart** tab → click button for **Print in black and white** → click **OK** → click **Close.**
Fill pie chart sectors with patterns	Click once on a sector then click again to select one sector only → double-click → a **Format Data Point** dialogue box opens → click **Fill Effects** button → **Fill Effects** window opens → click **Pattern** tab → select a pattern. To change the colour click the drop-down arrow for **foreground** → select colour → click **OK** → click **OK** again.

HOW TO…	METHOD
Insert headers and footers and use automatic fields	Click on the **Print Preview** icon → from Print Preview click on the **Setup** button → click on the **Header/Footer** tab → click on the **Custom Header** or **Custom Footer** button → click in one section → enter any text (e.g. your name and centre number) → click in another section → click on the icon(s) for the automatic field(s) to be displayed → click on **OK** → the Page Setup window will be displayed → make any other changes, then click **OK**.
Create a comparative bar chart	Select **only** the relevant range of cells (include row or column labels) → click the **Chart Wizard** icon → in **Step 1 of 4**, in the **Standard Types** tab, in the Chart types section → click on **Column** → in the **Chart sub-type** section, check that **Clustered Column** is selected → click **Next** → in **Step 2 of 4**, check the chart preview → if preview is correct, click **Next**, if incorrect, refer to **How to define the data series** on page 3 → **Step 3 of 4**, click the **Titles** tab → in the **Chart Title** box, enter the title → click in the **Category (X) axis** box → enter x-axis title → click in **Value (Y) axis** box → enter y-axis title → click the **Legend** tab → click to place tick in **Show legend** box → click **Next** → in **Step 4 of 4**, click button for **As new sheet** → click **Finish**.
Fill bars with pattern	Double-click on one bar → **Format Data Series** dialogue box displays → click the **Patterns** tab → click **Fill Effects** button → **Fill Effects** dialogue box displays → click **Pattern** tab → click on a pattern → click **OK** → click **OK** to close **Format Data Series** dialogue box.
Create a comparative line graph	Select **only** the relevant range of cells (include row or column labels) → click the **Chart Wizard** icon → in **Step 1 of 4**, in the **Standard Types** tab, in the Chart types section, click on **Line-column** → in **Chart sub-type** section, check that **Line-column with markers …** is selected → click **Next** → in **Step 2 of 4** → check the chart preview → if preview is correct, click **Next**, if incorrect, refer to **How to define the data series** on page 3 → in **Step 3 of 4**, click the **Titles** tab → in the **Chart Title** box, enter the title → click in **Category (X) axis** box → enter x-axis title → click in **Value (Y) axis** box → enter y-axis title → click the **Legend** tab → click to place tick in **Show legend** box → click **Next** → In Step 4 of 4, click button for **As new sheet** → click **Finish**.
Set the axis scale	Hover the mouse pointer on any number on an axis scale → double-click with mouse → **Format Axis** dialogue box displays → click **Scale** tab → enter the Minimum, Maximum and Major Unit values required → click the **Number** tab → format the numbers as required → click **OK**.
Remove the fill from the plot area (optional)	Hover the mouse pointer in grey plot area → double-click → **Format Plot Area** dialogue box displays → in Area section click **None** → click **OK**.
Format text	Select the relevant text area box → (highlight the relevant text in the box if required) → click the **Format** menu → click **Selected xxx** (the option will vary depending on which part of the chart is selected) → a **Format xxx** dialogue box will open → select the required formatting options → click **OK**.

(continued overleaf)

HOW TO...	METHOD
Set the text orientation on the x-axis	Hover with the mouse over the x-axis → double-click → a **Format Axis** dialogue box displays → click in the **Degrees** box and enter the required orientation → click **OK.**
Create a line-column graph	Select **only** the relevant range of cells (include row or column labels) → click the **Chart Wizard** icon → in **Step 1 of 4**, in the **Custom Types** tab, in the Chart types section, click on **Line-column** → click **Next** → in **Step 2 of 4** → check the chart preview → if preview is correct, click **Next**, if incorrect, refer to **How to define the data series** below → in **Step 3 of 4**, click the **Titles** tab → in the **Chart Title** box, enter the title → click in **Category (X) axis** box → enter x-axis title → click in **Value (Y) axis** box → enter y-axis title → click **Legend** tab → click to place a tick in **Show legend** box → click **Next** → in **Step 4 of 4**, click button for **As new sheet** → click **Finish.**
Format lines on a line graph	Hover with mouse on a line → double-click → a **Format Data Series** dialogue box displays → click **Patterns** tab → in **Line** section, click **Custom** button → click drop-down arrow next to **Style** → choose a style → click drop-down arrow next to **Weight** → choose a suitable line → to change colour, click drop-down arrow next to colour → click **OK.**
Format markers on a line graph	Hover with mouse on a marker → double-click → a **Format Data Series** dialogue box displays → click **Patterns** tab → in **Marker** section, click drop-down arrow next to **Style** → choose a style → to change marker colour, click drop-down arrow next to Foreground and/or Background and choose colour → click **OK.**
Define the data series	In the Chart Wizard **Step 2 of 4**, click the **Series** tab: To remove an unwanted series: in the **Series** section, click on the name of the unwanted series → click **Remove.** To select the correct data to be plotted on the x-axis: click on the **Collapse Dialog** button next to **Category (X) axis** labels → in the worksheet, select only the cells that should display on the x-axis (do not include the row/column labels) → click the **Expand Dialog** button. To select the correct data to be plotted on the y-axis: in the **Series** section, click on the name of a **Series** → click the **Collapse Dialog** button next to **Values** → select the correct range of cells to be plotted on the y-axis for that series (do not include the row/column label) → click the **Expand Dialog** button. Repeat this process for the remaining data series. To select the name for a legend item: in the **Series** section, click on the name displayed (e.g. this may be displayed as **Series1**) → in the **Name** section, delete any existing text → click on the **Collapse Dialog** button → in the worksheet click in the cell to be used as the name of the legend item → click the **Expand Dialog** button. Repeat this process for the remaining items to be displayed in the legend.

The files for the Build-up tasks can be found in a folder named **U2datafiles_buildtasks**. You will need the file **gcse_stat** to complete this task.

You have been asked to produce a report on GCSE statistics for a number of schools in the southern region.

Unless otherwise instructed you may use any readable font, alignment, emphasis and size to suit the data.

1　Open the file **gcse_stat** and save it in as an Excel file using the filename **stats1**

2　a　Use text wrap to display the column labels below on **2 lines** – do not split words.

　　School Measure
　　Compared to Benchmark

　b　Ensure that all data is displayed in full.
　c　Format the data items listed as follows:

LABEL	SIZE	COLUMNS
GCSE Achievement Statistics 2005	Large	Centred across all columns containing data Columns A–I Framed by a border
Value Added	Medium	A–B
Schools in South County	Medium	A–I Framed by a border

3　In the **Schools in South County** section, in the **Total column**, use a function to calculate the **Total** of the three **subjects**: English, Mathematics and Science for each of the schools.

4　a　In the **Schools in South County** section, in the **Average column**, use a function to calculate the **Average** of the three **subjects** for the first school.
　b　Replicate this formula for all the other schools.

5　In the **Value Added** section, name the cell containing the figure for GCSE as **value_added**

6　Save the spreadsheet keeping the filename **stats1**

1 You will need the following files for this task:

○ the file called **stats1** that you saved in Build-up task 1 (alternatively, you may use the file **stats1** provided in the worked copies folder)

○ the file **benchmark**.

2 a Open the file **benchmark** and save it in as an Excel file using the filename **nat_stats**

b Save using the new filename **stats2** the file **stats1**

3 In the **stats2** spreadsheet, a value added figure is to be taken into consideration for schools in the southern region due to the location of the schools.

a In the **Schools in South County** section, in the **School Measure** column, use a formula to calculate the figure to be used to indicate a school's performance. This figure is calculated as follows:

Add the average figure to the named cell **value_added**, then multiply the result by 105%.

b Replicate this formula for all the other schools.

4 The report needs to show how a school's results compare with the national benchmark. To calculate this figure you will need to link the two spreadsheets and use an absolute cell reference.

a In the **Schools in South County** section, in the **Compared to Benchmark** column, use a function to calculate whether a school's measurable value is higher or lower than the national benchmark.

This figure is calculated as follows:

IF the **School Measure** figure in the **stats2** spreadsheet is greater than the figure for the **GCSE Average** in the **nat_stats** spreadsheet, return the value **higher**, if it is not, return the value **lower**.

b Replicate this formula for the other schools.

5 a Format the figures in the **Total, Average** and **School Measure** columns as **integer** (zero decimal places) with no currency symbol.

b Format the column label and all the data in the **Compared to Benchmark** column to be centred horizontally.

6 a Insert your **name**, **centre number**, and an **automatic filename** as a header or footer.

b Set the page orientation to **landscape.**

c Save your spreadsheet keeping the filename **stats2**

d Ensure all data is displayed in full. Print a copy of the spreadsheet **stats2** showing all the figures.

7 You have been asked for a printout of the formulae of your spreadsheet **stats2**.

a In the **Schools in the South County** section, hide all the information in the columns from **Type** to **Science** (columns B to E).

    b In the **Value Added** section hide all the information in the rows from **Value Added** to **A2** (rows 3 to 6).

    c Display the formulae.

    d Check that the page orientation is **landscape**.

    e Display **gridlines** and **row and column headings**.

    f Ensure that all formulae are fully displayed **on one page** and clearly legible.

    g Save the file with the filename **statsform**.

    h Print the formulae on one page.

8 Close any open files.

BUILD-UP TASK ③ *Filter and sort data*

You will need the file **stats2** that you saved in Build-up task 2 to complete this task. (Alternatively, you may use the file **stats2** provided in the worked copies folder.)

You have been asked to present data about comprehensive schools only.

1 Open the file **stats2** and save it using the filename **comps**

2 Filter the data in the **Type** column to find all **Comprehensive** schools only.

3 Sort the data in the **School Measure** column in **descending** order ensuring that the corresponding data is sorted correctly.

4 In the **Value Added** section, delete the entire rows for **AS** and **A2**.

5 a Ensure all data is displayed in full.

    b Display **gridlines** and **row and column headings**.

    c Insert your **name, centre number** and an **automatic filename** as a footer.

6 a Save your spreadsheet keeping the filename **comps**

    b Print a copy of the filtered spreadsheet in **landscape** orientation showing all the filtered data in full.

7 Close any open files.

BUILD-UP TASK ④ *Create an exploded pie chart*

You will need the file **tests** to complete this task.

You have been asked by the Head of Faculty to produce an exploded pie chart showing the class average mark for tests done by students for the whole academic year.

1 a Open the datafile **tests** and save it in as an Excel file using the filename **marks**

    b Display all data in full.

2 Using the **CLASS AVERAGE** for the **five tests** from **INITIAL ASSESSMENT** to **END OF YEAR** create an exploded **pie chart**.

(continued overleaf)

   a Title the chart: **CLASS AVERAGE MARK FOR TESTS FOR ACADEMIC YEAR FOR THE LAST 10 YEARS**.

   b Each sector must be clearly labelled with a data label and the **actual value**.

   c Do not display a legend.

   d Create the chart on a sheet that is separate from the data source.

   e Pull out the smallest sector of the pie chart so that it is further away from the rest of the chart.

3 In the plot area, insert a text box with the words:

LOWEST MARK TERM 3

Ensure the text box does not overlap/touch any labels, values or sectors.

4 **a** Insert your **name, centre number** and an **automatic filename** as a header or footer.

    b Save the file.

    c Print one copy of the chart.

5 Close the file.

 BUILD-UP TASK 5 *Create a line-column graph*

The Head of Faculty has asked you to analyse some data on student test marks at the beginning and the end of the academic year.

1 Open your saved file called **marks**.

2 Create a **line-column graph** to plot the data for the **INITIAL ASSESSMENT** and the **END OF YEAR** test as **columns** against the data for the **CANDIDATE AVERAGE** from **2000 to 2005** inclusive.

   a Title the graph: **COMPARISON OF RESULTS AT BEGINNING AND END OF YEAR**

   b Label the x-axis: **YEAR**

   c Label the y-axis: **MARK**

   d Create the graph on a sheet that is separate from the data source.

3 Format the line as a thick, dark, solid line with markers.

4 Format the y-axis as follows:

minimum value: **50**
maximum value: **100**
interval: **10**

5 Insert your **name, centre number** and **filename** as a header or footer.

6 Save the file keeping the filename **marks**

7 Print one copy of the line-column graph.

Scenario

You are working in the administration office of Parchment Mail Order. The company sells office supplies to companies and individuals direct from its warehouse. All business transactions are conducted by mail order or via the Internet. Your Manager has created some outline spreadsheets. You have been asked to complete the spreadsheets and produce reports and graphs for your Manager.

You will need the following files which have been provided in .csv format:

TASK	FILENAME	DATAFILE INFORMATION
Task 1	**promwe17**	details of orders taken for promotional items
Task 2	**aveval**	details of the average value of sales
Task 3	**freqord**	data on customers that place orders most frequently
Task 4	**revprom**	details of the revenue from promotional sales
Task 5	**flashsls**	data on sales of flash drives

To perform your tasks, you will need to use application software that will allow you to:

- manipulate and format numeric data
- use live data from one spreadsheet in another
- produce graphs and charts.

Task 1

You will need the file **promwe17** to complete this task.

You have been asked to produce a report on income from promotional orders for the week ending 17 September 2005. Unless otherwise instructed you may use any readable font and size to suit the data.

1 Open the file **promwe17** and save it in your software's normal file type using the filename **promord**

2 a Use text wrap to display the column labels below on 2 lines; do not split words:

   Order Value
   Amount Due
   Sales Commission

   b Ensure that all data is displayed in full.
   c Format the data items listed as follows:

LABEL	SIZE	COLUMNS
Parchment Mail Order	Large	Centred across all columns containing data: Columns A–I Framed by a border
Promotion Orders for W/E 17 September 2005	Medium	Centred across all columns containing data: Columns A–I
Data	Medium	Centred across columns A–B Framed by a border
Summary	Medium	Centred across columns D–E Framed by a border
Orders	Medium	Centred across all columns containing data: Columns A–I Framed by a border

3 Some amendments need to be made to the spreadsheet.

   a Delete the entire column containing the data **Items** (Column F).

   b Insert a new column headed **Postage** between the columns labelled **Reduction** and **Amount Due**

4 In the **Data** section format the figure for Discount as percentage and integer (0 decimal places).

5 In the **Orders** section in the **Reduction** column you need calculate the discount to be given to each customer.

   a Enter a formula for the first order (PM5292):

     Multiply the figure for **Order Value** in the **Orders** section by the Discount figure (10%) in the **Data** section. You must use relative and absolute cell references in this formula.

   b Replicate this formula for the other items.

6 In the **Data** section name the cell containing the P&P figure of 4.5 as **delivery**

7 Postage is charged on orders under £50. Calculate whether a delivery charge is to be made

   a In the **Orders** section in the **Postage** column, use a function to calculate the postage to be charged:

     If the **Order Value** minus the **Discount** for the first order is less than 50, then return the value as the named cell **delivery**, otherwise return the figure 0.

   b Replicate this formula for the other orders.

8 The **Amount Due** for each customer needs to be calculated. In the Orders section in the Amount Due column:

   a Subtract the **Discount** from the **Order Value** then add the **Postage** for the first order.

   b Replicate this formula for the other orders.

9 In the **Orders** section, you need to calculate the **Sales Commission** figure for each order.

   a In the **Sales Commission** column, use a formula to calculate the figure for the first order by multiplying the **Amount Due** figure by **5%**.

   b Replicate this formula for the other orders.

10 In the **Orders** section:

   a Format the figures in the columns for **Amount Due** and **Sales Commission** to 2 decimal places with a currency symbol.

   b Format the figures in the columns for **Order Value**, **Reduction** and **Postage** to 2 decimal places with no currency symbol.

   c Make sure all 0 figures in the **Postage** column are also formatted to 2 decimal places.

11 a In the **Summary** section, in the cell to the right of the cell labelled **Average Value** use a function to calculate the **AVERAGE** of the **Order Value** column in the **Orders** section.

12 The sales commission for RP and PH needs to be calculated

   a In the **Summary** section, in the cell to the right of the cell labelled **Commission RP** use a function to total the **Sales Commission** if the value in the **Operator** column is **RP.**

   b Repeat this function to produce the results for **Commission PH.**

13 Format all the figures in the Summary section to 2 decimal places with a currency symbol.

14 a Set the page orientation to be **landscape** and display gridlines.

   b Insert your name, centre number, an automatic filename, and an automatic date as a header or footer.

   c Save your spreadsheet keeping the filename **promord**

   d Ensure all data will be displayed in full, on one page, when printed. You may need to adjust the margins to achieve this.

   e Print a copy of the spreadsheet **promord** showing all the figures.

15 You have been asked for a printout of the formulae of your spreadsheet **promord**.

   a Display the formulae.

   b Hide the entire columns containing the **Order Ref, Date Recd, Operator** and **Method** data (Columns A–D).

   c Display gridlines and row and column headings.

   d Ensure that all formulae are fully displayed on one page and clearly legible.

   e Save the file with the filename **proform**

   f Print the formulae on one page.

16 Close any open files.

Task 2

Before you begin this task ensure you have the file **aveval**

You have been asked to produce a graph to show whether there is a relationship between the value of orders and the number of orders placed.

1 a Open the datafile **aveval** and save it in your software's normal file format using the filename **valavegr**

b Ensure that all data is fully displayed.

2 Create an **xy scatter graph** to plot the data for **Average Order Value** against **Number of Orders**. Do not join the data points.

a Title the graph: **Average Order Value in Relation to Number of Orders**
b Label the x-axis: **Number of Orders**
c Label the y-axis: **Average Value of Order**
d Ensure the data is displayed against the appropriate axis.
e Do not display a legend.
f Create the graph on a sheet that is separate from the data source.
g Format the x-axis as follows:

minimum value:	**200**
maximum value:	**420**
interval:	**20**

h Format the y-axis as follows:

minimum value:	**150**
maximum value:	**390**
interval:	**20**

i In the chart area, insert a text box with the words:

Sales Period: September 2004 – September 2005
Ensure the text box does not overlap/touch any lines or data points.

3 Insert your name and centre number as a header or footer.

4 Save the file keeping the filename **valavegr**

5 Print one copy of the graph.

Task 3

You will need the file **freqord** to complete this task.

You have been asked to update the records of the most regular customers. One company has ceased trading so the details need to be deleted. The sales team want to target customers who have not placed an order in recent weeks. They need a report listing these customers.

1   a   Open the datafile **freqord** and save it in your software's normal file type using the filename **promlist**

   b   Ensure that all data is fully displayed.

   c   Delete the entire row for **Redfern Estates.**

   d   Amend the Record the **Customer** Avon Manor to be **Avon Manor Hotel**

2   Filter the data to find all products where the **Last Order** is **before 1 August 2005.**

3   Sort the data in ascending order of **Customer** ensuring that the corresponding data is sorted correctly.

4   Insert your name, centre number and an automatic filename as a header or footer.

5   Save your spreadsheet keeping the filename **promlist**

6   a   Display row and column headings.

   b   Print a copy of the filtered spreadsheet showing all the filtered data in full.

 PRACTICE TASK

Task 4

Before you begin this task ensure you have the files:

revprom

promord (that you created in Task 1)

The revenue generated from the September promotional offers needs to be recorded in the spreadsheet.

1   a   Open the datafile **revprom** and save it in your software's normal file type using the filename **salesrev**

   b   Ensure that all data is fully displayed.

2   You need to use a formula that will link the **salesrev** spreadsheet to the **promord** spreadsheet.

   a   Open the file **promord** (that you saved in Task 1).

   b   In the **salesrev** spreadsheet, in the cell next to **17/09/2005** use a function to calculate the total of the **Amount Due** column from the **promord** spreadsheet.

4   Insert your name, centre number and an automatic filename as a header or footer.

5   a   Ensure that all data will be fully displayed on one page and clearly legible when printed.

   b   Save the spreadsheet keeping the filename **salesrev**

   c   Print the **salesrev** spreadsheet, showing the figures, on one page.

6   a   Display the formulae.

   b   Display gridlines and row and column headings.

   c   Ensure that all formulae will be fully displayed on one page and clearly legible when printed.

   d   Save the file with the filename **saleform**

   e   Print the formulae on one page.

7   Close any open spreadsheet files.

Task 5

You have been asked by the Manager to produce an comparative bar graph showing a comparison between the number of flash drives sold in selected months.

1 a Open the datafile **flashsls** and save it in your software's normal file type using the filename **flashgra**
   b Ensure that all data is fully displayed.

2 a Select only the data for **128Mb, 256Mb, 512Mb** and **1Gb** Flash Drives for the three months:

   Jan
   Apr
   Sep

   b Create a comparative bar graph.
   c Title the graph:

   Comparison of Flash Drive Sales

   d Label the x-axis: **Flash Drive Capacity**
   e Label the y-axis: **Number Sold**
   f Ensure the data is displayed against the appropriate axis.
   g Ensure a legend is displayed showing the months

   Jan
   Apr
   Sep

   h Create the graph on a sheet that is separate from the data source.
   i Format the y-axis as follows:

   minimum value: **0**
   maximum value: **95**
   interval: **5**

3 Insert your name and centre number and an automatic filename as a header or footer.

4 Save the file keeping the filename **flashgra**

5 Print one copy of the graph.

   Ensure that all data is distinctive and can be clearly identified when printed.

6 Close the file and exit the software.

7 Check all your printouts and files for accuracy.

Definition of terms

Absolute cell reference A cell address that does not change in relation to the position of the formula in the spreadsheet. Both the row number and column letter are preceded by a $ sign (e.g. $A$1).

Active cell A single cell that is currently selected, displays with a darker border.

Active window The window in which the current task is being performed.

Adjacent Cells which are next to each other.

Alignment The position of data within a cell.

Amend To make changes to data.

Automatic fields A code that can be inserted, by the click of an icon, that instructs Excel to insert items in the document automatically, for example the date, filename, page numbers.

AutoSum An automatic function that calculates the total value of a range of adjacent cells.

AVERAGE A function that calculates the mean (medium) value of a range of cells.

Bar chart A chart that displays data as vertical bars to show data changes over a period of time, comparisons between individual items or comparisons between data.

Brackets Used in a formula to force Excel to perform calculations in a particular order. A range of cells in a function is enclosed in brackets.

Category axis x-axis of a chart (usually the horizontal axis).

Category labels Labels displayed on the x-axis that describe the data.

Cell A spreadsheet consists of rows and columns, a cell is formed where they cross. Data is entered into a cell.

Cell reference (Cell address) The address of a cell, consisting of the column letter followed by the row number. A cell reference identifies the location of values to be used in a calculation.

Chart A pictorial representation of numerical data.

Chart heading Chart title.

Chart location Where a graph is displayed, it can be on the worksheet (spreadsheet) or as a separate sheet.

Chart title The chart heading, provides information about the chart content.

Chart Wizard An automated feature for producing charts easily. It guides the user through a series of windows to create a chart.

Clear contents Deleting the contents of the cells. If entire rows/columns are cleared, the row/column remains but all cells in the row/column are empty (blank).

Column A line of cells running vertically down a spreadsheet, identified by letters.

Column chart Excel's name for a vertical bar chart.

Column headings The letters used to identify columns.

Column labels The titles that identify the data in a column.

Contiguous data Cells that are next to each other. When a block of cells can be selected for the creation of a chart, this is referred to as contiguous data.

Co-ordinate Applies to the data used for xy scatter graphs: a co-ordinate is made up of an x value and a y value.

COUNT A function that counts the number of cells containing numeric data.

COUNTA A function that counts the number of cells that contain data (numeric or alphabetic).

COUNTIF A function that counts the number of cells that meet a specified condition.

Criterion A selection condition used to find specific data.

.csv Comma separated value or comma separated variable. Tabular data saved in a format that can be read by a number of applications. A comma usually separates the data in each column. Only the data (text and numbers) is preserved, formatting will be lost.

Currency format Numbers are displayed with a monetary symbol in front of them to show the currency used in a country (e.g. £).

Customised Changes made to the 'default' settings to suit the individual user.

Datafile File that contains data (which can be in any format). In this unit a datafile is provided for use when creating spreadsheets and graphs.

Data label The name (description) of each data point.

Data series A set of related data points to be plotted on a chart.

Decimal places The number of figures displayed after the decimal point.

Default The setting that a computer program (or system) will use unless it is changed or 'customised'.

Delete row/column Removing the cells completely, the remaining row numbers or column letters are automatically re-numbered/re-labelled.

Drag The action of clicking and holding a selected item and sliding it to a new position by moving the mouse.

Fill handle A square on the bottom right corner of a cell that enables copying of the cell contents or formula to adjacent cells.

Find A method of searching for specified data.

Find and Replace A method of searching for specified data and replacing it with a specified alternative everywhere it appears.

Folder An area created to store and organise files.

Format The display on a spreadsheet (e.g. column labels, numbers, etc.) or on a chart (e.g. data points, lines, text labels, etc.).

Formatting Changing the layout and appearance of text and/or numbers and/or cells.

Formula A calculation in a spreadsheet, can use values and/or cell references.

Formula bar A bar above the main worksheet area that displays the actual content of the active cell.

Formulae More than one formula. Sometimes referred to as formulas.

Function A pre-defined formula that carries out a specific calculation, for example SUM, COUNT, AVERAGE.

Generic file type (Generic file format) A file saved in a format that can be read by most computer systems and in a large number of software applications.

Headers and footers The area in the top and bottom margin of the page. Items placed in headers and footers will appear at the top and bottom of every page. See also automatic fields.

Hover To position the mouse over an object/area on the screen.

IF A function that returns one value if a condition is met and another value if the condition is not met.

Insert row/column A new row or column is inserted between existing data in a spreadsheet. Row numbers or column letters are automatically re-numbered/re-labelled when the new row/column is inserted.

Integer A whole number i.e. no (zero) decimal places.

Interval The gap between numbers on a value axis.

Label In a spreadsheet: the row or column titles. In a graph: text entries that describe the contents of areas of the chart (e.g. title, legend, etc.).

Legend A key, it is a text box in the chart area that identifies the patterns or colours for each data series in a chart.

Line graph A graph that displays data series as a line.

Maintaining integrity of data Ensuring that all data that belongs together, stays together when data is manipulated or a sort is performed.

Major unit Excel's term for interval.

Markers The data points on a line graph.

Marquee A flashing dashed border around selected cell(s).

Mathematical operator One of four mathematical symbols: * / + - (multiply, divide, add, subtract).

MAX A function that returns the largest number from a range of cells.

Menu A list of items.

MIN A function that returns the smallest number from a range of cells.

Mixed cell reference A cell reference where one of the components is relative and the other is absolute. For example: $A1 – the reference will always be made to the column (A) but the row reference will change in relation to the position of the formula in the spreadsheet.

Name box Appears on the left of the formula bar, displays the cell address or the name given to a cell.

Named cell A cell that has been given a name.

Named cell reference A reference to a named cell. The values in the named cell will always be used in calculations regardless of the position the named cell occupies in the spreadsheet.

Named range A range of cells that has been given a name.

Native file type (native file format) The default format that datafiles will be saved in, unless an alternative format is selected. For example, the native file format for a file saved in Microsoft Excel would be .xls.

Negative number A number below zero, usually preceded with a minus sign.

Non-contiguous data Non-adjacent data.

Non-generic file type Also referred to as 'native' or 'normal' file type. The file type in which the file will be saved by 'default' (unless you change it!).

Normal file type The file type in which documents will be saved, unless the user specifies an alternative format. The 'normal' file type for an Excel file is .xls.

Orientation The way paper is displayed, can be portrait (shortest side at the top) or landscape (widest side at the top).

Print Preview Displays on screen how a spreadsheet or graph/chart will look like when printed.

Range A group (series) of cells. In a spreadsheet formula a range of adjacent cells is enclosed in brackets with a colon in between the first and last cell in the range (e.g. (F3:H3)).

Relative cell reference A cell reference that changes in relation to the position of the formula in the spreadsheet. When a formula is copied over cell(s), the formulas change automatically. The calculation is performed on cells relative (next to) the copied formula.

Replicate To copy.

Row A line of cells running horizontally across a spreadsheet, identified by numbers.

Row headings The grey row numbers.

Scale The minimum and maximum values (numbers) displayed on an axis.

Sector A slice on a pie chart.

Sort Re-ordering of data in ascending or descending order. When sorting, ensure that all associated data is also sorted, this is referred to as maintaining the integrity of data.

Spellcheck A tool in Excel that automatically checks words against a large dictionary.

Spreadsheet Is used to manipulate figures, a spreadsheet program processes tabular information, usually numbers. All tasks involving the use of numbers can be done on a spreadsheet.

Subfolder A folder within a folder.

Submenu A further list of choices available from some menu items.

Subscript Text that appears smaller and in a lower position than the rest of the text on a line.

SUM A function that adds all the values in a range of cells.

SUMIF A function that adds all the values of cells that meet a specified condition.

Superscript Text that appears smaller and in a higher position than the rest of the text on a line.

Tab (in a window) A marker (like a file marker) to indicate that more options are available by clicking on the tab. A window may have a number of tabs, these are the different sections of the window. To view the options in that section, click on the tab name.

Taskbar A bar usually at the bottom of the screen, running the length of the Desktop, it shows which tasks the computer is performing.

Text orientation The angle of the data labels.

Title bar Is displayed at the top of a program window, it shows the program icon, name and filename.

Tool tip When the mouse hovers over an item the program displays a tip, usually with a yellow background, showing the name of an object on the screen.

Truncate Data not displayed in full.

User area The workspace on a computer for the storage of files. Examples are: the My Documents folder, a network drive, a floppy disk or hard disk drive.

Value A number entered into a cell or a result of a calculation.

Value axis The y-axis on a chart (usually the vertical axis).

Values (chart values) Numbers displayed next to pie chart sectors or on the y-axis of a bar chart or line graph.

Workbook A file that contains one or more worksheets (spreadsheets). A workbook allows all related spreadsheets and graphs to be stored in one file.

Worksheet Excel term for a spreadsheet. The main sheet that is used in Excel to store and work with data. A worksheet consists of cells that are organised into columns and rows. In Excel a worksheet is always stored in a workbook.

x-axis The horizontal axis on a bar chart or line graph.

x-axis title The name displayed on the category axis.

y-axis The value axis on a chart (value axis).

y-axis title The name displayed on the value axis.

Assessment guidelines for Unit 2

1 Your tutor will provide you with all the files you need for the assessment.

2 Before an assessment you should create a new folder just for the assessment.

TIP!

Before you start, copy the folder containing the files into another folder in case you need to open an original file again

3 You will usually be provided with 5 files in .csv format.

The order of tasks will vary from paper to paper. For all tasks you will need to open a .csv file and save it as an Excel file (.xls). During the assignment you will need to apply formatting and enter formulae into at least two spreadsheets, link two spreadsheet files, produce two graphs and filter and sort data. You will also be required to edit the data in at least one task. In some assignments, you will format and enter formula in a spreadsheet at the beginning of the assessment, in others the first task may be to produce a graph or to filter and/or sort data.

During the assessment, you will need to complete about 5 tasks

General assessment tips

○ After opening a .csv file widen all columns to familiarise yourself with the data (you may also wish to print) then close the file without saving. Reopen the file to begin a task.

○ Follow each instruction in the correct sequence. Do not leave an instruction intending to do it later.

○ Do not enter any text in bold unless instructed, the text is presented in bold to help you to identify filenames, text to be entered and instructions.

○ When asked to insert an automatic date, an automatic filename, and/or an automatic page number, do not type the date, filename or page number – you must use the automatic date, automatic page number and automatic filename option in Excel.

○ Remember the saving tip. Read through the whole of a task and save a file with the new filename before you start working through the task to prevent accidental overwriting of a file.

○ Always re-save a .csv file as an Excel file before making any amendments. This will prevent you from accidentally saving a formatted spreadsheet with formulae as a .csv file and losing your work.

Filenames:

You are advised to enter filenames using the same case as in the assignment. However, you will not be penalised if you use different case for filenames. Do not enter a full stop after a filename.

Headers and footers:

Unless there is a specific instruction, you may use any font size, font type and alignment for headers and footers, but do make sure that the information in headers or footers does not overlap any page items. A small font size is usually best.

Spreadsheet tasks

There will usually be three tasks covering spreadsheet skills.

You will need to:

- open .csv files and save them as .xls files
- apply text and numeric formatting
- edit at least one spreadsheet
- enter formula and functions
- link two spreadsheets
- filter and/or sort data
- format and print spreadsheets and spreadsheet selections displaying figures and the formulae to a specified number of pages.

Your tutor will provide you with all the files that you need to complete the tasks.

Spreadsheet assessment tips

Formatting

- You may use any font style unless otherwise instructed.
- You may need to use different font sizes as a guide:
  - small: 10 – 12
  - medium: 14 – 16
  - large: 18+
- Use the 'find' facility to locate data.
- Apply text wrap **before** you widen the columns to display data in full.
- If you cannot reduce the column width to wrap text without hiding data you can force the text to wrap by using Alt + Enter in front of the word you want to display on a new line.
- Remember that monetary amounts are not always displayed with the currency symbol or to two decimal places – read the instructions carefully to ensure you apply the correct formatting. Always use the formatting function – never key in the currency symbol or zeros after the decimal place.
- Make sure negative numbers are displayed with the minus sign (not just in red).
- When you are required to format to currency you should always use the currency symbol appropriate to the country in which you are working. In the UK this will be a £. In Southern Ireland it will be a €.

○ Use the Merge and Centre icon to merge cells and centre the data across the merged columns in one action.

○ When asked to apply a border select a Thick Box Border – check the display in print preview.

Editing the spreadsheet

○ When inserting a row click in any cell in the row immediately *below* the position in which you want the new row to be inserted.

○ When inserting a column, click in any cell in the column to the *right* of the position you want the new column to be inserted.

○ Double check to make absolutely sure that you have entered all numbers **100%** accurately.

○ When deleting a row/column make sure you delete the entire row/column, not just the data contained in the row/column

○ Use Find and Replace when asked to replace data – if you make a mistake go to Edit and Undo!

○ Take great care when copying and pasting, existing data will be overwritten when you paste the new data. If you make a mistake, click on the Undo icon.

○ Check that formulae have been updated after editing the spreadsheet.

Entering formulae

○ Use range references (whenever appropriate) in your formulas, rather than specifying individual cells (eg =SUM(B2:D2) rather than =B2+C2+D2).

○ When requested to delete a row/column ensure you delete the entire row/column not just the data in the row/column.

○ If the instruction is to use a function you MUST use a function, e.g. SUM, AVERAGE. Do not use a formula even though this may also give a correct result.

○ When constructing formulae always use the cell reference of the data in the spreadsheet – do not enter the data contained in the cell manually.

○ When asked to replicate, make sure that the formulae in the rest of the row/column is constructed in the same way as the source formulae.

○ Remember to clear any formulae from cells that should be blank.

○ You may need use brackets when entering formulae, you will not be instructed to do so as you are expected to know when to use brackets.

○ Think carefully about whether you need to use a relative, an absolute or a mixed cell reference – you will not always be instructed to do so as you are expected to know when and how to use cell references appropriately. Remember, a single formula may require the use of different types of cell reference for each part of the formula.

○ Look at the figures generated by the formula to check that they make sense.

Sorting and Filtering

- To filter on just one column, highlight the data to be filtered before clicking on the Data menu and selecting **AutoFilter** only one filter button (down arrow) will appear.

- When sorting check that the integrity of data has been maintained.

Printing

- To switch from the spreadsheet view to formulae view and vice versa, press the Ctrl + ` key.

- If you have been asked to display gridlines and/or row and column headings check that they are shown in print preview (remember, you may choose to have these displayed on any print even if they have not been requested).

- Use print preview before printing to check that the data in all cells is fully displayed

- Check that all headers and footers are correct (check for the updated filename) and do not overlap any data in the spreadsheet.

- On spreadsheet printouts, check that wrapped cells are still wrapped as specified in the assignment, and that data in the wrapped cells is displayed in full (remember, you can adjust the height of the row as well as the width of the column).

- If you are printing the formulae of a file containing links, open the source file (the spreadsheet that you linked to) first. This will prevent the linked formula from being too long.

GRAPH TASKS

There will usually be two tasks covering skills in creating graphs.

You will need to:

- select a variety of data sets for display in graphical format
- select the appropriate chart type (exploded pie, comparative bar/line, xy scatter)
- enter titles, data labels and axis titles
- enter and amend axis intervals and set upper and lower limits
- apply and remove legend
- ensure comparative data is distinctive
- insert and position a text box
- print graphs/charts on a sheet separate from the data source.

Your tutor will provide you with all the files that you need to complete the tasks.

Creating graphs

- Make sure that you select the correct data. Take care *not* to highlight any extra cells when creating a chart. If you do, click in a blank cell to deselect and select the correct data.

- In Step 1 of the Chart Wizard click on the Press and Hold to View Sample button to check that the results are as you would expect.
- Always create the graph as a new sheet.
- A legend should only be displayed on a pie chart if the data labels are not displayed next to each sector.
- For any chart that displays a legend, make sure that the data is clearly distinctive.
- For comparative charts, to create a legend automatically, select the row/column labels.
- For line bar graphs ensure that the line is clearly visible against the bars and is also distinctive in the legend.
- Look at the figures in the original spreadsheet to make sure that data points on the chart have been plotted correctly – take particular care when creating xy scatter graphs!
- When setting axis scales remember to remove the tick in the auto boxes.
- Do not rely solely on print previews, check your prints very carefully to ensure that all data in your chart is clearly identifiable.

Good Luck!

Contents

In Unit 3, you need to create a new database, enter approximately 10 records, create a report, create labels, import a generic datafile of about 100 records, update it, create queries and reports from it.

This book is divided into six sections:

○ in Section 1 you will learn how to create a new database

○ in Section 2 you will learn how to create tabular reports and how to create labels

○ in Section 3 you will learn how to import a csv file and modify the field characteristics. You will then learn how to delete a record, replace data and amend data

○ in Section 4 you will learn how to create queries using logical, range and wildcard criteria

○ in Section 5 you will learn how to create a grouped report and how to format reports

○ in Section 6 you will learn how to create columnar and tabular reports displaying selected fields.

You will use a software program called Microsoft Office Access 2003 which is part of Microsoft Office 2003. Access is a program that saves data as it is entered, allows different views of data and lets you search for and present data in many different ways. We will refer to it as Access from now on.

Preparing your work area

You are advised to prepare your user area so that you can keep your files organised.

○ Create a folder for your CLAiT Plus work.

○ In this folder, create a subfolder for all the CLAiT Plus units that you will be doing.

○ In each unit subfolder, create further subfolders. For example:

• **U3 DB working** (your working folder in which all working files will be saved)

• **L2U3DB_files** (the source files folder from the CD-ROM)

• **L2U3DB_workedcopies** (the worked copies folder also copied from the CD-ROM).

Files for this book

To work through the tasks in this book, you will need the files from the folder called **L2U3DB_files**. This folder is on the CD-ROM provided with this book. Copy this folder into your user area before you begin.

▶▶ How to...   *copy the folder* **L2U3DB_files** *from the CD-ROM*

1 Insert the CD-ROM into the CD-ROM drive of your computer.

2 Close any windows that may be open.

3 From the desktop, double-click on the **My Computer** icon to display the **My Computer** window.

4 Double-click on the **CD drive** icon.

5 A dialogue box will open displaying the contents of the CD-ROM. Click once on the folder **L2U3DB_files**. The folder will be highlighted (usually blue).

6 In the **File and Folder Tasks** section, click on **Copy this folder**.

7 The **Copy Items** dialogue box will be displayed. In this dialogue box, click on the user area where you want to copy the folder **L2U3DB_files** to.

8 Click on the **Copy** button. The folder **L2U3DB_files** will be copied to your user area.

TIP!

It is advisable to copy and paste a second copy to another folder in your user area as backup.

Mouse terms

Unless otherwise instructed, always click using the left mouse button.

TERM	ACTION
Point	Move the mouse on the mousemat until the pointer appears at the required position on the screen
Click	Press and release the left mouse button once
Double-click	Quickly press the left mouse button twice, then release it
Right-click	Press and release the right mouse button once. A menu will be displayed
Hover	Position the cursor over an icon or menu item and pause. A Tool tip or a further menu item will appear
Click and drag	Used to move items. Click on an item with the left mouse button, hold the mouse button down and move the item to the required location. Release the mouse button

LEARNING OUTCOMES

In this section you will learn how to:

- ○ create a new blank database
- ○ create a new table in design view
- ○ enter field names, set the data type and the field properties
- ○ save and name a table
- ○ enter records in datasheet view
- ○ widen a field.

▶▶ How to...   *create a new blank database*

1 Load Microsoft Access 2003.

2 Click on the **File** menu, click on **New**.

3 The task pane will be displayed on the right (Figure 3.1).

4 Click on **Blank database...**. The **File New Database** dialogue box will be displayed (Figure 3.2).

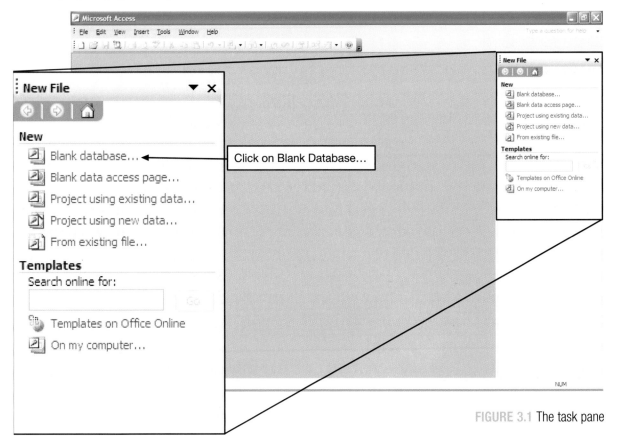

FIGURE 3.1 The task pane

5 Click on the drop-down arrow next to **Save in** and go to the databases working folder in your user area.

6 In the **File Name** box, delete **db1** and type in an appropriate filename.

7 Click on **Create**.

8 The **Database window** will be displayed (Figure 3.3). Check that **Tables** is selected in the **Objects** section on the left.

9 On the right, double-click on **Create table in Design view**.

10 The table Design view will be displayed.

11 Maximise this window.

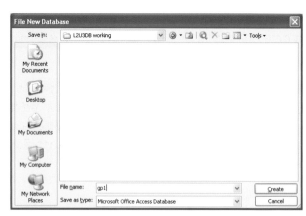

FIGURE 3.2 The File New Database dialogue box

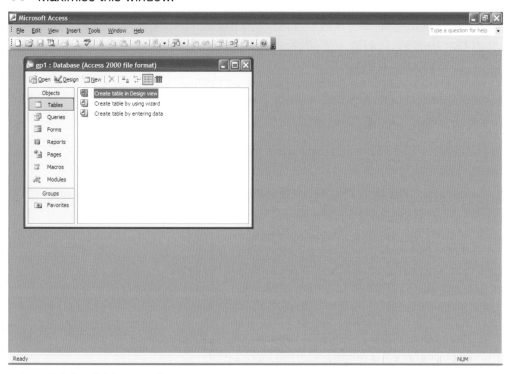

FIGURE 3.3 The Database window

Check your understanding *Create a blank database*

1 Load Access.

2 Create a blank database in your working folder called **gp1**.

3 Go to the table **Design view**.

Understanding how to create a database table

A database table is the basic component of a database, and it contains the data (records) on which all queries, reports and forms will be based. Therefore, it is very important that the table is designed correctly.

A new table is created in Design view and records are entered using either a data entry form or in Datasheet view. You will learn how to enter records in Datasheet view.

When you create a new database, you need to enter the field heading (field name) and set the data type for each field (e.g. text, number, date, currency, logic (yes/no)). A field can only have one data type. You must also set the correct field properties for each field. You will be expected to know what field properties to set.

Understanding the use and purpose of data types

Text

Text is used when you want to display text, a combination of text and numbers, and certain numbers that will not be used for calculations (e.g. telephone numbers). A text field will accept any letters and numbers. Codes are often used in databases to represent data. This helps to save space, thus improving the efficiency of the database, and it also helps to save time spent entering data. The field property can be set to accept certain codes only. This is referred to as *data validation*.

Date

A date field will only accept valid dates. Dates may be entered in any format in the table, Access will automatically convert the format to the format set in Design view when the table was designed. If you are in the UK, then, in order to provide accurate information, dates must always be set in any UK English format (day, followed by month, followed by year).

Number

Numbers might be used in a calculation. They can be displayed as whole numbers or with decimal places. Number fields will only accept numbers, letters cannot be entered into a number field.

Currency

Currency is used to display monetary amounts. The currency symbol represents the type of money used in a particular country (e.g. in the UK the currency is £ or €). Currency fields will only accept numbers. When entering data, the currency symbol need not be entered as Access will automatically display the symbol that was selected when the table was designed.

Logic

This is a Yes/No field. Access displays a logic field with a square check box – a tick represents a 'Yes' value, a blank box represents 'No'.

Understanding the Design view of a table

The first column in the top half of Design view is used to enter the field names (field headings), and the second column is used to select the appropriate data type for each field from a drop-down list. A description of the field may be entered in the third column but this is not displayed in Table, Query or Report view, therefore the description may be left blank.

The lower left half of the screen is used to set the field properties for each field. The lower right part of the screen displays more detailed information about the field properties. It is important that you take care when designing a table.

 **How to...** *enter field names, set the data type and the field properties*

1 In the table **Design view** (Figure 3.4), check that the cursor is in the first row in the **Field Name** column.

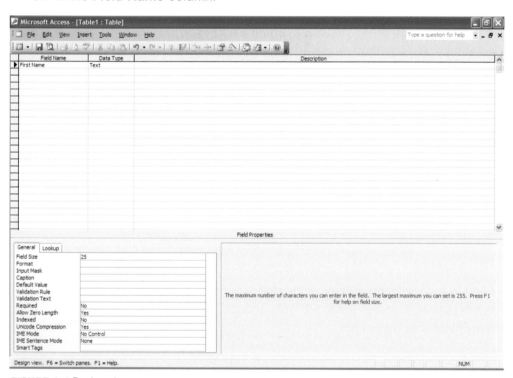

FIGURE 3.4 Design view

2 Enter the first field heading in the **Field Name** column (Figure 3.4).

3 Press the **Tab** key to move to the **Data Type** column (or click in the **Data Type** column).

4 Click on the drop-down arrow to select the data type (e.g. Text, Currency, Date/Time or Yes/No).

5 In the **Field Properties** section, set the properties as shown in the **Field Properties** table.

DATA TYPE	FIELD SIZE	FORMAT	DECIMAL PLACES
Text	Delete the default size and enter the required number based on the number of characters in the data that is to be entered in the field	–	–
Number	Click on the drop-down arrow. Select **Single** or **Double**	Click on the drop-down arrow. Select **Fixed**	Click on the drop-down arrow. Select the required number. Do not leave the setting on Auto
Date	–	Click on the drop-down arrow. Select an option (e.g. Short Date)	–

Field properties

6 Do not change any other field properties.

7 When you have entered the field name, set the data type and the field properties for the first field. Click in the second row in the **Field Name** column and repeat the process for all remaining fields (Figure 3.5).

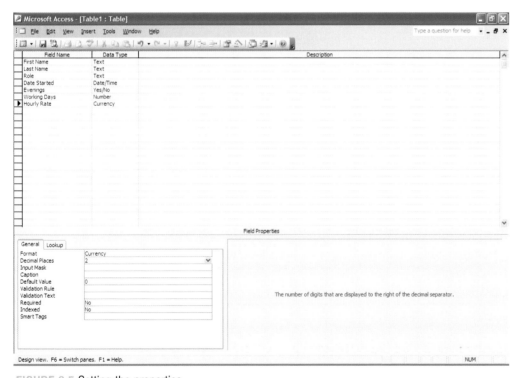

FIGURE 3.5 Setting the properties

In your database **gp1**, enter the field headings and set the data types and field properties as shown below.

FIELD HEADING	DATA TYPE	FIELD PROPERTIES
First Name	Text	25
Last Name	Text	25
Role	Text	5
Date Started	Date (Date/Time)	Short Date
Evenings	Logic field (Yes/No)	
Working Days	Number	Single, fixed, 0 decimal places
Hourly Rate	Currency	Currency, two decimal places

▶▶ How to... *save and name the table*

1 When you have created the structure of your database table, click on the **Save** icon. The **Save As** dialogue box will be displayed (Figure 3.6).

FIGURE 3.6 The Save As dialogue box

2 Type in the required table name.

3 Click on **OK**.

4 Access will display a box asking you if you want to create a primary key. Click on **No** (primary keys are needed for databases with more than one table).

5 Click on the **View** icon ▦ ▾ on the toolbar to switch to **Datasheet view**.

6 The field headings will be displayed as column headings, a check box will be displayed in any logic fields (a yes/no field), a zero will be displayed in any numeric fields and the £ sign will be displayed with zeros in any currency fields.

1 Save your table using the filename **surgery staff**

2 Do not create a primary key.

3 Switch to Datasheet view.

Data can be entered, edited or deleted in the table in Datasheet view or by using a *form*. Any changes made to the data using a form are automatically updated in the table. Only one record can be viewed at a time in a form.

To use a form, click on the **Forms** option in the **Objects** section in the Database window. Double-click to open the form (if a form has been created) and enter data.

You will add records directly into the table in Datasheet view. These will be automatically saved on entry.

1 Check that the cursor is flashing in the first field of row one. Enter the required data.

2 Press the **Tab** key to move to the next field and enter the required data.

3 To place a tick in a logic field box, click in the box with your mouse or press the **spacebar**.

4 In the numeric and currency fields, enter the required data. The zeros will be overtyped.

5 Press the **Tab** key to move to the next record (Figure 3.7).

Ensure that you enter all data, especially numbers and dates, with one hundred per cent accuracy.

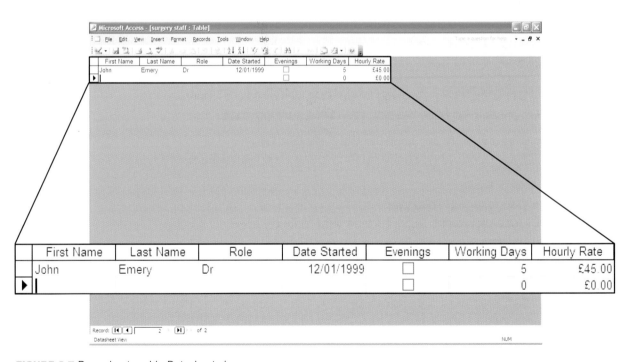

FIGURE 3.7 Record entered in Datasheet view.

1 Position the cursor on the line to the right of the field heading. The cursor will turn into a double-headed arrow ┿ . Double-click.

2 Access will adjust the column width to fit the longest line of data that is visible on the screen within the field.

Check your understanding *Enter records in Datasheet view*

1 In your database table **surgery staff**, enter the following records.

First Name	Last Name	Role	Date Started	Evenings	Working Days	Hourly Rate
John	Emery	Dr	12/01/1999	No	5	£45.00
Amy	Innes	SN	19/03/2004	Yes	3	£9.50
Robina	Darwan	OT	01/04/2001	No	2	£11.50
James	Reed	Dr	20/08/2000	Yes	1	£52.00
Elaine	Shaw	SN	12/02/2002	No	4	£14.00
Jane	Murphy	SN	06/10/2004	No	5	£10.00
Sue	Campbell	Rec	13/02/1999	Yes	5	£7.25
Idris	Adam	Phrm	20/06/2003	No	3	£19.00
Eileen	Morgan	OT	15/11/2003	No	2	£19.00
Ruth	Clarke	Rec	12/01/1999	No	5	£8.00

2 Ensure that all field headings and records are displayed in full.

3 Click on the **Spelling** icon on the toolbar to check the spelling.

4 Save your updated table keeping the name **surgery staff**.

5 For your information, the codes in the **Role** field are:

Dr   Doctor
SN   Staff Nurse
OT   Occupational Therapist
Rec Reception Staff
Phrm Pharmacist

ASSESS YOUR SKILLS – Create a new database

By working through Section 1 you will have learnt the skills listed below. Read each item to help you decide how confident you feel about each skill:

○ create a new blank database

○ create a new table in Design view

○ enter field names, set the data type and the field properties

○ save and name a table

○ enter records in Datasheet view

○ widen a field.

If you think that you need more practice on any of the skills in the above list, go back and work through the skill(s) again.

If you feel confident, move on to Section 2.

2: Create a tabular report and create labels

LEARNING OUTCOMES

In this section you will learn how to:

○ create a tabular AutoReport

○ switch to the report Design view

○ sort data

○ delete the page number or date

○ insert your name and centre number

○ set the page orientation

○ insert report headers and footers

○ enter a report title

○ save a report with a specified filename

○ print a report

○ close a report

○ open a saved table

○ create labels

○ display headers and footers on a label report.

Simple tabular reports

A tabular report displays field names (column headings) at the top of the page with records in rows across the page. There are a number of ways to create reports. To create a tabular report in which all the records and field headings need to be displayed, the quickest method is to create an AutoReport.

If you need to create a tabular report from a small database, you are advised to follow the method below to create a tabular AutoReport. Other methods of creating reports are covered in Sections 5 and 6.

TIP!

If you have used the New Object: AutoForm icon once, the next time it may display as the last object used (e.g. **New Object: Report** ▾ or **New Object: Query** ▾).

▶▶ How to... *create an AutoReport*

1 With the table open in **Datasheet view**, on the toolbar, click on the drop-down arrow next to **New Object: AutoForm** ▾.

2 A drop-down list will be displayed (Figure 3.8). Click on **Report**.

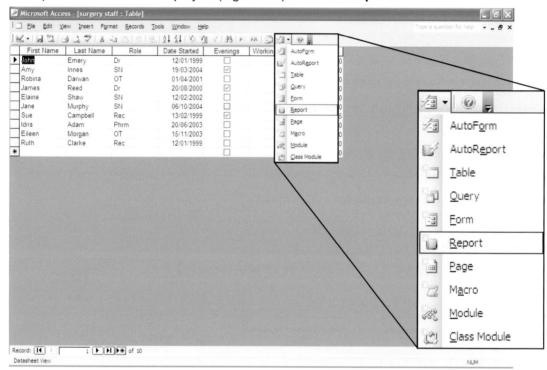

FIGURE 3.8 Selecting Report

3 The **New Report** dialogue box will be displayed (Figure 3.9).

4 Click on **AutoReport: Tabular**.

5 Click on **OK**.

6 Access will create the report automatically and will display it in Print Preview (Figure 3.10). Zoom in to the report to check that all the data is displayed in full. If any data is truncated click on the view icon ▾ to switch to the report Design view and refer to **How to... widen a field** in Section 5 on page 230.

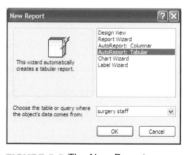

FIGURE 3.9 The New Report dialogue box

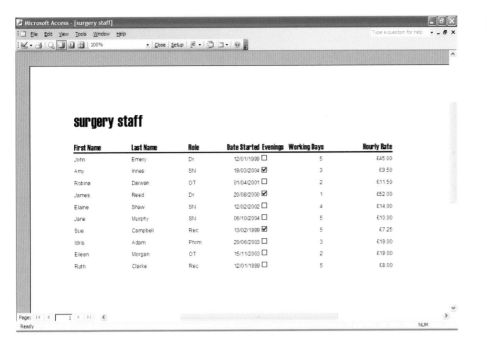

FIGURE 3.10 The report displayed in Print Preview

Check your understanding *Create a tabular AutoReport*

1 Open your database table **surgery staff**.

2 Create a tabular AutoReport to display all the fields and all records in the same order as in the table.

▶▶ How to... *switch to the report Design view*

1 In the Print Preview of the report, click on the **View** icon on the toolbar.

2 The report will be displayed in Design view (Figure 3.11).

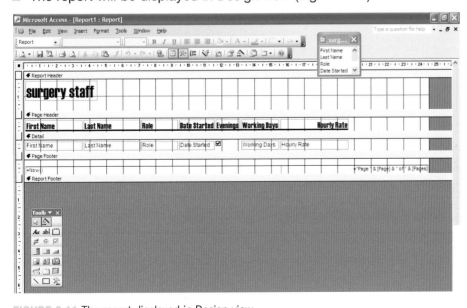

FIGURE 3.11 The report displayed in Design view

▶▶ How to... *sort data*

1 In Design view, click on the **Sorting and Grouping** icon ⌷≡ . The **Sorting and Grouping** dialogue box will be displayed. The cursor will appear in the first row of the **Field/ Expression** column (Figure 3.12).

2 Click on the drop-down arrow in the first row. A list of field headings will be displayed. Select the field to be sorted.

3 Click in the first row of the **Sort Order** column, click on the drop-down arrow. Select **Ascending** or **Descending** (Figure 3.13).

4 Click on the cross to close the Sorting and Grouping dialogue box.

5 Click the **Print Preview** icon 🔍 to check that data has been sorted.

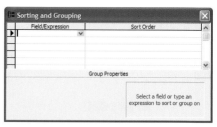

FIGURE 3.12 The Sorting and Grouping dialogue box

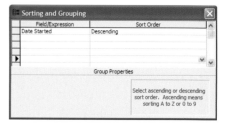

FIGURE 3.13 Sorting the field

Check your understanding *Sort data in a report*

In your **Report1** titled **Surgery Staff**, sort the data in ascending order of **Last Name**.

Headers and footers in reports

Access automatically displays the date and the number of pages in a report. Therefore you will not have to insert these but, when you preview the report, you should check that these are displayed. In Design view, the date displays as =*Now()* in a control box and the page numbers display as ="Page" & [Page] & "of" & [Pages] in a control box.

▶▶ How to... *delete the page number or date*

1 In Design view, click once in the control box to be deleted. Square handles will be displayed around the control box.

2 Press the **Delete** key.

▶▶ How to... *insert your name and centre number*

You can use label boxes in Design view to enter your name and centre number. To enter text labels, the Page Header/Page Footer and the Toolbox need to be displayed (Figure 3.14).

1 If the Page Header/Page Footer are not displayed, click on the **View** menu, click on **Page Header/Footer**.

2 If the Toolbox is not displayed, click on the **View** menu, click on **Toolbox** (Figure 3.14).

TIP!

A *control* is a label box or a text box in a report. If you are unsure which control (box) is a label or a text box, click on the box and then press the F1 key. A tool tip will be displayed with an explanation of the type of box (control).

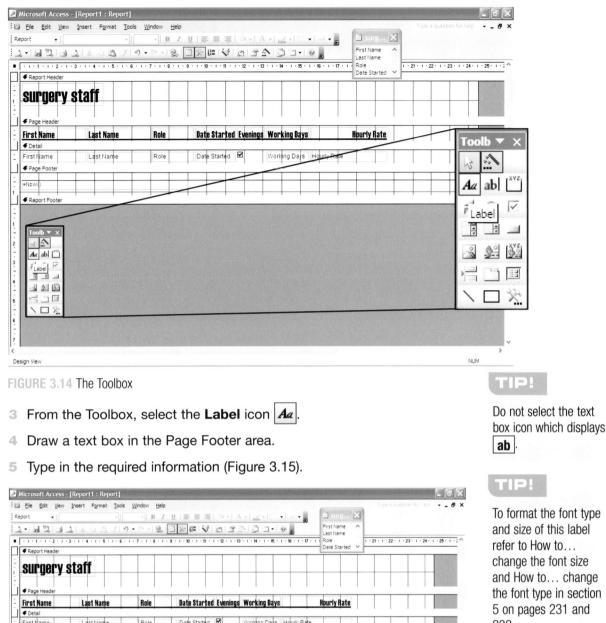

FIGURE 3.14 The Toolbox

3 From the Toolbox, select the **Label** icon Aa.

4 Draw a text box in the Page Footer area.

5 Type in the required information (Figure 3.15).

TIP!

Do not select the text box icon which displays ab.

TIP!

To format the font type and size of this label refer to How to… change the font size and How to… change the font type in section 5 on pages 231 and 232.

FIGURE 3.15 Drawing a text box and entering data

1 In the footer of your **Report1**, titled **surgery staff**, check that the date field is displayed.

2 Delete the page number.

3 Create a label box and enter your name and centre number in the footer.

▶▶ How to... *set the page orientation*

1 Click on the **File** menu, click on **Page Setup**.

2 The **Page Setup** dialogue box will be displayed.

3 Click on the **Page** tab and select **Portrait** or **Landscape**.

4 Margins can also be changed in the Page Setup dialogue box. Click on the **Margins** tab. Change the top, bottom, left and right margins as required.

5 Click on **OK**.

Check your understanding *Set the orientation*

Set the orientation of your **Report1** titled **surgery staff** to **landscape**.

▶▶ How to... *widen the report title control box and enter a report title*

1 In the report Design view, click on the report title. Square handles will be displayed around the control box.

2 Click and drag the square handle on the right of the control box further to the right to widen the control box.

3 Click in the box for the report title. A cursor will be displayed.

4 Delete the existing title and enter the new title (Figure 3.16).

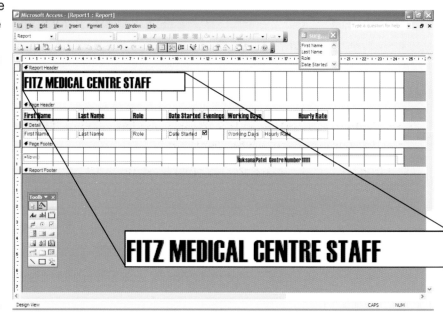

FIGURE 3.16 Entering the new title

 **How to...** *save a report with a specified name*

1. Click on the **File** menu, click on **Save**.

2. The **Save As** dialogue box will be displayed (Figure 3.17).

FIGURE 3.17 The Save As dialogue box

3. Delete the existing name and enter the required report name.

4. Click on **OK**.

 **How to...** *print a report*

1. Before you print, always use Print Preview. Zoom in to various parts of your report to check that all the data is fully displayed.

2. Click on the **Print** icon on the toolbar (from Print Preview or Design view).

3. Always check your printout to make sure that all the data is fully displayed even if you have used Print Preview.

How to... *close a report*

1. Click on the **File** menu, click on **Close**.

Check your understanding *Save and print a report*

1. In your **Report1** titled **surgery staff**, delete this title.

2. Widen the report title control box and enter the title **FITZ MEDICAL CENTRE STAFF**

3. Save your report using the filename **FITZ MEDICAL CENTRE STAFF**

4. Use Print Preview to make sure the title, field headings and all the records are fully displayed.

5. Print your report entitled **FITZ MEDICAL CENTRE STAFF**.

6. Close the report.

How to... *open a saved table*

1. In the **Database window**, in the **Objects** section, click on **Tables**. The tables in your database will be displayed.

2. Double-click on the table name to open it (Figure 3.18).

TIP!

Instead of double-clicking you can click once to select the table (do not click if the table name is already highlighted), then click on **Open** Open .

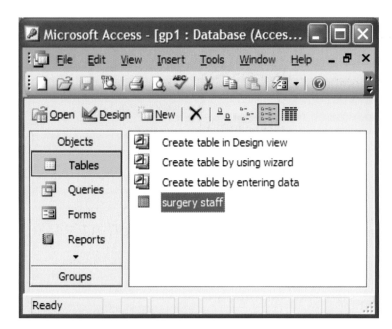

FIGURE 3.18 Opening a saved table

▶▶ How to... *create labels*

1 With the table (or query) open in **Datasheet** view, on the toolbar, click on the drop-down arrow next to **New Object** .

2 A drop-down list will be displayed. Click on **Report**. The **New Report** dialogue box will be displayed (Figure 3.19).

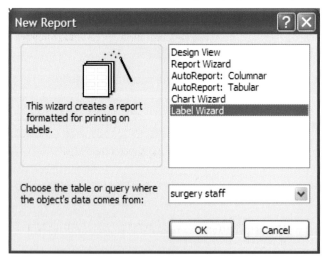

FIGURE 3.19 The New Report dialogue box

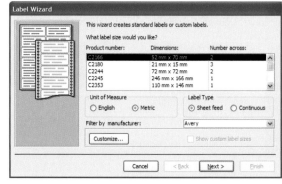

FIGURE 3.20 The Label Wizard

TIP!

If you have used this icon already, it may display as **New Object: Report** .

3 Click on **Label Wizard**. Click on **OK**.

4 The **Label Wizard** dialogue box will be displayed (Figure 3.20). If required, select the appropriate label dimensions and, if appropriate, select the correct manufacturer.

TIP!

Choose Avery 2 across, as this usually allows all the data to be fully displayed without the need to change the Page Setup.

5 Click on **Next**. In step 2, select an appropriate font name and font size (Figure 3.21). Click on **Next**.

6 In step 3, double-click in turn on each of the field headings required (Figure 3.22).

TIP!

Instead of double-clicking, you can click once on the field name, then click on the **Add** button [>].

7 To display two fields on one line, press the spacebar after you have displayed the first field. Press **Enter** to display the next field on a new line. Click on **Next**.

8 In step 4, double-click on the field(s) to be sorted (Figure 3.23).

9 Click on **Next**.

10 In step 5, enter the name of the label report (Figure 3.24). Click on **Finish**. The labels will be displayed in Print Preview.

11 To display headers and footers, click the view icon to switch to the label report Design view.

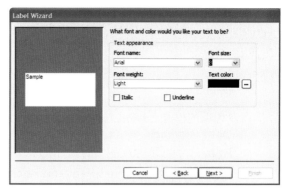

FIGURE 3.21 Selecting a font name and size

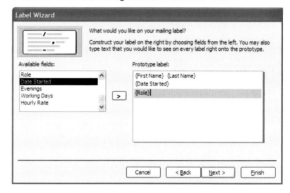

FIGURE 3.22 Selecting the field headings

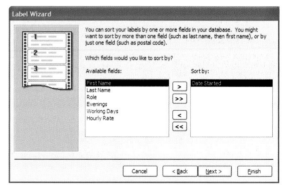

FIGURE 3.23 Selecting the fields to be sorted

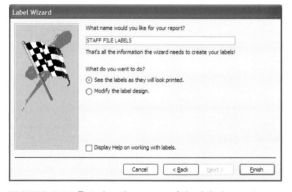

FIGURE 3.24 Entering the name of the label report

TIP!

Unlike other reports, the report title does not display on a label report.

1   Using your database table **surgery staff**, create labels to be used for the staff files.

2   Display the following fields on the labels:

First Name   Last Name (separated by at least one space, on one line)
Date Started
Role

3   Sort the data in ascending order of **Date Started**.

4   Save the report using the name **STAFF FILE LABELS**

▶▶ How to...   *display headers and footers on a label report*

1   In **Design view**, click on the **View** menu, click on **Page Header/ Footer**, then click on the **View** menu again, click on **Page Header/ Footer** (or, if the page header and page footer are already displayed, drag the grey bar to reduce/increase the page header and/or footer) (Figure 3.25).

2   If the Toolbox is not displayed click on the **View** menu, click **Toolbox**.

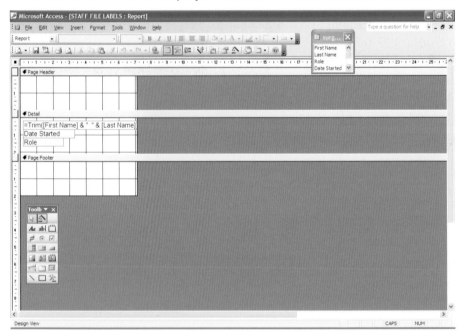

FIGURE 3.25 The Label Report Design view

3   From the Toolbox, select the **Label** icon **Aa**.

4   Draw a box in the page footer area (or in the header area if required).

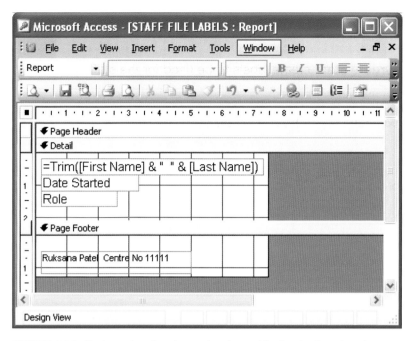

FIGURE 3.26 Footer entered and page header and footer depth reduced

5   Type the required information into the text box (Figure 3.26).

6   Use Print Preview to ensure that all the labels fit on one page and that all the data is displayed in full.

FIGURE 3.27 Some data may not be displayed

7   When you click on the Print Preview icon, the message shown in Figure 3.27 may be displayed. Click on **OK** then, in Print Preview or Design view, click on the **File** menu, click on **Page Setup**, select the **Margins** tab. Reduce the left and/or right margins.

8   Optional: click on the **Columns** tab and reduce the **Column Spacing**.

9   Click on **OK**.

10   Use Print Preview again.

11   If any data is not displayed in full, click the **View** icon to go to the Design view.

12   Click on a control box in the **Detail** section, then on the **Formatting toolbar**, click on the drop-down arrow next to the **Font Size** box and select a smaller size.

13   Reduce the width of the control box and the page width.

14   Use Print Preview again.

15   Click the **Save** icon to save the updated label report.

1   In the footer of your label report titled **STAFF FILE LABELS**, create a label box and enter your name and centre number. Use Print Preview to ensure that all the data will be fully displayed on the printout.

2   Save the updated report keeping the filename **STAFF FILE LABELS**

3   Print the labels on one page. Check your printout to ensure that all the data is fully displayed.

4   Close the label report and the database table **surgery staff**.

5   Close the database **gp1**.

ASSESS YOUR SKILLS – Create a tabular report and create labels

By working through Section 2 you will have learnt the skills listed below. Read each item to help you decide how confident you feel about each skill:

○ create a tabular AutoReport

○ switch to the report Design view

○ sort data

○ delete the page number or date

○ insert your name and centre number

○ set the page orientation

○ insert report headers and footers

○ enter a report title

○ save a report with a specified filename

○ print a report

○ close a report

○ open a saved table

○ create labels

○ display headers and footers on a label report.

If you think that you need more practice on any of the skills in the above list, go back and work through the skill(s) again.

If you feel confident, move on to Section 3.

LEARNING OUTCOMES

In this section you will learn how to:

- import a csv file (generic datafile)
- modify field characteristics
- compact the database
- create a backup copy
- add a new record
- find a record
- delete a record
- amend existing data
- replace data in a field
- delete a field.

CSV

The abbreviation *csv* stands for 'comma separated values' or 'comma separated variables'. A csv file is a generic datafile, which means it can be opened and read by most software, not just by the software it was created in.

▶▶ How to... *import a csv file*

1 Load Access and create a new blank database, using a suitable filename.

2 Click on the **File** menu, click **Get External Data**, click **Import** (Figure 3.28).

TIP!

Maximise the Database Window.

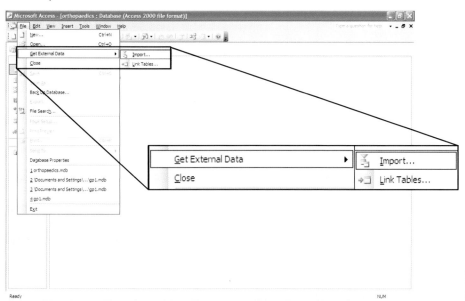

FIGURE 3.28 Importing a csv file

3   The **Import** dialogue box will be displayed.

4   Click on the drop-down arrow next to the **Look in** box. Locate the user area where the csv file is saved. There may be no files displayed at this point.

5   Click on the drop-down arrow to the right of the **Files of type** box. Scroll down the list and select **Text Files** (Figure 3.29).

6   In the main window, click on the csv file to be imported (you must ensure that the filename is highlighted) (Figure 3.30).

7   Click on **Import**. The **Import Text Wizard** will be displayed.

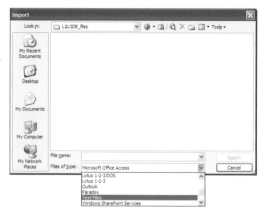

FIGURE 3.29 The Import dialogue box

FIGURE 3.30 The highlighted csv file

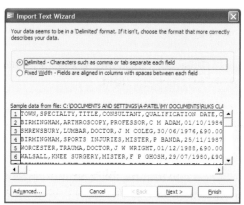

FIGURE 3.31 Step 1 of the Import Text Wizard

8   In step 1 of the Import Text Wizard, ensure **Delimited** is selected (Figure 3.31). Click on **Next**.

9   In step 2, ensure the **Comma** option is selected. Click on the drop-down arrow to the right of the **Text Qualifier** box. Select "(double speech marks). Click in the check box for **First Row Contains Field Names** (Figure 3.32).

10   Click on **Next**.

11   In step 3, check that the option for **In a New Table** is selected (Figure 3.33). Click on **Next**.

TIP!

You must select the text qualifier *before* you click in the check box.

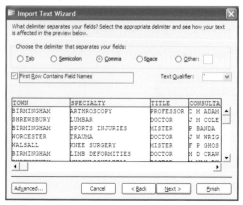

FIGURE 3.32 Step 2 of the Import Text Wizard

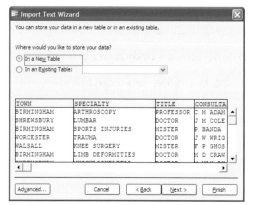

FIGURE 3.33 Step 3 of the Import Text Wizard

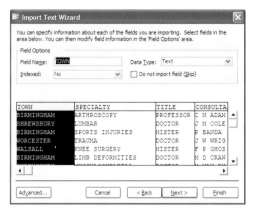

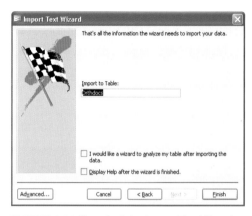

FIGURE 3.34 Step 4 of the Import Text Wizard

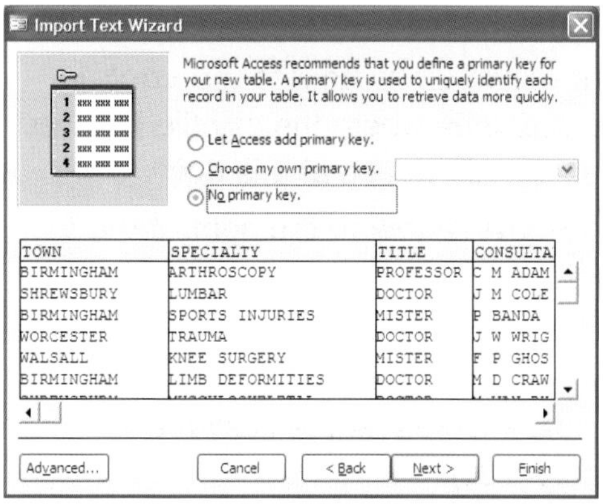

FIGURE 3.35 Step 5 of the Import Text Wizard

12 In step 4, click on **Next** (do not make any changes here) (Figure 3.34).

13 In step 5, click on the button for **No Primary Key** (Figure 3.35). Click on **Next**.

14 In step 6, click on **Finish** (the name of the csv file will be displayed in the **Import to Table** box) (Figure 3.36).

15 In step 7, the message **Finished importing file...** should be displayed. Click on **OK** (Figure 3.37).

TIP!

If the window displays a message that there are import errors, click on **OK**, then select the table in the Database window. Click on the **Delete** key. Select the **Import Errors** table and click on the **Delete** key. Start the import process from the beginning following each step carefully.

FIGURE 3.36 Step 6 of the Import Text Wizard

FIGURE 3.37 Step 7 of the Import Text Wizard

Check your understanding *Import a csv file*

To do this task you will need the csv file **orthdocs**.

1 Load Access and create a new blank database.

2 Save the database into your working folder using the filename **orthopaedics**

3 Import the csv file **orthdocs**. Save the table keeping the name **Orthdocs**

4 Open the database table **Orthdocs**.

5 Maximise the Database window.

6 Widen all the fields to ensure that all the data is fully displayed.

7 Save the updated database table.

▶▶ How to... *modify field characteristics*

TIP!

Refer to How to...
enter field names,
set the data type and
the field properties in
Section 1 if you need
to (page 188).

When a table is imported into Access, the Access default field properties
are set. A text field size is set to 255 characters. To improve the efficiency
of the database and to decrease the file size, you should view the data in
the imported table, and then switch to the table Design view to modify the
default characteristics. Ensure that you do not set incorrect field properties
as this may cause errors in the table – you must maintain the integrity of
the data.

1 Go to the Design view of the database table. Click in the **Data Type**
   column of the field to be modified. In the **Field Properties** section,
   amend the properties as required.

2 Click in the **Data Type** column of the next field to be modified. In the
   Field Properties section, amend the properties as required.

3 Repeat this process for all the other fields.

4 Click the **Save** icon.

5 Click the **View** icon to return to table Datasheet view.

Check your understanding *Modify field characteristics*

1 Modify the field properties in your database table **Orthdocs** as follows.

FIELD NAME	DATA TYPE	FIELD SIZE
TOWN	Text	25
SPECIALTY	Text	20
TITLE	Text	10
CONSULTANT	Text	25
QUALIFICATION DATE	Date	Short Date format (e.g. 30/11/1987)
CONSULTATION FEE	Currency	Currency with currency symbol, zero decimal places
WAITING DAYS	Number	Number, double, fixed format, zero decimal places

2 Save the amended database table.

▶▶ How to... *compact the database (optional)*

1 In the Database window, click on
   the **Tools** menu, click **Database
   Utilities**, click **Compact and Repair
   Database**.

2 A security warning message may
   be displayed (Figure 3.38). Click on
   Open.

FIGURE 3.38 Security
warning message

TIP!

Before you proceed,
create a backup copy
of your imported,
modified database.

1 Compact and repair the database after you have amended the field properties.

2 Open the database table.

▶▶ How to... *create a backup copy of a database (optional)*

1 Click on the **File** menu, click **Back Up Database**.

2 The **Save Backup As** dialogue box will be displayed. Access will save in the same folder as the database you are working on and will suggest the original name followed by the date in American format (year, month, date).

3 In the **Save Backup As** dialogue box, click on **Save**.

4 A warning message may be displayed again. Click on **Open**.

5 The original database will reopen in the Database window.

6 In the **Objects** section, check that **Tables** is selected and that the table name is highlighted. Click on **Open**.

▶▶ How to... *add a new record*

New records can be added easily to a database table. However, these can only be added at the end of the table, below the last record.

1 Click on the **New Record** button in the **Record Navigation** buttons at the bottom left of the screen or click in the first column of the last row (the blank row).

2 Enter the required data in the first field. Press the **Tab** key to move to the next field.

3 Enter the required data.

4 Access automatically saves new or amended data. Only changes to the layout of a database table need to be saved.

▶▶ How to... *find a record in a large database and delete it*

In a large database, it is advisable to use the Find facility to find a record to be deleted instead of trying to scroll through the table to locate a record.

1 Click anywhere in the field in which you want to find the data.

TIP!

Although you can only add records at the end of a database table, you may find that when you close a table and open it again, the order of records may have changed (e.g. new records may no longer be displayed at the bottom). Access does this automatically. This is acceptable.

2 Click on the **Edit** menu, click **Find**. The **Find and Replace** dialogue box will be displayed (Figure 3.39).

3 In the **Find What** box, enter the data to be found.

4 Click on the drop-down arrow next to **Match**. A drop-down list will be displayed. Select the option for **Any Part of Field**.

5 Click on the **Find Next** button.

6 Close the **Find and Replace** dialogue box. Ensure that the cursor is displayed in the record to be deleted.

7 Click on the **Edit** menu, click **Delete Record**.

8 Access will display a message prompting you to confirm the delete.

9 Click on **Yes**.

FIGURE 3.39 The Find and Replace dialogue box

TIP!

In Access you cannot undo an action, so always check to make sure you have found the correct record – there may be several records containing similar data.

Check your understanding *Delete a record*

1 Open the imported database table **Orthdocs** if it is not already open.

2 Maximise the Table Window.

3 Widen all the fields to ensure that all the data is fully displayed.

4 Delete the record for the CONSULTANT **F S WILCOCK**

▶▶ *How to...* amend existing data

1 Ensure that all the data and the field headings are fully displayed by double-clicking between each of the field headings.

2 Click in the field to be amended. Delete the existing contents. Enter the new data.

3 Access saves an amendment automatically when you move out of the field.

4 When you have made all amendments, click in a blank row to avoid any accidental changes to data.

5 Click on the **Save** icon to save any changes to the layout of the table.

▶▶ *How to...* replace data in a field

1 Click anywhere in the field in which the data needs to be replaced.

2 Click on the **Edit** menu, click **Replace**. The **Find and Replace** dialogue box will be displayed (Figure 3.40).

3 In the **Find What** box, enter the data to be replaced. In the **Replace With** box, enter the new data.

FIGURE 3.40 The Find and Replace dialogue box

4   Check that the **Match** box displays **Whole Field** or **Any Part of Field** as appropriate for the data in the field. (If not, press the drop-down arrow and select the option required).

5   Click to place a tick in the box for **Match Case**.

6   Click on the **Replace All** button.

7   Access displays a message prompting you to confirm the replace. Click on **Yes**.

TIP!

Do not click on the **Replace** button. This will replace only one instance of the data.

Check your understanding *Replace data*

1   In your database table **Orthdocs**, amend the SPECIALTY for DR T G WOODS to **GENERAL ORTHOPAEDICS** and the WAITING DAYS to **5**

2   In the **TITLE** field, replace **all** the entries as follows:

Replace PROFESSOR with **PROF**
Replace MISTER with **MR**
Replace DOCTOR with **DR**

▶▶ How to... *delete a field*

1   Switch to the table Design view.

2   Click in the row in the field to be deleted (click in the **Field Name** or **Data Type** column).

3   Click on the **Edit** menu, click **Delete Rows**.

4   Access displays a message prompting you to confirm the delete. Click on **Yes**.

ASSESS YOUR SKILLS – Import a datafile and update a database

By working through Section 3 you will have learnt the skills listed below. Read each item to help you decide how confident you feel about each skill:

- ○ import a csv file (generic datafile)
- ○ modify field characteristics
- ○ compact the database
- ○ create a backup copy
- ○ add a new record
- ○ find a record
- ○ delete a record
- ○ amend existing data
- ○ replace data in a field
- ○ delete a field.

If you think that you need more practice on any of the skills in the above list, go back and work through the skill(s) again.

If you feel confident, move on to Section 4.

In this section you will learn how to:

- understand range criteria, logical operators and wildcards
- understand comparison operators
- create a new query
- select field names and drag them into the Query grid
- display selected fields
- sort data in a query
- enter the selection criteria
- run the query
- create a query using two criteria
- save a new query with a specified name
- return to Query Design view
- save an existing query
- create a calculated field.

Understanding queries

A query is used in a database to ask questions about the data in the database table in order to find specific information. To find the specific information, appropriate *selection conditions* are entered into a query design. The term used to describe the selection conditions is *criteria*. A single criteria is referred to as a criterion.

The advantage of a query over other methods of finding specific information (e.g. filters) is that, when a database table is amended or updated, a saved query is also automatically updated. This is referred to as *live data handling*. Once a query is created and saved it can be used again, updated and resaved. Any amendments to the data in a query will automatically update the database table. Queries are often used to create reports that present information in a professional manner.

There are many ways of creating queries. Two frequently used ways are as follows:

- Creating a query using the wizard.
- Creating a query in Design view. You will learn how to create queries in Design view.

There are a number of ways to go to Design view. One frequently used method is as follows.

1 Close the database table.

2 From the Database window, click on **Queries** in the **Objects** section.

3 Click on **Create query in Design view**.

4 Click on **Open**. The **Show Table** dialogue box will be displayed.

5 Click to select the table name.

6 Click on **Add**.

7 Click on **Close**.

However, using the icons on the toolbars allows you to perform actions much more quickly (e.g. Save, Print). Similarly, it is quicker to use the **View** button on the toolbar to go to Design view. You will learn how to the use the quicker way.

Understanding query expression criteria

Range criteria

Range criteria are used to find records that are between a certain value. The range could be dates, numbers or text:

BETWEEN 30/11/85 and 20/03/87	finds all records between and including these dates.
Tip	Access will insert a # (hash) before and after each date: **#30/11/85# and #20/03/87#**
BETWEEN 30 and 45	finds all records between and including these numbers.

Logical operators

AND	Use AND to combine search criteria within one field: LONDON AND BIRMINGHAM.
	AND is also used between two values in the BETWEEN criteria: BETWEEN 30/11/85 AND 20/03/87.
OR	Use OR to find records that match any of the criteria specified: HEATHROW OR STANSTEAD OR LUTON.

Wildcard criteria

Wildcard criteria are used to find records that do not have an exact match in a field. Wildcards are used to 'pattern search':

*	Matches any number of characters. It can be used as the first or last character in the character string: ***grey***. This would find any shade of grey (e.g. silver grey, grey blue, metallic grey).
?	Matches any single alphabetic character: **b?ll**. This would find 'ball', 'bell', 'bill'.
#	Matches any single numeric character: **2#1**. This would find 201, 211, 221, 231, etc.

TIP!

Any of these operators can be combined in a query.

When you move out of a field, Access will automatically enter the word *Like* in the Criteria row and will insert speech marks before and after the criteria.

Understanding comparison operators

Where numbers or dates are used in tables, comparison operators in a query allow you to search for specific numbers or dates.

COMPARISON OPERATORS IN NUMERIC FIELDS	
>	Greater than
>=	Greater than or equal to
<	Less than
<=	Less than or equal to
<>	Not equal to or exclude

For example, <> "SALOON" and <> "ESTATE" finds all cars except SALOON and ESTATE models. <> cannot be used in wildcard searches. *Not like* should be used to exclude data if wildcard criteria are used.

COMPARISON OPERATORS IN DATE FIELDS	
>	After
>=	On or after
<	Before
<=	On or before
<>	Not equal to or exclude

TIP!

If you click in another field after entering the date criteria, you will see that Access displays a **#** (hash) sign before and after the date.

For example, **<> 01/01/2006** finds all dates except 01/01/2006. <> cannot be used in wildcard searches. *Not like* should be used to exclude data if wildcard criteria are used.

▶▶ How to... *create a new query*

1 In **Datasheet view** (with the table open), click on the drop-down arrow next to the **New Object** icon.

2 A drop-down list will be displayed. From the list, click on **Query**.

3 The **New Query** dialogue box will be displayed. Check that **Design view** is highlighted.

4 Click on **OK**.

If you have used this icon already to create a query, Access changes the icon and the tool tip to New Object: Query 📑 ▼ or New Object: Report 📄 ▼ .

Query Design view

Figure 3.41 shows the Query Design view.

Field List box

The Field List box displays the table name in the title bar (the shaded area, usually blue) and the list of field headings in the database table.

Query grid

The Query grid consists of six rows:

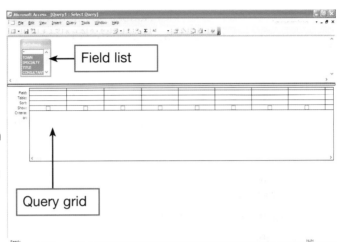

FIGURE 3.41 Query Design view

- The *Field* row displays the field name (field heading).

- The *Table* row displays the name of the database table.

- When clicked in, the *Sort* row displays a drop-down arrow with three sort options.

- If the *Show* row is ticked, the field (column) will be displayed in the query result.

- The selection condition should be entered into the *Criteria* row

- More selection conditions may be entered into the *OR* row. You are advised not to enter any criteria in this row as there is a greater chance of error when you create queries using multiple criteria.

▶▶ How to... *select field names and drag them into the Query grid*

1 Position the cursor on the database table name (usually blue) in the Field List box. Double-click. All the field names will be highlighted.

2 Click and drag the highlighted field names to the **Field** row of the first column. All the field names will be displayed in the **Field** row, the table name will be displayed in the **Table** row in all the columns, and a tick will be displayed in the **Show** row in each box (Figure 3.42).

This method of selecting fields ensures that no fields are left out (e.g. field names that are at the bottom of the list).

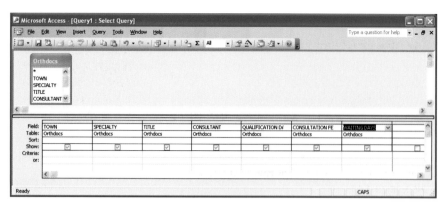

FIGURE 3.42 Field names dragged into the Query grid

TIP!

Another way to select fields to drop into the Query grid is to double-click on each field name.

▶▶ How to... *display selected fields*

Click in the **Show** box to remove the tick for the fields that you do not want to display.

▶▶ How to... *sort data in a query*

1 Click in the **Sort** row of the field to be sorted. A drop-down arrow will be displayed.

2 Click on the drop-down arrow. A list will be displayed.

3 Click on **Ascending** or **Descending**.

TIP!

In a query or a report, you do not need to show a field in which you entered selection criteria.

▶▶ How to... *enter the selection (query) criteria*

1 Click in the **Criteria** row of the field to be queried. Enter the required criteria.

2 You must enter the criteria with one hundred per cent accuracy. See the section **Understanding query expression criteria** on page 213 for information on what range, logical and wildcard criteria are and how to enter these criteria in a query. See the section **Understanding comparison operators** on page 214 for information on what comparison operators are and how to use these in queries.

TIP!

In the Criteria row, text can be entered in upper or lower case.

TIP!

Increase the field width before you enter the query criteria so that the criteria are fully displayed. You can also increase the width after you enter the criteria.

▶▶ How to... *run the query*

1 Click on the **Run** icon ⚡ on the toolbar. The results of the query will be displayed as a table in Datasheet view.

2 The number of records found in the query will be displayed in the **Record Navigation** buttons at the bottom left of the screen.

▶▶ How to... *create a query using two criteria*

1 Click in the **Criteria** row of the first field to be queried. Enter the selection criteria.

2 Click in the **Criteria** row of the second field to be queried.

3 Click in the **Criteria** row of any other fields and enter the selection criteria.

TIP!

Notice that Access displays **#** (hash) signs before and after some selection criteria (e.g. dates) when you move out of a field.

TIP!

When creating queries with multiple criteria, enter the criteria in one field, then click on the **Run** icon 🖊 to run the query. This will enable you to check that the criterion entered is correct and that the correct records are found. Click on the **View** button on the toolbar to return to Query Design view and enter the next criterion. Click on the **Run** icon again to check the accuracy of the second criterion, and so on.

▶▶ How to... *save a new query with a specified name*

1 Click on the **File** menu, click **Save**. The **Save As** dialogue box will be displayed.

2 Delete any existing text and enter the required query name.

3 Click on **OK**.

Check your understanding *Create a query using range and logical criteria*

1 In your database table **Orthdocs**, create a new query.

2 Using **range** criteria, find all the consultants whose WAITING DAYS are **between 5 and 15**

3 Using **logical** criteria, find all the consultants whose SPECIALTY is **LUMBAR or GENERAL ORTHOPAEDICS**

4 Save the query as **Lumbar + GenOrth 5-15 days**

5 Run your query.

6 Check that the records found match the criteria you entered. The query result should display 26 records. If necessary, return to Query Design view (see **How to... return to Query Design view** on page 219).

7 Your query criteria should be similar to that shown in Figure 3.43.

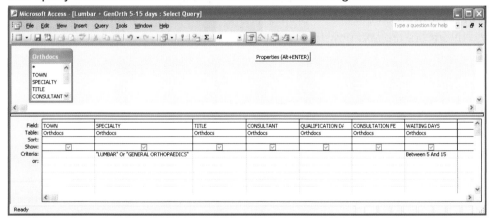

FIGURE 3.43 The query Lumbar + GenOrth 5-15 days in Design view

8 Save and close the query.

1   In your database table **Orthdocs**, create a new query.

2   Using **range** criteria, find all the consultants whose CONSULTATION FEE is **less than or equal to £140** (remember, you should not enter the currency symbol in the query criteria).

3   Using **logical** criteria, find all the consultants whose SPECIALTY is **MUSCULOSKELETAL or SPORTS INJURIES**

4   Using **wildcards**, find all the consultants whose QUALIFICATION DATE was in the **1970s**.

5   Save the query as **Sports + Musc <=140 1970s**

6   Run your query.

7   Check that the records found match the criteria you entered. The query result should display 9 records. If necessary, return to query Design view (see **How to... return to Query Design view**).

8   Your query criteria should be similar to those shown in Figure 3.44.

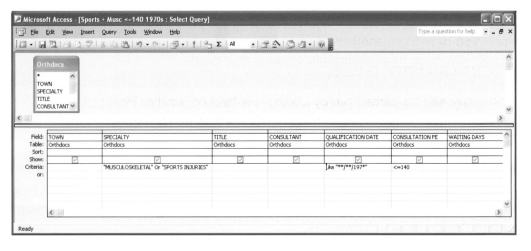

FIGURE 3.44 The query Sports + Musc <=140 1970s in Design view

9   Save and close the query.

Checking query results in Datasheet view

Once you have run your query, you should look at the records and check that those found meet the selection criteria. If you need to make changes, return to Query Design view.

1 With the query open in Datasheet view click on the **View** button . You will be returned to Query Design view. Make any changes to the query criteria.

2 To return to Datasheet view, click on the **View** button 🔲 ▾ again or click the **Run** icon ❗ .

▶▶ How to... *save an existing query*

Click on the **File** menu, click **Save**.

Calculated fields

A calculated field is a new field with a new field name. It is created in order to carry out a calculation in an existing database. Any of the four mathematical operators can be used in a calculation. In a calculated field, a field name must be enclosed in square brackets **[ ]**

A calculation may be carried out by adding, subtracting, multiplying or dividing one field to/by/from another.

e.g. DISCOUNT: [QUANTITY]-[SALES]

A calculation may also be carried out by adding, subtracting, multiplying or dividing one field by a figure or a percentage. Note percentages must be entered in decimal format (e.g. 25% would be entered as 0.25)

e.g. DISCOUNT: [QUANTITY]*0.1

▶▶ How to... *create a calculated field using two fields in a database table*

Calculations in databases are carried out in a Query Design view.

1 In Query Design view, drag all the fields to the Query grid.

2 Scroll to the right of all the existing fields and click in the **Field** row of the first blank field.

3 Enter the new field name, followed by a colon **:**

Then enter a square opening bracket **[**

4 Enter the existing field name exactly as it appears in the database table.

5 Enter a square closing bracket **]** then enter the appropriate mathematical operator, enter a square opening bracket **[**, then enter the second field name and a square closing bracket **]**

6 Run the query to check the results of the calculation.

TIP!

Ensure that you enter the field name with one hundred per cent accuracy.

1   In your database table **Orthdocs** create a new query.

2   Create a new field called **FIRST VISIT** and calculate the first visit fee by subtracting the **WAITING DAYS** from the **CONSULTATION FEE**.

3   Save the query as **INITIAL FEE**

4   Run the query.

5   Return to Query Design view and make any amendments, if required.

6   Your calculated field should be displayed as shown in Figure 3.45.

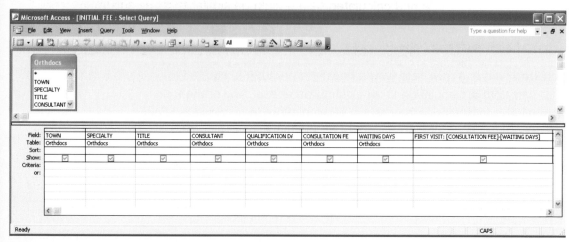

FIGURE 3.45 The query INITIAL FEE with a calculated field

7   Save and close the query.

▶▶ How to...   *create a calculated field using one field and a number*

1   In Query Design view, drag all the fields to the Query grid.

2   Scroll to the right of all the existing fields and click in the **Field** row of the first blank field. Enter the new field name, followed by a colon **:** then enter a square opening bracket **[**

3   Enter the existing field name exactly as it appears in the database table.

4   Enter a square closing bracket **]** and the appropriate mathematical operator.

5   Enter the number.

6   Run the query to check the results of the calculation.

TIP!

Do not enter a space before or after the mathematical operator.

TIP!

You cannot enter a number followed by a percentage sign. To calculate a percentage, enter the number in decimal format.

1. In your database **Orthdocs**, create a new query.

2. Find all the consultants whose SPECIALTY is **TRAUMA**

3. Create a new field called **WAITING** and calculate the WAITING by subtracting **2** from the WAITING DAYS.

4. Save the Query as **Trauma Priority**

5. Run the query. The query result should display 12 records.

6. Return to Query Design view and make any amendments, if required.

7. Your query criteria and calculated field should be similar to those shown in Figure 3.46.

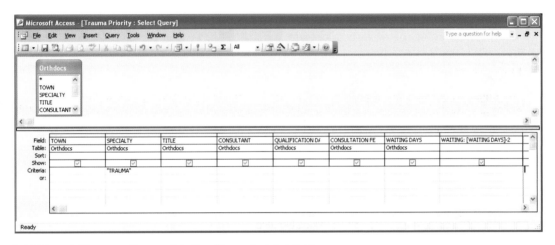

FIGURE 3.46 The query Trauma Priority with a calculated field

8. Save and close the query.

▶▶ How to... *print a query*

Before you print a query, use Print Preview to check whether all the fields and records fit on the required number of pages and check to ensure that all the data is fully displayed.

1. Click on the **File** menu, click **Print**. The **Print** dialogue box will be displayed.

2. Click on **OK**.

▶▶ How to... *close a query*

Click on the **File** menu, click **Close**.

TIP!

Always check your printout to ensure that all the data is fully displayed.

TIP!

A quick way to print is to click on the **Print** icon on the toolbar.

ASSESS YOUR SKILLS – Create queries

By working through Section 4 you will have learnt the skills listed below. Read each item to help you decide how confident you feel about each skill:

- understand range criteria, logical operators and wildcards
- understand comparison operators
- create a new query
- select field names and drag them into the Query grid
- display selected fields
- sort data in a query
- enter the selection criteria
- run the query
- create a query using two criteria
- save a new query with a specified name
- return to Query Design view
- save an existing query
- create a calculated field.

If you think you that need more practice on any of the skills in the above list, go back and work through the skill(s) again.

If you feel confident, move on to Section 5

LEARNING OUTCOMES

In this section you will learn how to:

- open a saved query
- create a grouped report
- understand the parts of a grouped report
- sort data in a grouped report
- delete unwanted labels
- edit existing labels
- create a new label
- add automatic fields
- adjust the width of a report
- select control boxes
- move controls in a report
- widen a field
- change the margins
- change the font size
- change the font type
- format numeric data
- fit a report to a specified number of pages.

Reports

Reports can be based on a database table or a query. You will create reports based on queries. To create a report based on a table, use the same method.

▶▶ *How to...* *open a saved query*

1 In the **Database window**, in the **Objects** section, click on **Queries**. The saved queries in your database will display on the right.

2 Double-click on the query name to open the saved query.

▶▶ *How to...* *create a grouped report*

Records in a report can be grouped so that records containing the same information in a field (e.g. TOWN) can be displayed together. Data can then be sorted within the grouped records. Another advantage of a grouped report is that summaries can be displayed for each group (e.g.

TIP!

Instead of double-clicking, you can click once to select the query, then click on **Open**.

the total, average, minimum or maximum figures in each group). Labels describing what the summaries are can be displayed automatically, or custom labels can be entered.

You will create a report using the Report Wizard. Access will open a series of Report Wizard windows.

FIGURE 3.47 The New Report dialogue box

1 With the query open in Datasheet view, click on the drop-down arrow next to the **New Object:** icon [icon] ▾.

2 A menu will be displayed. Click on **Report**. The **New Report** dialogue box will be displayed. Click on **Report Wizard**, click **OK** (Figure 3.47). The **Report Wizard** will open.

3 In step 1 of the Report Wizard (Figure 3.48), in the **Available Fields** section, double-click on each of the field headings to be displayed in the report. Any fields you double-click will be displayed in the **Selected Fields** section (Figure 3.49).

4 Ensure that you select the fields in the order specified for the report, not in the order the fields are displayed in the list. If you select an incorrect field, click on the **Remove** button [<]. Click on **Next**.

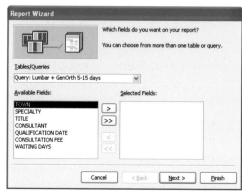

FIGURE 3.48 Step 1 of the Report Wizard

TIP!

Another method of selecting a field is to click on the field name, then click on the **Add** button [>].To select all the fields, click on the **Add All** button [>>].)

5 In step 2 of the Report Wizard, in the left section, select the field(s) to be grouped. Double-click or click on the **Add** button. Check that the field you have selected to be grouped on is displayed in the preview on the right of the window (Figure 3.50). Click on **Next**.

6 In step 3 (Figure 3.51), do *not* select any fields to be sorted. You will sort the fields in Design view later.

TIP!

If you sort at this stage, Access will display the sorted field(s) as the first field(s). Changing the field order in Design view is time consuming.

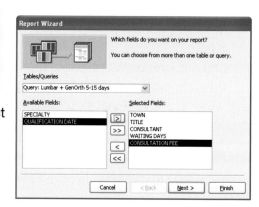

FIGURE 3.49 Selected Fields

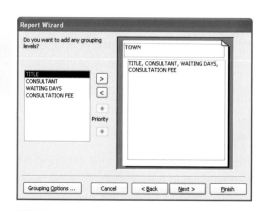

FIGURE 3.50 Step 2 of the Report Wizard

7 Click on the **Summary Options** button. The **Summary Options** dialogue box will be displayed (Figure 3.52). Only the selected fields containing numeric data will be displayed in this dialogue box. In the field row for the relevant field, click in the relevant check box.

- To display a **total**, click on **Sum**.
- To display an **average**, click on **Avg**.
- To display the **minimum number**, click on **Min**.
- To display the **maximum number**, click on **Max**.

8 Check that the option for **Detail and Summary** is selected. Click on **OK** to close the Summary Options dialogue box. Click on **Next**.

9 In step 4, select the required orientation. Select a layout for your reports. Check that there is a tick in the box for **Adjust the field width so all fields fit on a page** (Figure 3.53).

TIP!

Select the **Stepped** layout for grouped reports.

10 Click on **Next**.

11 In step 5, select a style for the report (Figure 3.54).

TIP!

Select the **Compact** style.

12 Click on **Next**.

13 In step 6, enter the report title (Figure 3.55). Click on **Finish**.

The grouped report displays in Print Preview. In Print Preview, click on the **Multiple Pages** icon and select the **2 x 3 Pages** option to see how many pages the report fits on.

Zoom in to various parts of the report (the title, field headings, records) to check if any data is not displayed in full. Make a note of any changes that need to be made.

14 Click the view icon to go to the Report Design view.

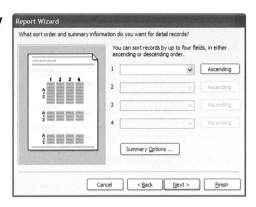

FIGURE 3.51 Step 3 of the Report Wizard

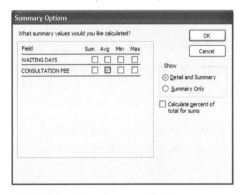

FIGURE 3.52 The Summary Options dialogue box

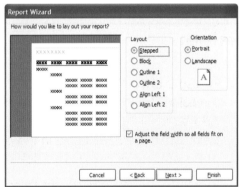

FIGURE 3.53 Step 4 of the Report Wizard

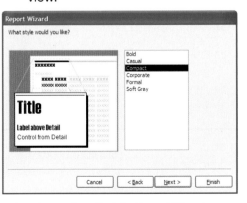

FIGURE 3.54 Step 5 of the Report Wizard

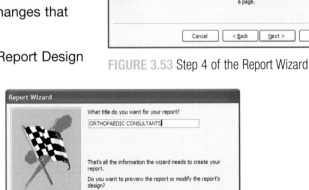

FIGURE 3.55 Step 6 of the Report Wizard

1 Open your saved query **Lumbar + GenOrth 5-15 days**.

2 Create a grouped report to display the following fields in the following order: **TOWN**, **TITLE**, **CONSULTANT**, **WAITING DAYS**, **CONSULTATION FEE**.

3 Group the report by **TOWN**.

4 Display the **AVERAGE** CONSULTATION FEE for each group.

5 Set the orientation to **portrait**.

6 Title the report **ORTHOPAEDIC CONSULTANTS**

7 Save the report using the filename **ORTHOPAEDIC CONSULTANTS**

Understanding the parts of a grouped report in Design view

Figure 3.56 shows the various parts of a grouped report in Design view.

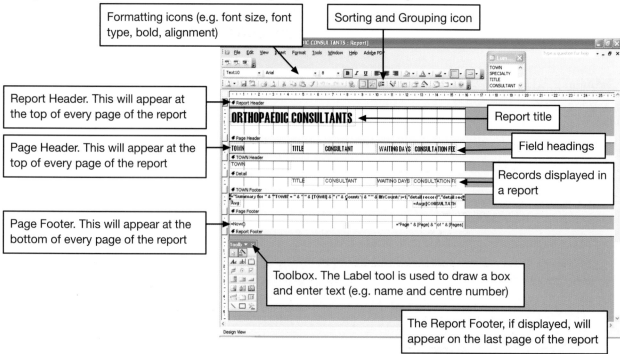

Formatting icons (e.g. font size, font type, bold, alignment)

Sorting and Grouping icon

Report Header. This will appear at the top of every page of the report

Report title

Page Header. This will appear at the top of every page of the report

Field headings

Records displayed in a report

Page Footer. This will appear at the bottom of every page of the report

Toolbox. The Label tool is used to draw a box and enter text (e.g. name and centre number)

The Report Footer, if displayed, will appear on the last page of the report

FIGURE 3.56 The parts of a grouped report in Design view

▶▶ How to... *sort data in a grouped report*

1 Click on the **View** icon to switch to Design view (if required).

2 Click on the **Sorting and Grouping** icon ▯ . The **Sorting and Grouping** dialogue box will be displayed (Figure 3.57). The field heading for the grouped field(s) will be displayed in the top row(s) of the **Field/Expression** column on the left. Do not make any changes to these fields.

3 Click in the first blank row below the existing field heading(s). A drop-down arrow will be displayed in this row. From the list of fields displayed, click on the field name of the field to be sorted. The field heading will be displayed in the row.

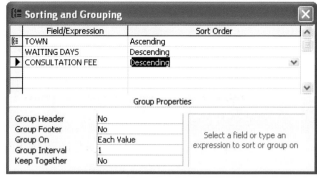

FIGURE 3.57 The Sorting and Grouping dialogue box

4 Click in the same row of the field you selected in the second column for **Sort Order**.

5 Click on the drop-down arrow. Select **Ascending** or **Descending**.

6 Repeat this process if you need to sort on a second field.

7 Click on the cross to close the dialogue box. The records will be sorted.

8 Switch to Print Preview to check.

Check your understanding *Sort data in a grouped report*

In your report entitled **ORTHOPAEDIC CONSULTANTS**, sort the report in descending order of **WAITING DAYS**, then in descending order of **CONSULTATION FEE**.

Making amendments to a report in Design view

▶▶ *How to...* delete unwanted detail

1 Click on the detail box. Ensure that square handles are displayed around the detail box (control) (Figure 3.58).

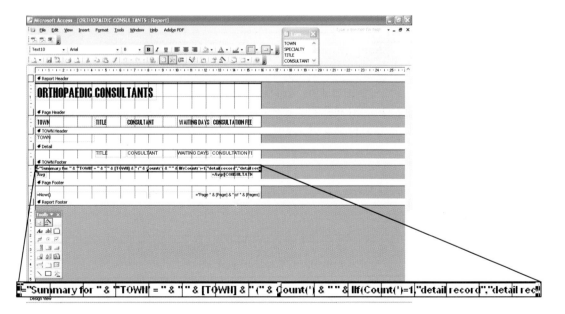

FIGURE 3.58 Deleting unwanted details

2 Press the **Delete** key.

In your report titled **ORTHOPAEDIC CONSULTANTS**, delete the whole of the following label from the **TOWN** footer area:

="Summary for " & "'TOWN' = " & " " & [TOWN] & " (" & Count(*) & " " & Ilf(Count(*)=1,"detail record","detail records") & ")"

Ensure that you delete the entire control box, not just the contents.

▶▶ How to... *edit existing labels*

1 Click in the label. A warning icon may be displayed. Click on the drop-down arrow next to the warning icon and select **Ignore Error**.

2 Increase the width of the existing label control by dragging the handle to the right.

3 Click in the label box (not in the box showing the formula =...). The cursor will display.

4 Delete the existing text.

5 Enter the required label (Figure 3.59).

TIP!

Use Print Preview to check the new label is displayed correctly.

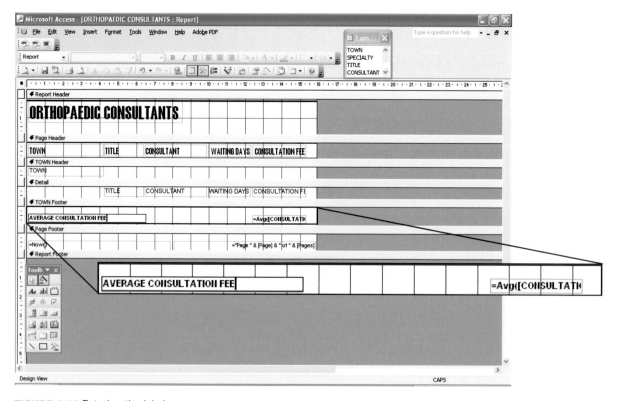

FIGURE 3.59 Entering the label

In the your report titled **ORTHOPAEDIC CONSULTANTS**, edit the existing label **Avg** to be **AVERAGE CONSULTATION FEE**

▶▶ *How to...* create a new label

1 Click and drag the grey bar below the **Page Footer** area to increase the depth of the footer area.

2 To display the Toolbox, click on the **View** menu, click on **Toolbox**.

3 From the Toolbox, select the **Label** icon.

4 Draw a text box in the **Page Footer** area. Type the required information in the text box.

5 Use Print Preview to ensure that all the labels fit on one page and that all the data is displayed in full.

▶▶ *How to...* add automatic fields

Access automatically displays the date and page number on every report. These can be moved if required or, if deleted, can be inserted again.

To insert page numbers:

1 Click on the **Insert** menu, click on **Page Numbers**.

2 Click on the drop-down arrow under **Alignment** to choose the required alignment, if required.

To add an automatic date:

1 Click on the **Insert** menu, click on **Date and Time**. The **Date and Time** dialogue box will be displayed.

2 Click on the button to choose a date format.

3 Click on **OK**.

In the footer of your report titled **ORTHOPAEDIC CONSULTANTS**, display:

An automatic date
Automatic page numbers
Your name
Your centre number

1 Position the cursor at the edge of the right-hand side of the report and click. The cursor will change to a double-headed arrow ⟷.

2 Click and drag the arrow to the right to increase the width or to the left to decrease the width.

▶▶ *How to...* select control boxes

1 Click once on the control for the first control box. Square handles will be displayed around the box.

2 Hold down the **Shift** key and click on any other control box(es). Square handles will be displayed around the control boxes.

3 When you have selected the relevant fields, release the Shift key.

▶▶ *How to...* move controls in a report

1 Position the cursor anywhere in the boxes you have selected. The cursor changes to a hand.

2 Click and drag the mouse to move the selected boxes. To move the control boxes very slightly press the **Ctrl** and **arrow** keys.

3 Release the mouse.

TIP!

Once you have made your selection, do not click on any part of the screen – you may deselect any boxes (controls) if you click.

TIP!

The field order in a report can be moved by selecting the control box for the field heading and the field content as described in How to... move controls in a report.

Check your understanding *Move controls in a report*

1 In your report titled **ORTHOPAEDIC CONSULTANTS**, in the **TOWN** footer area, move all the control boxes further up in the TOWN footer section so that there is no unwanted space in this section. Ensure that you drag the grey bar up to reduce the white space.

2 Move the control boxes for the field headings and field details for **WAITING DAYS** and **CONSULTATION FEE** further to the right.

3 Move the control box for the **Avg([CONSULTATION FEE])** so that the figure is aligned in the column.

4 Save your report.

▶▶ *How to...* widen a field

1 Select the relevant field heading(s) and the field detail for each field heading selected using the method described in How to... select control boxes.

2 Drag the arrow to the right. Both the field heading and the content (the records) will be widened.

3 Use Print Preview to ensure that all the data is fully displayed.

4 If necessary, switch to Design view and make any further amendments.

1 In your report titled **ORTHOPAEDIC CONSULTANTS**, widen the field heading and field detail control boxes for the **CONSULTANT** field.

2 Adjust any other field widths as required.

3 Use Print Preview to ensure that the names of all the consultants and all data are fully displayed.

Formatting a report in Design view

▶▶ How to... *change the margins*

1 Click on the **File** menu, click on **Page Setup**, click the **Margins** tab (Figure 3.60).

2 Change the top, bottom, left and right margins as required.

3 Click on **OK**.

FIGURE 3.60 Changing the margins

TIP!

Use Print Preview to check that the data now fits on the required number of pages.

In your report titled **ORTHOPAEDIC CONSULTANTS**, change the margins in your report as follows:

Top and bottom margins **25 mm**

Left and right margins   **15 mm**

▶▶ How to... *change the font size*

1 Select the control box. Ensure that square handles are displayed around the control.

2 Once you have selected the required controls, click on the drop-down arrow next to **Font Size**. From the drop-down list, select the required font size.

TIP!

To select more than one control box, use the **Shift** key.

TIP!

Use Print Preview to check the new font size.

In your report titled **ORTHOPAEDIC CONSULTANTS**, change the font size for your name and centre number to **9**.

1 Select the control box. Ensure that square handles are displayed around the control.

2 Once you have selected the required controls, click on the drop-down arrow next to **Font Name**.

3 From the drop-down list, select the required font type.

TIP!

To select more than one control box, use the **Shift** key.

TIP!

To display a font name quickly, enter the first few letters of the font name in the **Font** box.

TIP!

Use Print Preview to check the new font type. Ensure that all the text is clearly legible. The emphasis (bold, italics) can be changed by clicking on the relevant icon on the Formatting toolbar.

Check your understanding *Change the font type of a label in a report*

In your report titled **ORTHOPAEDIC CONSULTANTS**, change the font type for your name and centre number to **Arial**.

▶▶ **How to...** format numeric data

1 Click in the control box which holds the numeric value (not the label for that value).

2 Ensure that square handles are displayed around the control.

3 Right-click in the control box. A menu will be displayed. Select **Properties** (Figure 3.61). The **Text Box** dialogue box will be displayed (Figure 3.62).

4 Select the **Format** tab.

5 Click in the **Format** row. A drop-down arrow will be displayed. Click on the arrow to view the list of available formats.

TIP!

If you are unsure which box it is, click on the control and press **F1**.

TIP!

You may need to scroll down the list.

TIP!

Do not choose the **General** option.

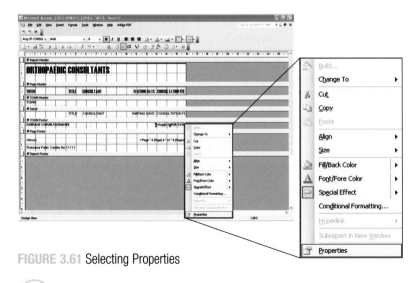

FIGURE 3.61 Selecting Properties

FIGURE 3.62 The Text Box dialogue box

6   Click on the required format.

7   Click in the **Decimal Places** row.

8   Select the number of decimal places required.

9   Click on the cross to close the Text Box dialogue box.

TIP!

To display numbers to a set number of decimal places the **Format** must be set to **Fixed** or **Currency**.

TIP!

Use Print Preview to view your report. Click on the **Multiple Pages** icon and select **2 x 3 Pages** to view all the pages. Make a note of any changes that need to be made. Click on the **View** icon to return to Design view and then make any further adjustments. Remember to use Print Preview again before printing.

Check your understanding *Format numeric data in a report*

In your report titled **ORTHOPAEDIC CONSULTANTS**, format the figure for the **AVERAGE CONSULTATION FEE** to currency with two decimal places.

▶▶ *How to...* fit a report to a specified number of pages

In Access there is no setting to fit to a specified number of pages. In Design view, use the following techniques to fit a report as required.

1   Change the margins.

2   Change the font size of various controls (e.g. report title, field headings, labels).

3   Change the depth of various parts of the report (e.g. report title, labels).

TIP!

Use Print Preview after making each amendment.

Check your understanding *Fit a report to a specified number of pages*

1   Ensure that the report titled **ORTHOPAEDIC CONSULTANTS** fits on to two pages.

2   Save your report.

3   Print your report. Check that all the data is fully displayed.

4   Close the report.

ASSESS YOUR SKILLS – Create a grouped report and format a report

By working through Section 5 you will have learnt the skills listed below. Read each item to help you decide how confident you feel about each skill:

- open a saved query
- create a grouped report
- understand the parts of a general report
- sort data in a grouped report
- delete unwanted labels
- edit existing labels
- create a new label
- add automatic fields
- adjust the width of a report
- select control boxes
- move controls in a report
- widen a field
- change the margins
- change the font size
- change the font type
- format numeric data
- fit a report to a specified number of pages

If you think that you need more practice on any of the skills in the above list, go back and work through the skill(s) again.

If you feel confident, move on to Section 6.

6: Create a columnar and a tabular report

LEARNING OUTCOMES

In this section you will learn how to:

- create a columnar report
- create a tabular report displaying selected fields.

▶▶ How to... *create a columnar report*

A columnar report displays data in two columns. The first column displays the field headings. These headings are repeated for every record. The second column displays the actual records. Columnar reports are generally used to display a smaller number of records.

1   With the query open in Datasheet view, click on the drop-down arrow next to the **New Object: AutoForm** icon.

2   A menu will be displayed. Click on **Report**. The **New Report** dialogue box will be displayed.

3   Click on **Report Wizard**, click **OK**. The **Report Wizard** will be displayed.

4   In the **Available Fields** section, double-click on each of the field headings to be displayed in the report. Any fields you double-click will be displayed in the **Selected Fields** section.

5   Ensure that you select the fields in the order specified for the report, not in the order the fields are displayed in the list. If you select an incorrect field, click on the **Remove** button ⎣ < ⎦.

6   Click on **Next**. In step 2, Click on **Next**.

7   In step 3, do *not* select any fields to be sorted. You will sort the fields in Design view later. Click on **Next**.

8   In step 4, in the Layout section, click on **Columnar**. Select the required orientation (Figure 3.63). Click on **Next**.

9   In step 5, select a style for the report.

10 Click on **Next**.

11 In step 6, enter the Report title. Click on **Finish**. The columnar report will be displayed in Print Preview. In Print Preview, click on the **Multiple Pages** icon 🔢 to check how many pages the report fits on. Zoom in to various parts of the report (the title, field headings, records) to check if any data is not displayed in full. Make a note of any changes that need to be made.

TIP!

If you have used this icon already, it converts to **New Object: Report** 📓 ▾

TIP!

Another method of selecting the available fields is to click on the field name, then click on the **Add** button ⎣ > ⎦. To select all fields, click on the **Add All** button ⎣ >> ⎦.

TIP!

Select the **Compact style**.

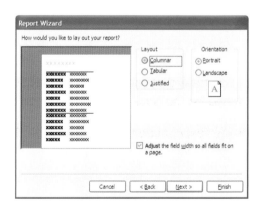

FIGURE 3.63 Step 4 of the Report Wizard

1 Open your saved query **Trauma Priority**.

2 Create a columnar report in portrait orientation to display the following fields in the following order: **TOWN, WAITING, CONSULTATION FEE**.

3 Title the report **WAITING PERIOD FOR TRAUMA PATIENTS**

4 Sort the report in ascending order of **WAITING**.

5 Left align all the control boxes for all three fields.

6 In the footer, display only your **name, centre number** and the **date**.

7 Fit the report to one page.

8 Save the report using the filename **WAITING PERIOD FOR TRAUMA PATIENTS**

9 Print your report. Check that all the data is fully displayed.

10 Close the report.

▶▶ How to... *create a tabular report displaying selected fields*

In Section 2 you learnt how to create a tabular AutoReport to display all the fields. You will now learn how to create a tabular report that displays selected fields by using the wizard.

AutoReports apply limited formatting to a report whereas the Report Wizard allows you more flexibility when creating reports. Tabular reports display data in columns with the field headings displayed at the top of each column. Field headings are displayed at the top of every page of a report.

1 With the query open in Datasheet view, click on the drop-down arrow next to the **New Object:** icon.

2 A menu will be displayed. Click on **Report**. The **New Report** dialogue box will be displayed. Click on **Report Wizard**, click **OK**. The **Report Wizard** dialogue box will be displayed.

3 In the **Available Fields** section, double-click on each of the field headings to be displayed in the report. Any fields you double-click will be displayed in the **Selected Fields** section.

4 Ensure that you select the fields in the order specified for the report, not in the order the fields are displayed in the list. If you select an incorrect field, click on the **Remove** button [<]. Click on **Next**.

5 In step 2, click on **Next**.

6 In step 3, do not select any fields to be sorted. You will sort the fields in Design view later. Click on **Next**.

7 In step 4, click on the button to select **Tabular**. Select the orientation. Click on **Next**.

8 In step 5, select a style for the report.

9 Click on **Next**.

10 In step 6, enter the Report title. Click on **Finish**. The tabular report displays in Print Preview. In Print Preview, click on the **Multiple Pages** icon to see how many pages the report fits on. Zoom in to various parts of the report (the title, field headings, records) to check if any data is not displayed in full. Make a note of any changes that need to be made.

TIP!

Select the **Compact style**.

Check your understanding *Create a tabular report using the Report Wizard*

1 Open your saved query **Sports + Musc <=140 1970s**.

2 Create a tabular report displaying the following fields in the following order:

SPECIALTY
WAITING DAYS
TITLE
CONSULTANT
TOWN

3 Set the orientation to **landscape**.

4 Enter the report title **SPORTS INJURIES EXPERIENCED CONSULTANTS**

5 Sort the report in descending order of **QUALIFICATION DATE**.

6 In the footer, enter your name. Make sure the date is displayed. Do not display the page number.

7 Make sure that all the data is fully displayed.

8 Save the report using the name **SPORTS INJURIES EXPERIENCED CONSULTANTS**

9 Print the report.

10 Close the report.

11 Close any open tables or queries and exit Access.

ASSESS YOUR SKILLS – Create a columnar and a tabular report

By working through Section 6 you will have learnt the skills listed below. Read each item to help you decide how confident you feel about each skill:

○ create a columnar report

○ create a tabular report displaying selected fields.

If you think that you need more practice on any of the skills in the above list, go back and work through the skill(s) again.

If you feel confident, do the Build-up and Practice tasks on pages 247–256.

QUICK REFERENCE – Create a new database, create a tabular report and labels

Keep a copy of this page next to you. Refer to it when working through tasks and during any assessments.

HOW TO	METHOD
Create a new blank database	Load Microsoft Access 2003 → click on the File menu, New → the task pane is displayed on the right → click on Blank Database → the File New Database dialogue box will be displayed → click on the drop-down arrow next to Save in and go to your user area → in the File Name box delete db1 and type in an appropriate filename → click on Create → the Database window will be displayed → check that Tables is selected in the Objects section on the left → on the right, double-click on Create table in Design view → Table Design view will be displayed.
Enter field names, set the data type and the field properties	In Table Design view, check that the cursor is in the first Field Name row → enter the first field heading in the Field Name column → press the Tab key to move to the Data Type column (or click in the Data Type column) → click on the drop-down arrow to select the data type → in the Field Properties section set the properties → click in the second row in the Field Name column and repeat the process for all remaining fields.
Save and name the table	Click on the Save icon → the Save As dialogue box will be displayed → type in the table name → click on OK → Access will display a message asking you if you want to create a primary key → click on No → click on the View icon to switch to Datasheet view.
Enter records	In Datasheet view check that the cursor is flashing in the first field → enter the required data → press the Tab key to move to the next field and enter the data → to place a tick in a logic field box, click in the box with your mouse or press the spacebar → in numeric and currency fields, enter the data (the zeros will be overtyped) → press the Tab key to move to the next record
Widen a field	Position the cursor on the line to the right of the field heading → the cursor will turn into a double-headed arrow → double-click → Access will adjust the column width to fit the longest line of data on the screen within the field.
Create an AutoReport	With the table/query open in Datasheet view (as a table), click on the drop-down arrow next to New Object: → a menu will be displayed → click on Report → the New Report dialogue box will be displayed → click on AutoReport: Tabular → OK.
Switch to report Design view	Click on the View icon → the report will display in Design view.

(continued overleaf)

HOW TO	METHOD
Sort data	In Design view, click on the Sorting and Grouping icon → the Sorting and Grouping dialogue box will be displayed → the cursor will be displayed in the first row of the Field/Expression column → click on the drop-down arrow in this row → a list of field headings will be displayed → select the field to be sorted → in the Sort Order column, click on the drop-down arrow and select Ascending or Descending → click on the cross to close the Sorting and Grouping dialogue box.
Delete the page number or date	In Design view, click once in the box for the page numbers → square handles will be displayed around the control box → press the Delete key (the date can be deleted using the same method).
Insert name and centre number	In Design view, click on the View menu, Page Header/Footer → to display the Toolbox, click on the View menu, Toolbox → from the Toolbox, select the Label icon → draw a text box in the page footer area → type the information in the text box.
Set the page orientation	Click on the File menu → Page Setup → Page tab → select Portrait or Landscape.
Change the margins	In the Page Setup window, click on the Margins tab → change the top, bottom, left and right margins → click on OK.
Widen the report title control box and enter a report title	In Report Design view, click on the report title → square handles will be displayed around the control box → click and drag the square handle on the right of the control box further to the right to widen the control → click in the box for the report title → a cursor will be displayed → delete the existing title and enter the new title.
Save a report with a specified name	Click on the File menu, Save → the Save As dialogue box will be displayed → delete the existing name and enter the report name → click on OK.
Close a report	Click on the File menu → Close.
Open a saved table	In the Database window, in the Objects section, click on Tables → the tables in your database will be displayed → double-click on the table name to open it.
Create labels	In table Datasheet view, click on the drop-down arrow next to New Object: AutoForm → click on Report → the New Report dialogue box will be displayed → click on Label Wizard, OK → the Label Wizard will be displayed → select the label dimensions and manufacturer → click on Next → in step 2 select the font name and font size → click on Next → in step 3 double-click in turn on each of the Field Headings required → to display two fields on one line press the space bar between two fields → press Enter to display the next field on a new line → click on Next → in step 4 double-click on the field(s) to be sorted → click on Next → in step 5 enter the name of the label report → click on Finish → to display headers and footers, switch to label report Design view.
Display headers and footers on a label report	In Design view, click on the View menu, Page Header/Footer, then click on the View menu again, Page Header/Footer (or if page headers and footers are already displayed, drag the grey bar to an appropriate height for the header and footer) → click on the View menu, Toolbox → from the Toolbox, select the Label icon → draw a text box in the page footer area (or header area) → type the information in the text box.

QUICK REFERENCE – Import a datafile, update a database, create queries and create a report

Keep a copy of this page next to you. Refer to it when working through tasks and during any assessments.

HOW TO	METHOD
Import a csv file	Load Access → create a new blank database → click on the File menu, Get External Data, Import → click on the drop-down arrow next to Look in → go to the user area where the csv file is saved → click on the drop-down arrow to the right of Files of type → select Text Files → in the Look in box click on the csv file to be imported → ensure the filename is highlighted → click on Import → in step 1 ensure the Delimited option is selected → click on Next → in step 2 ensure the Comma option is selected → click on the drop-down arrow to the right of Text Qualifier → select '' (double speech marks) → click in the check box for First Row Contains Field Names → click on Next → in step 3 check that the option for In a New Table is selected → click on Next → in step 4 click on Next → in step 5 click the button for No Primary Key → click on Next → in step 6 click on Finish → in step 7 you should see the message Finished importing file... → click on OK.
Modify the field characteristics	Switch to Table Design view → click in the Data Type column of the field to be modified → in the Field Properties section amend the properties → repeat for all other the fields → click on the Save icon.
Add a new record	Click on the New Record icon in the Record Navigation buttons or click in first column of a blank row → enter the new data → use the Tab key to move from field to field and to move to the next record.
Find a record in a large database and delete it	Click anywhere in the relevant field → click on the Edit menu, Find → the Find and Replace dialogue box will be displayed → in the Find What box enter the data → click on the drop-down arrow next to Match → select the option for Any Part of Field → click on the Find Next button → close the Find and Replace dialogue box → ensure the cursor is displayed in the record to be deleted → click on the Edit menu, Delete Record → Access will display a message prompting you to confirm the delete → click on Yes.
Amend existing data	Click in the field (cell) to be replaced → delete the unwanted data → enter the new data.
Replace data	Click anywhere in the relevant field (column) → click on the Edit menu, Replace → the Find and Replace dialogue box will be displayed → in the Find What box, enter the data to be replaced → in the Replace With box, enter the new data (the code) → check that the Match box displays Whole Field or Any Part of Field (as required) → click to place a tick in the Match Case box → click on Replace All → Access will display a message asking you to confirm the replace → click on Yes → click on the cross to close the Find and Replace dialogue box.
Delete a field	Switch to table Design view → click in the row in the field to be deleted (click in the Field Name or Data Type column) → click on the Edit menu, Delete Rows → Access will displays a message prompting you to confirm the delete → click on Yes.

(continued overleaf)

HOW TO	METHOD
Go to Query Design view	*Method 1 (quicker method)* With the database table open, click on the drop-down arrow next to the New Object: icon → a drop-down menu will be displayed → click on Query → the New Query dialogue box will be displayed → check that Design view is selected → click on OK. *Method 2* Close the table → in the Database window, click on Queries in the Objects section → click on Create query in Design view, Open → the Show Table Dialogue box will be displayed → click to select the table name → click on Add, Close.
Select all fields to place them in the Query grid	Double-click on the table name in the Field List box in the top section of Query Design view → all field headings (field names) will be highlighted → position the cursor in the highlighted field names → click and drag the field names to the Query grid → release the mouse button in the field row of the first column → all the field headings will be placed in separate columns.
Select certain fields and place them in the Query grid	In the Field List box, double-click on each field name (field heading) required → each field will be placed in the Query grid.
Enter the selection criteria	Click in the Criteria row of the field to be queried → enter the required criteria.
Enter comparison operators for numbers	> more than >= more than and equal to < less than <= less than and equal to between between a range of numbers
Enter comparison operators for dates	> after >= after or on < before <= before or on between between a range of dates
Enter selection criteria in two fields	In the Query grid, click in the Criteria row of the field to be queried → enter the criterion → click in the next field → enter the criterion.
Sort data in queries	Click in the Sort row of the field to be sorted → a drop-down arrow will be displayed → click on the drop-down arrow → select Ascending or Descending.

HOW TO	METHOD
Display selected fields	Click in the Show box to remove the tick for the fields (columns) that should not be displayed.
Run a query	Click on the Run icon in Design view → the results of the query will be displayed as a table in Datasheet view → the number of records found are displayed in the Record Navigation buttons at the bottom left of Datasheet view.
Save a query with a specified name	Click on the File menu, Save → the Save As dialogue box will be displayed → delete the text Query1 → enter the query name → click on OK.
Return to Query Design view to make amendments	Click on the View button → make the changes in the Query grid → click on Run to run the query.
Save an existing query	Click on the File menu, Save.
Prepare to print a query	Click on Print Preview → use Zoom to zoom in to different parts of the table → check the longest line in each column is fully displayed → check that all the fields (columns) fit on one page → click on the Close button to close Print Preview → make any changes to the layout in Datasheet view → use Print Preview again (change the orientation if required – see Set the page orientation).
Print a query	Click on the File menu, Print → in the Print dialogue box, click on OK (or click on the Print icon).
Close a query	Click the File menu → click Close.
Create a calculated field using two fields in a database table	In Query Design view, drag all the fields to the Query grid → scroll to the right of all the existing fields and click in the Field row of the first blank field → enter the new field name followed by a colon : → enter a square opening bracket [→ enter the existing field name exactly as it appears in the database table → enter a square closing bracket]→ enter the appropriate mathematical operator → enter a square opening bracket → enter the second field name → enter a square closing bracket → run the query to check the results of the calculation.
Create a calculated field using one field and a number	In Query Design view, drag all the fields to the Query grid → scroll to the right of all the existing fields and click in the Field row of the first blank field → enter the new field name followed by a colon : → enter a square opening bracket [→ enter the existing field name exactly as it appears in the database table → enter a square closing bracket] → enter the appropriate mathematical operator → enter the number (to calculate a percentage, enter the number in decimal format) → run the query to check the results of the calculation.
Open a saved query	In the Database window, in the Objects section, click on Tables → the saved queries in the database will be displayed on the right → double-click on the query name to open it.

(continued overleaf)

HOW TO	METHOD
Create a grouped report	Open the query in Datasheet view → click on the drop-down arrow next to the New Object icon → a menu will be displayed → click on Report → the New Report dialogue box will be displayed → click on Report Wizard, OK → the Report Wizard will be displayed → in the Available Fields section, double-click on the field headings in the order they need to appear in the report → click on Next → in step 2, in the left section, select the field(s) to be grouped → double-click → click on Next → in step 3 do *not* select any fields to be sorted → click on the Summary Options button → the Summary Options dialogue box will be displayed → in the field row for the relevant field, click in the relevant check box → check that the option for Detail and Summary is selected → click on OK → click on Next in the Report Wizard box → in step 4 select the required orientation → select a layout → check there is a tick in the box for Adjust the field width so all fields fit on a page → click on Next → in step 5 select a style → click on Next → in step 6 enter the report title → click on Finish.
Sort data in a grouped report	Click on the View icon to switch to report Design view → click on the Sorting and Grouping icon → the Sorting and Grouping dialogue box will be displayed → the field heading for the grouped field(s) will be displayed in the top row(s) of the Field/Expression column on the left (do not make any changes to these fields) → click in the first blank row below the existing field heading(s) → a drop-down arrow will be displayed in this row → click on the drop-down arrow and select the field name of the field to be sorted → the field heading will be displayed in this row → click in the same row of the field you selected in the second column for Sort Order → click on the drop-down arrow and select Ascending or Descending → repeat this process if you need to sort on a second field → click on the cross to close the window.
Delete unwanted labels	Click on the label → ensure that square handles are displayed around the label box (control) → press the Delete key.
Edit existing labels	Click in the label → a cursor will be displayed in the control box → a warning tag may display → click on the drop-down arrow next to the warning icon and select Ignore Error → increase the width of the existing label control by dragging the handle to the right → click in the label box → delete the existing text → enter the label.
Create a new label	Click and drag the report footer section to increase the depth of the page footer → to display the Toolbox, click on the View menu, Toolbox → from the Toolbox, select the Label icon → click and drag the grey bar below the page footer area to increase the depth of the footer area → draw a text box in the page footer area → type the information in the text box.
Adjust the width of a report	Position the cursor at the edge of the right-hand side of the report and click → the cursor will change to a double-headed arrow → click and drag the arrow to the right to increase the width or to the left to decrease the width.
Select control boxes	Click once on the control for the first control box → square handles will be displayed around the box → hold down the Shift key and click on any other control box(es) → square handles will be displayed around the control boxes → when you have selected the relevant fields, let go of the Shift key.

HOW TO	METHOD
Move controls in a report	Position the cursor anywhere in the boxes that you selected → the cursor changes to a hand symbol → click and drag the hand symbol to move the selected boxes → release the mouse.
Widen a field	Select the relevant field heading(s) and the field detail for each field heading selected using the method described above → drag the arrow to the right → both the field heading and the content (the records) will be widened.
Add automatic fields	*Note*: Access automatically displays the date and page number on every report. Therefore you may not need to insert the date and page number. To insert page numbers, click on the Insert menu, Page Numbers → to add an automatic date, click on the Insert menu, Date and Time → the Date and Time dialogue box will be displayed → choose a date format → click on OK.

QUICK REFERENCE – *Format a report in Design view, create a columnar and a tabular report*

Keep a copy of this page next to you. Refer to it when working through tasks and during any assessments.

HOW TO	METHOD
Change the margins	Click on the File menu, Page Setup, Margins tab → change the margins as required → click on OK.
Change the font size	Select the control box → ensure that square handles are displayed around the control box → to select more than one control box use the Shift key → click on the drop-down arrow next to the Font Size box → from the drop-down list, select the font size.
Change the font type	Select the control box → ensure that square handles are displayed around the control box → click on the drop-down arrow next to the Font Name box → from the drop-down list, select the font type.
Format numeric data	Click on the control box which holds the numeric value (not the label for that value) → ensure that square handles are displayed around the control box → right-click in the control box → a menu will be displayed → select Properties → the Text Box dialogue box will be displayed → select the Format tab → click in the Format row → a drop-down menu will be displayed → click on the drop-down arrow → a list of available formats will be displayed → click on the required format → click in the Decimal Places row → select the number of decimal places required → click on the cross to close the Text Box dialogue box.
Create a columnar report	Open the query in Datasheet view → click on the drop-down arrow next to the New Object icon → a menu will be displayed → click on Report → the New Report dialogue box will be displayed → click on Report Wizard, OK → the Report Wizard will be displayed → in the Available Fields section, double-click on the field headings required in the order they need to appear in the report → click on Next → in step 2 click on Next → in step 3 do *not* select any fields to be sorted → click on Next → in step 4 select Columnar → select the orientation → click on Next → in step 5 select a style → click on Next → in step 6 enter the report title → click on Finish.
Create a tabular report displaying selected fields	Open the query in Datasheet view → click on the drop-down arrow next to the New Object icon → a menu will be displayed → click on Report → the New Report dialogue box will be displayed → click on Report Wizard, OK → the Report Wizard will be displayed → in the Available Fields section, double-click on each of the field headings required → click on Next → in step 2 click on Next → in step 3 do *not* select any fields to be sorted → click on Next → in step 4 select Tabular and select the orientation → click on Next → in step 5 select a style → click on Next → in step 6 enter the report title → click on Finish.

Scenario

You work for a distribution company that specialises in selling books. You have been asked to create a small database to hold details of the company sales representatives.

1 Open a database software application.

2 Create a new database called **reps**

3 In a new table, set up the field headings and data types as shown below. Ensure that the field lengths are long enough to display all the information in full.

FIELD HEADING	DATA TYPE
FIRST NAME	Text
LAST NAME	Text
REGION	Text
HOURS	Number, 0 decimal places
PAY RATE	Currency, 2 decimal places with currency symbol
COMPANY CAR	Logic field
START DATE	English date format (day, month, year)

4 Enter the records shown below into your database table. You may use a data entry form to enter this data.

FIRST NAME	LAST NAME	REGION	HOURS	PAY RATE	COMPANY CAR	START DATE
WILLIAM	GABAR	NORTH EAST	35	16.75	YES	05/05/1970
ARTHUR	MARINO	NORTH WEST	40	16.00	YES	03/01/1983
DYLAN	JONES	WALES	20	21.50	NO	25/07/1998
VERDA	OLNICK	MIDLANDS	25	21.50	NO	06/04/2004
JASMINE	SPARGO	SOUTH EAST	35	23.75	NO	14/08/2002
DONALD	JANAI	SOUTH WEST	40	16.00	YES	26/09/1996
JANINE	WINSTON	SCOTLAND	25	16.75	YES	03/03/2000
GILL	O'SULLIVAN	IRELAND	35	16.50	YES	12/04/2005
SIMRAN	KHAN	LONDON	20	25.00	NO	01/02/1989

5 Check your data for accuracy and save the table.

BUILD-UP TASK ❷ *Create a calculated field in a query*

You have been asked to calculate the weekly wages for each of the sales representatives.

1   In a query, create a new field called **WAGE** and calculate the wage for each sales representative by multiplying the **HOURS** by the **PAY RATE**.

2   Save the query using the name **REPS PAY**

BUILD-UP TASK ❸ *Format and print a tabular report*

1   Using the query **REPS PAY** you saved in Build-up task 2, produce a **tabular** report, in **landscape** orientation, displaying all the records.

2   Display all the fields in the following order:

FIRST NAME
LAST NAME
REGION
HOURS
PAY RATE
COMPANY CAR
START DATE
WAGE

3   Title the report **WEEKLY PAYMENTS TO SALES REPS**

4   Sort the data in descending order of **WAGE**.

5   Format the figures in the **WAGE** column to be displayed to **two** decimal places with a currency symbol.

6   Ensure the figures in the **PAY RATE** column are also displayed to **two** decimal places with a currency symbol.

7   In the footer display:

an automatic date field
your name
your centre number

> **TIP!**
>
> You may change the font type, size and alignment.

8   Ensure all data will be fully displayed on the printout.

9   Save the report as **WEEKLY PAYMENTS TO SALES REPS**

10 Print the report on **one** page in **landscape** orientation.

BUILD-UP TASK ④ Create and print labels

The sales representatives will be attending a conference. Name labels need to be printed for each of the representatives.

1 Display the following fields on the labels:

FIRST NAME   LAST NAME (on one line, separated by at least one space)
REGION

2 Sort the data in ascending order of **LAST NAME**.

3 Do not display field headings on the labels.

4 In the footer, display your **name** and **centre number**.

5 Ensure all the data will be fully displayed on the printout.

6 Print the labels on **one** page.

7 Save and close the database.

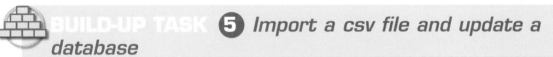

BUILD-UP TASK ⑤ Import a csv file and update a database

A datafile of books (in csv format) has been created. You have been asked to import this file into your database software and update the database. You will need the datafile **DBBOOKS**. (*Note*: some entries in the **AUTHOR** field are intentionally blank – i.e. do not contain data.)

1 Create a new database using the name **stockbks**

2 Import the csv file **DBBOOKS** and save it as a new table in your database software's file format.

3 Modify the field characteristics as shown below.

FIELD HEADING	DATA TYPE
ISBN NO	Text
TITLE	Text
AUTHOR	Text
PUBLISHER	Text
YEAR	Number, 0 decimal places
PRICE	Currency, 2 decimal places with currency symbol
DELIVERY	Text
PAGES	Number, 0 decimal places
TYPE	Text

4 You need to amend the following data. Delete the records with ISBN NO **1842242105** and AUTHOR **Hudson Bob**.

5 In the **Type** field, replace *all* the entries for **Paperback** with **PB** and **Hardback** with **HB**

6 Save the database table.

BUILD-UP TASK ⑥ Create a query using logical and comparison operators

You have been asked to query the database to provide specific reports for the manager. A customer has asked for a list of books that could be recommended to students.

1 In a query, find all the titles where the **PRICE** is **£29.95 or less** and the **DELIVERY** is **STOCKED** or **1 DAY** or **2 DAYS** or **3 DAYS**.

2 Save the query as **UNDER 30 QUICK DELIVERY**

BUILD-UP TASK ⑦ Create and format a tabular grouped report

1 Use the query **UNDER 30 QUICK DELIVERY** created in Build-up task 6 to produce a tabular report in landscape orientation entitled **POSSIBLE BOOK RECOMMENDATIONS**.

2 Display the following fields in the following order: **PUBLISHER**, **ISBN NO**, **TITLE**, **DELIVERY**, **PRICE**.

3 Group the report by **PUBLISHER**

4 Sort the data in the **PUBLISHER** field in **ascending** order, then sort the data within each group in **descending** order of **PRICE**.

5 For each group, display the **Total** figure for **PRICE** and also display the **Overall Total** figure.

6 Enter the label **COST IF ORDERED FOR LIBRARY** for the figure for each group.

7 Enter the label **TOTAL COST IF ALL BOOKS RECOMMENDED** for the overall total figure.

8 Format the **PRICE** figures and all the **Total** figures to be displayed to **two** decimal places with a currency symbol.

9 Align the **Total** figures under the **PRICE** column.

10 In the footer display:

an automatic date field
automatic page numbers
your name
your centre number

11 Ensure all the data is fully visible.

12 Save the report as **POSSIBLE BOOK RECOMMENDATIONS** and print the report in **landscape** orientation to fit on no more than **three** pages.

BUILD-UP TASK ⑧ *Create a query using logical, range and wildcard criteria*

The manager wants to promote publications with CD-ROMS and shorter publications.

1 In a query, find all the titles where the **TYPE** includes a **CD-ROM** or is **PB** or **HB** and where the **PAGES** are between **36** and **200**.

2 Save the query as **PROMOTIONS**

BUILD-UP TASK ⑨ *Create and format a columnar report*

1 Use the query **PROMOTIONS** created in Build-up task 8 to produce a columnar report in portrait orientation entitled **BOOK PROMOTIONS**

2 Display the following fields in the following order: **TITLE**, **TYPE**, **PRICE**.

3 Sort the data in **ascending** order of **PRICE**.

4 In the footer display:

your name
your centre number

5 Ensure all the data is fully visible.

6 Save the report as **TITLES FOR PROMOTION** and print the report in **portrait** orientation to fit on no more than **one** page.

Task 1

Scenario

You work as a Customer Support Assistant in a travel agency that specialises in low-cost holidays in the sun. Your duties include the creating, updating and querying the company databases. You have been asked to create a small database of holiday representatives who are available for work during the summer season.

1 Open a database software application.

2 Create a new database called **holiday reps**

3 In a new table, set up the field headings and data types as shown below. Ensure that the field lengths are long enough to display all the information in full.

FIELD HEADING	DATA TYPE
FAMILY NAME	Text
GIVEN NAME	Text
DOB	English date format (day, month, year)
CONTACT NUMBER	Text
FIRST SEASON	Logic field
PREFERENCE	Text
WORK DAYS	Number, 0 decimal places
WEEKLY WAGE	Currency, 2 decimal places with currency symbol

4 Enter the records shown below into your database table. You may use a data entry form to enter the data.

FAMILY NAME	GIVEN NAME	DOB	CONTACT NUMBER	FIRST SEASON	PREFERENCE	WORK DAYS	WEEKLY WAGE
BRETT	SIMON	04/02/1978	0796 621 8997	YES	TURKEY TUNISIA	5	350.00
ABSOLM	JODI	30/09/1986	0203 546 1374	NO	SPAIN	6	195.75
FALLATHI	ALI	28/01/1980	0203 671 8993	NO	CYPRUS TURKEY	5	375.50
HOKER	ANGELA	14/09/1987	0530 824 4433	YES	BALERIC ISLANDS	6	225.50
SAVINE	DENISE	21/03/1986	0797 540 6213	YES	FRANCE SPAIN	5	180.00
BROOKS	SAM	05/05/1985	0204 311 7968	NO	GREECE	6	195.75
SIMMS	LISA	09/12/1986	0114 236 3800	YES	GREECE	6	195.75
PATEL	KAYUREE	11/05/1986	0771 406 3501	YES	TURKEY	4	300.75
PREET	KIRAN	27/11/1987	0797 914 6336	YES	SPAIN	6	225.50

5 Check your data for accuracy and save the table.

PRACTICE TASK

Task 2

1   Using the database table saved in Task 1 produce a **tabular** report, in **landscape** orientation, displaying all records.

2   Display all fields in the following order:

FAMILY NAME
GIVEN NAME
DOB
CONTACT NUMBER
FIRST SEASON
PREFERENCE
WORK DAYS
WEEKLY WAGE

3   Title the report **SUMMER SEASON HOLIDAY REPS**

4   Sort the data in **descending** order of **DOB**.

5   In the footer display:

an automatic date field
your name
your centre number

6   Ensure all the data will be fully displayed on the printout.

7   Save and print the report on **one** page in **landscape** orientation.

8   Labels for the files of each representative need to be printed. Display the following fields on the labels:

GIVEN NAME   **FAMILY NAME** (on one line, separated by at least one space)
PREFERENCE
WORK DAYS

9   Sort the data in **descending** order of **WORK DAYS** then in **ascending** order of **FAMILY NAME**.

10 Do not display field headings on the labels.

11 In the footer, display your **name** and **centre number**.

12 Ensure all the data will be fully displayed on the printout. Save the labels report.

13 Print the labels on **one** page.

14 Save and close the database.

Task 3

A datafile (in csv format) of available holidays has been created. You have been asked to query this data to provide specific reports for customers. You will need the csv file **holiday**.

1 Create a new database using the name **summer 2007**

2 Import the file **holiday** and save it as a new table in your database software's file format.

3 Modify the field characteristics as shown in the following table.

FIELD HEADING	DATA TYPE
COUNTRY	Text
STAR RATING	Number, 0 decimal places
TYPE	Text
PROPERTY	Text
SUITS	Text
COST	Currency, 0 decimal places with currency symbol
CHILD DISCOUNT	Logic
AIRPORT	Text
DATE	English date (day, month, year) in any format
DAYS	Number, 0 decimal places

4 One of the hotels has been found to be unsatisfactory. Delete the record for **Tunisia** with a STAR RATING of **2** leaving from **London Gatwick** AIRPORT.

5 The price of one holiday has been reduced. Amend the record for **France** with a STAR RATING of **4** in a **Villa** PROPERTY to have a COST of **999** instead of 1020.

6 In the **TYPE** field replace entries for:

Self Catering with **SC**
Half Board with **HB**
Full Board with **FB**
Bed and Breakfast with **BB**
All Inclusive with **AI**

7 Save the database table.

8 You have been asked to calculate the child discounts for holidays in late July where a child discount is available. In a query, find all the holidays where the **CHILD DISCOUNT** is **YES** and the **DATE** is **Between 21/07/07 and 28/07/07**.

9 In the same query, create a new field called **REDUCTION PER CHILD** and calculate the amount of the reduction by multiplying the **COST** by **40%** (COST*0.4).

10 Save the query using the name **CHILD REDUCTIONS**

Task 4

1 Use your saved query called **CHILD REDUCTIONS** to produce a **columnar** report in **portrait** orientation. Title the report **LATE JULY CHILD DISCOUNTS**

2 Display the following fields in the following order:

DATE
DAYS
COUNTRY
STAR RATING
TYPE
COST
REDUCTION PER CHILD

3 Sort the data in **descending** order of **REDUCTION PER CHILD**.

4 Format the figures in the **COST** column to be displayed to **integer** (no decimal places) with a currency symbol.

5 Format the figures in the **REDUCTION PER CHILD** column to be displayed to **integer** (no decimal places) with a currency symbol.

6 In the footer display:

an automatic date field
automatic page numbers
your name
your centre number

7 Ensure all the data is fully visible and fits on no more than **two** pages. You may alter the margins and the format of the report to achieve this.

8 Save the report as **CHILD DISCOUNTS IN JULY**

9 Print the report in **portrait** orientation to fit on no more than **two** pages.

Task 5

1 A customer has asked for a list of holidays to suit their preferences and budget. In a query, find all the holidays where the STAR RATING is **4 or more**, leaving from *any* **London** AIRPORT and the PROPERTY is a **Villa** or **Hotel** or **Resort**.

2 Save the query as **4* PLUS LONDON**

3 Use the query **4* PLUS LONDON** to produce a **tabular** report in **landscape** orientation titled **LUXURY HOLIDAYS FROM LONDON AIRPORTS**

4 Display the following fields in the following order: **COUNTRY**, **DATE**, **DAYS**, **TYPE**, **PROPERTY**, **STAR RATING**, **COST**.

5 Group the report by **COUNTRY**.

6 Sort the data in the **COUNTRY** field in **ascending** order, then sort the data within each group in **ascending** order of **DATE**.

7 For each group, display the **Minimum** figure for **COST**.

8 Enter the label **LEAST EXPENSIVE HOLIDAY** for the figure for each group.

9 Format the **COST** figures and the **Minimum** figures to be displayed as **integer** (no decimal places) with a currency symbol.

10 Align the **Minimum** figures under the **COST** column.

11 In the footer display:

an automatic date field
automatic page numbers
your name
your centre number

12 Ensure all the data is fully visible.

13 Save the report as **LUXURY HOLS FROM LONDON** and print the report in **landscape** orientation to fit on no more than **two** pages.

Definition of terms

Amend To change or to edit.

Back up To create a spare copy.

Calculated field A new field created in Query Design view in order to carry out a calculation.

Click and drag A mouse technique used to move items. The mouse button is held down so that the cursor can be moved to reposition an item.

Codes Abbreviations that stand for longer words, often referred to as 'encoding data'. Codes help to maintain database efficiency.

Comparison operator Used in queries to search for information in numeric and date fields. Information from the database is compared with the criteria entered, and matching results are displayed.

OPERATOR	IN NUMERIC FIELDS	IN DATE FIELDS
>	more than	after
<	less than	before
>=	more than and equal to	on or after
<=	less than and equal to	on or before

Control A label or text box that controls the display of information in a report.

Criteria More than one criterion. The selection conditions used in one or more fields.

Criterion A selection condition used in a query to find specific records.

csv file 'Comma separated values' or 'comma separated variables'. A generic file format that can be opened and read by a wide range of software.

Data file A file in any file format that contains data.

Data type The type of data in a field (e.g. text, number, date, currency).

Database An organised list of information.

Database window A window that lists all the objects currently in the database. Clicking on an object in the Objects sections allows a user to view the objects in that section (e.g. tables, queries, reports).

Datasheet view View of a table or query in rows and columns showing all the data in all the records. The field names appear as column headings and the records as rows.

Decimal places The number of figures displayed after the decimal point.

Default The automatic setting(s) in Access. The setting that a computer program (or system) will use unless it is changed or 'customised'. For example, the default font for a table in Access may be Arial. Unless you change this, tables will always be displayed in this font.

Delete a record Removing the contents of a record completely. The remaining record numbers are automatically renumbered.

Design view View of a table, query or report showing how it is designed. A user can make amendments in Design view.

Field A separate item (block) of data that makes up a record.

Field heading A field name (column heading).

Field name A column heading that describes the data in that column. Referred to as a 'field heading'.

Field properties The formatting for the data type (e.g. currency with two decimal places or a field length of 25 characters for a text field).

Find and replace A technique where the computer searches for a particular word or character in a table and replaces instances of that word or character with alternative words or characters.

Folder An area created to store and organise files.

Form A display on the screen which allows a user to enter records into the table. A form may also be used for viewing data.

Formatting How data is displayed (e.g. with a currency symbol, in bold, in a particular font type or font size).

Grouped report A grouped report combines data into groups. A grouped report can include calculations such as totals, averages and maximum and minimum values.

Grouping Records with the same information in a field are displayed together.

Hover To position the cursor over an object/area on the screen.

Import To insert prepared data into an Access table.

Label A text box displaying data that will not change.

Labels This is a type of report designed to be printed on label sheets. A label report does not display a report title.

Logical operator AND, OR and NOT. Used in queries to combine search criteria.

Object An element within the database (e.g. a table, query, form or report).

Orientation The way paper is displayed. The orientation can be portrait (shortest side at the top) or landscape (widest side at the top).

Print Preview Displays on-screen what a table, query or report will look like when printed.

Query A method of questioning a database to find specific information.

Query Design view The view in which queries are created. It is divided into two sections. The top section displays a field list box which displays the table name and the field headings. The lower section is the Query grid (see *Query grid*).

Query grid The lower part of the query window where criteria are entered, data is sorted and the display of fields is selected.

Range A set of values that have a lower and upper limit.

Read only A property set on a file which does not allow the user to make any changes to the file. To amend a file, the user must remove the read-only property.

Record A set of related data. Similar to a row in a table.

Record Navigation buttons Buttons at the bottom left of the screen in Datasheet view. Allow a user to move between records in a table or query. They display the number of records in a table or query.

Report A more professional way of displaying information from a table or query.

Run (a query) Finds all the records that meet the criteria entered into the Query grid.

Sort Reordering of data in ascending or descending order.

Spellcheck A tool in Access that automatically checks the spelling of words against a large dictionary.

Subfolder A folder within a folder.

Summary (group summary) The sum, average, minimum or maximum can be displayed for each group in a grouped report. Summaries can only be displayed for numeric fields.

Tab (in a window) A window may have a number of tabs. These are the different sections of the window. To view the options in that section, click on the tab name.

Table A means of storing and displaying data in rows and columns.

Text box A text box is a control that displays the value of a database field or the value of a calculation.

Text qualifier " (speech marks – double or single) that surround text fields in a data file. A text qualifier is required if one or more field contains a comma.

Tool tip When the cursor hovers over an item the program displays a tip, usually with a yellow background. A tool tip shows the name of an object on the screen.

Truncate Data is not displayed in full.

User area The workspace on a computer for the storage of files. Examples are the My Documents folder, a network drive, a floppy disk or the hard disk drive.

Wildcard character *, ?, #. Used to carry out a pattern search.

Wizard A help feature that guides a user through a series of steps in order to create reports or queries in a database.

1   Your tutor will provide you with the file you need for the assessment.

2   Before an assessment you should create a new folder just for the assessment.

3   You will usually be provided with one file – a datafile in csv format that you will import into your database software during the course of the assessment.

The order of the tasks may vary from paper to paper. In some assignments, you may be required to create a small database at the beginning of the assessment. In others, the first task may be to import the csv file into your database software and to modify the field properties to prepare it for use. You may be required to create and run queries and reports on both the newly created database and the database that you import into your database software (Access).

DURING THE ASSESSMENT, YOU WILL NEED TO COMPLETE ABOUT 5 TASKS

General assessment tips

○   Follow each instruction in the correct sequence. Do not leave an instruction with the intention of doing it later.

○   Do not enter any text in bold unless instructed – the text is presented in bold to help you to identify filenames, text to be entered and instructions.

○   When asked to display an automatic date and automatic page numbers in a report, remember that Access will automatically display these items (except on a label report), so you do not need to enter them again – you just need to check that they are displayed on the report.

○   When entering your name and centre number in a report, make sure that you make the label box wide enough to display all the details.

○   Always check in Print Preview before printing and check your printouts to ensure all the data is displayed in full. Pay particular attention to dates and numbers with decimal places. In text fields, look at the longest entry in the actual database table and compare this to your printout to ensure that this entry is displayed in full.

Create a new database

You will need to create a small database of about 10 records with 7–10 fields.

You will need to:

1 Create a new database.

2 Create a new table in Design view.

3 Create field names and define field types in a table.

4 Format data types.

5 Save and name a table.

6 Enter records.

- Read through the scenario so that you understand the type of data you will be working with.

- Read through the entire task *before* you start.

- Look at the data you will be entering into the database before designing your database.

- Make a note of how many characters there are in the longest entry in each field so that you know the **minimum** setting for the field length.

- For fields that will contain telephone numbers, set the Data Type to Text to ensure any leading 0s will be displayed.

- Format numeric fields as **Fixed** and always set the number of decimal places.

- Check that date fields are in English format (day, followed by month, followed by year). You do not need to create a primary key.

- When entering data in Datasheet view, widen each column sufficiently to see all the data in full.

Create a tabular report displaying all fields

You will probably be required to create a tabular report showing all the fields in the database you have created.

You will need to:

1 Create a simple tabular report.

2 Insert report headers and footers.

3 Enter a report title.

4 Widen fields.

5 Save the report with a specified filename.

6 Sort data in a specified order.

7 Print the report.

Assessment tips – create a tabular report

- Read through the task and check to see if the fields are to be presented in the same order as they have been entered in the table. If they are, then use the **AutoReport** facility to create a tabular report. If not, use the Report Wizard (see the section 'Create a variety of reports displaying selected fields' below).

- Zoom in to the report and check that all the data is displayed in full (compare it to the data in table view). Make a note of any fields that are truncated and adjust them in Design view – remember to check the report in Print Preview again after any adjustments have been made.

- Check that the date fields are displayed in full and are in English format (day, followed by month, followed by year).

- Check that numbers are displayed with the number of decimal places stated in the assignment (e.g. if one decimal place is specified, the figure 4 should be displayed as 4.0). If necessary, amend the field properties in report Design view.

- Sort the report using the **Sorting and Grouping** option in report Design view. You will probably need to amend the title of the report in Design view. Make sure you enter the title exactly as shown in the assignment.

- Remember that the date and page number(s) will be displayed automatically – you just need to check these in Print Preview. You may delete any automatic fields that are not requested but, unless there is an instruction to remove them, you will not be penalised if you leave them in.

- Make sure the label field is wide enough to display your name and centre number in full.

Create and print labels

You will need to create labels either from the database table that you have created or from a query in the database that you have imported.

You will need to:

1 Create labels.

2 Display specified fields.

3 Sort in labels in a specified order.

4 Print labels.

Assessment tips – create labels

- Use the Label Wizard to create labels.

- Select Avery 2 across as the label type.

- Make sure you have inserted the space(s) between fields on the same line.

- Remember, unlike other reports, labels can be sorted in the fourth step of the Label Wizard.

- You may need to enlarge the header/footer to display your name (**View menu**, **Page Header/Footer**).

- If an error message appears stating that the labels do not fit on the page, reduce the left and right page margins.

View the labels in Print Preview and check that all the data is displayed in full. Make a note of any fields that are truncated and adjust them in Design view – remember to check the report in Print Preview again after any adjustments have been made.

Import a datafile, save it as a new table and modify the field characteristics

You will be provided with a datafile, usually in csv format, that you will be required to import into Access and save as new table.

You will need to:

1 Create a new database.

2 Import a generic file and save it as a new table.

3 Modify the field characteristics.

Assessment tips – import a datafile

○ In step 2 of the Import Text Wizard ensure the **Comma** option is set and select the Text Qualifier to be '' (double speech marks). Then click in the check box for **First Row Contains Field Names**.

○ In step 5 no primary key is required.

○ If an error message is displayed after the file has been imported, delete the table and try again.

○ Open the imported table, widen the fields and look at the data in the database to familiarise yourself with the information contained within each field.

○ You will probably need to modify some field characteristics in Design view.

○ Format numeric fields as **Fixed** and always set the number of decimal places. Check that date fields are in English format (day, followed by month, followed by year).

○ When modifying field lengths, make sure the field lengths are wide enough to display all the data in full, otherwise, data will be lost.

Amend a database

You will be required to make some amendments to the database. The requested amendments will vary from assignment to assignment. For example, in some assignments you may be asked to delete records; in others you may be asked to add a record or change the data in a record. Most assignments will require you to find and replace data.

You will need to:

1 Find a record.

2 Delete record(s).

3 Add records(s).

4 Amend records.

5 Find and replace data.

Assessment tips – amend a database

○ Click in the field in which you want to find the data before using the Find facility.

○ Look carefully at the data to be replaced to see if you need to select the **Any Part of Field**, **Whole Field** or **Start of Field** options – in most cases you will need to use the **Any Part of Field** option.

- Check the record(s) to be deleted very carefully as there may be several records containing similar data – remember that you cannot undo a delete action!

- When making amendments, widen the fields to display all the data.

- After making amendments, click in the last blank row to avoid accidental amendments.

Create queries

You will need to create queries on the imported database and in some assignments you may also need to create queries on the database you create.

You will need to:

1 Use comparison operators.

2 Use range criteria.

3 Use logical criteria.

4 Create a calculated field.

5 Use wildcard criteria.

6 Combine criteria to create a query.

7 Save the query with a specified name.

Assessment tips – create queries

- Read the entire step relating to the query before you start.

- Look at the data in the table to see how the data has been entered (for example, if you are asked to find all the records that contain SUN, is SUN the only data if the field, or will you need to use a wildcard?).

- Take care to enter the criteria with one hundred per cent accuracy. However, you do not need to match case when entering criteria in a query.

- When queries contain multiple criteria, run the query at each stage to check that the correct data has been found.

- Remember using the criteria BETWEEN *includes* the number/dates entered.

- When calculating percentages in calculated fields, you must enter the number in decimal format (e.g. 0.05 for 5%).

Create a variety of reports displaying selected fields

You will need to create a variety of reports in both landscape and portrait orientation. Most reports will be based on the queries you have created. At least one report will require you to group data on at least one field, and you will probably be required to display a group summary. Most reports will require the data in at least one field to be sorted.

You will need to:

1 Create tabular reports.

2 Create columnar reports.

3 Create grouped reports.

4 Display group summaries.

5 Set the report orientation.

6 Create text labels and enter text.

7 Select and move controls.

8 Insert report headers and footers.

9 Enter a report title.

10 Widen fields.

11 Save the report with a specified filename.

12 Sort data in a specified order.

13 Print the report.

Assessment tips – create reports

○ Read through the entire step/task before using the wizard to create the report.

○ Make sure you select the correct query/table on which to base the report.

○ Take care when selecting the fields to be displayed – make sure that all the requested fields (and no more) are selected.

○ Do not sort reports in the Report Wizard – perform any sorting using the **Sorting and Grouping** option in report Design view.

○ When sorting grouped reports, take care *not* to remove any grouping options.

○ When summaries are displayed, additional unrequested information may also be displayed – these unwanted labels may be deleted in report Design view. However, unless you are instructed to remove additional data, you will not be penalised if this information is also displayed.

○ Zoom in to the report and check that all the data is displayed in full (compare it to the data in the open query). Make a note of any fields that are truncated and adjust them in Design view – remember to check the report in Print Preview again after any adjustments have been made.

○ Check that the date fields are displayed in full and are in English format (day, followed by month, followed by year).

○ Check that numbers are displayed with the number of decimal places stated in the assignment (e.g. if one decimal place is specified, the figure 4 should be displayed as 4.0). If necessary, amend the field properties in Report Design view.

- You will probably need to amend the title of the report in Design view. Make sure you enter the title exactly as shown in the assignment.

- Remember that the date and page number(s) will be displayed automatically – you just need to check these in Print Preview. You may delete any automatic fields that are not requested but, unless there is an instruction to remove them, you will not be penalised if you leave them in.

- Make sure that any label fields are wide enough to display the information in full.

- Check that the report will be printed on no more than the specified number of pages (printing on fewer than the number of pages specified is fine, but do check that you have all the required records). The page margins may be adjusted to display more records on a page and/or the font size of the report headings/field headings or data may be changed.

- Always make a final check in Print Preview before printing the report.

Good luck!

Preparation for the assessment

General assessment guidelines for all units

Before the assessment

You are advised to obtain a copy of the syllabus from the OCR website. Read through all the assessment objectives to ensure that you have the necessary skills before you begin the assessment.

Before you start a live assessment, complete at least two 'mock exams' in assessment conditions, without any help from your tutor or classmates.

The assessment

- Level 2 assessments are usually split into five or six tasks.
- You are allowed a notional duration of 3 hours for each assessment.
- Before you begin, read through the paper to see what you will need to do.
- You may want to allow yourself about 2½ hours to complete the tasks and then 30 minutes to check all your final printouts and your saved files.
- Your tutor may allow you to complete an assessment over several consecutive sessions (lessons).
- Once you start an assessment your tutor cannot give you further teaching, and is not allowed to help you, so make sure that you are ready for the assessment before you start it.
- Your tutor will provide you with a photocopy of the assignment.
- Printing can be done after the assessment, however, you are advised to print your work whenever there is an instruction to print.

> **TIP!**
>
> When you have printed your work, do not move straight on to the next instruction or task! Check your printout against the instructions in the assignment to make absolutely sure that you have carried out each instruction correctly and that the printout matches what you have on the screen.

Your name

You will be asked to enter your name. It is good practice to enter your first and last name.

Filenames/query names/report names

You are advised to enter filenames/query names/report names using the same case as in the assignment. However, you will not be penalised if you use a different case for these names. Do not enter a full stop after a file or folder name.

Headers and footers

Unless there is a specific instruction, you may use any font size, font type and alignment for headers and footers, but do make sure that the information in headers or footers does not overlap any page items. A small font size is usually best.

During the assessment

○ During the assessment you are allowed to use:

  - the textbook that you worked through for your learning
  - the Quick Reference Guides from the Heinemann book that you have been using
  - your own notes
  - handouts from your tutor that cover general IT skills
  - any books that cover general IT skills.

○ You are not allowed to use any books, notes, handouts, etc. that are referenced to the assessment objectives of the syllabus.

○ You cannot ask your tutor or anyone else for help.

○ If there is a technical problem, e.g. something wrong with the computer or printer then you should inform your tutor/the invigilator.

○ Read through the whole task before you start.

○ All the instructions are numbered, and many have sub-steps (a, b, c, etc.). Read through the whole step before you start doing anything.

○ Follow each instruction in the correct sequence. Do not leave out an instruction, even if you intend to do it later.

○ Tick each instruction when you have completed it.

○ Check that you have completed a step fully and correctly before moving on to the next step.

○ Don't rush!

○ Enter all data in the same case as in the assignment.

○ Enter all data as it is presented in the assignment.

○ Any data that you have to type in is presented in bold to help you see what you have to key in. You should not use bold emphasis unless you are told to do so in the assessment.

○ Remember that if you find an error, you can correct it, but if you leave the checking to your tutor, they cannot give you your work back to correct any errors that they have found.

○ If you notice an error, you can make changes to your work and print again.

○ Remember, you can print as many draft copies as you wish, but you must remember to destroy any incorrect copies or unwanted drafts.

○ You will be asked to enter your centre number. You can enter this in any format, e.g. Centre Number 11111, Centre No 11111, Centre 11111, 11111.

At the end of the assessment

○ Check your printout against the assessment paper. Use a different colour pen/pencil to tick each instruction on the copy of the assessment.

○ Make sure that you have saved all your files.

- Make sure that you have used the correct filename/query name/report name.
- Make sure that all your files are saved in the correct user area.
- Make sure every printout has your first and last name on it.
- Arrange your prints in the order that they are listed in the assessment.
- Destroy any printouts that you do not wish to be marked (or hand these to your tutor making sure that your tutor knows these are not to be marked!).
- Hand to your tutor:
  - your final printouts in the correct order, you may wish to staple these to keep them secure
  - the copy of the assessment paper
  - the disk where you have saved your files (if you save on disk); if not, tell the tutor where your files are saved on the computer.

Index

absolute cell references 89–90, 98–9, 118
alignment
  of tab stops 24–5
  of text in cells 81
amending data
  database fields 210–11
  documents 30–2
  spreadsheets 88–9
archiving files 43–5
AutoFilter 120–2
automatic fields
  database reports 229
  documents 14–15
  spreadsheets 111
AutoReports, creating 194–5
axis values, formatting 139–40

backing up databases 209
bar charts 134, 135–6
borders
  spreadsheets 83
  tables in documents 26–7
brackets in spreadsheet formulae 96–8
bulleted lists 16

calculated fields, queries 219–21
cell references 89–90, 95–6, 98–101, 118–19
Chart Wizard 127
charts 124–5
  bar charts 134, 135–6
  comparative charts 134–6
  pie charts 127–31
  see also graphs
columnar reports, creating 235
columns
  clearing contents 92
  display headings 112
  hiding/unhiding 114–15
  inserting/deleting 89–91
compacting databases 208
comparative charts 134–6
comparison operators 103, 214
compressed folders, archiving to 44
contiguous data, selecting 126
COUNT functions 106–7
criteria, database queries 213–14, 216–17

csv (comma separated values) files 76–7
  importing 205–7
  opening in Excel 77
  saving as Excel file 77–8
currency format 85
cut and paste, moving data 93

data points (plot points) 148, 151
data series, graphs 137–9
data sources, mail merge 39–40
data types 187
databases
  backing up 209
  compacting 208
  creating new 185–6
datafiles 76–7
  importing 205–7
  opening/saving 77–8
  viewing 125–7
datasheet view
  queries 218–19
  tables 191
dates 86, 187, 213, 214, 229
decimal places format 84–5, 86
design view
  queries 215–17
  reports 195, 226
  tables 188–9
displaying reports 194–5
distinctive data 131–2
documents
  data files, inserting 18–19
  editing 30–3
  formatting 11–13
  graphs, inserting 17–18
  images, inserting 17
  mail merge 33–7
  password protecting 37–8
  printing 15–16
  spell checking 31–2
drag and drop, moving data 94

editing data
  database fields 210–11
  spreadsheets 88–9
  word documents 30–1
e-documents see documents
exploded pie charts 128–31